18th

To Paul
Have a good read.
With all good wishes

Richard Powell

Raging Against Time

by

Arnold Powell

authorHOUSE®

AuthorHouse™ UK Ltd.
500 Avebury Boulevard
Central Milton Keynes, MK9 2BE
www.authorhouse.co.uk
Phone: 08001974150

This book is a work of non-fiction. Unless otherwise noted, the author and the publisher make no explicit guarantees as to the accuracy of the information contained in this book and in some cases, names of people and places have been altered to protect their privacy.

First published by AuthorHouse 5/29/2007

ISBN: 978-1-4343-1581-6 (sc)
ISBN: 978-1-4343-1580-9 (hc)

Printed in the United States of America
Bloomington, Indiana

This book is printed on acid-free paper.

I dedicate this book to Stacey-Louise Balcombe, an excellent mother and chef and to Robin and Melanie Powell and James Fraiman all fine parents and physicians, who contrary to my advice entered a difficult but honoured medical profession.

To attain our aspirations we walk paths made accessible by forbears, to whom we owe a great debt of thanks.
In time these are repaid by the encouragement and opportunity we grant to those who follow us.

To preserve anonymity patient's names have been changed.

Table of Contents

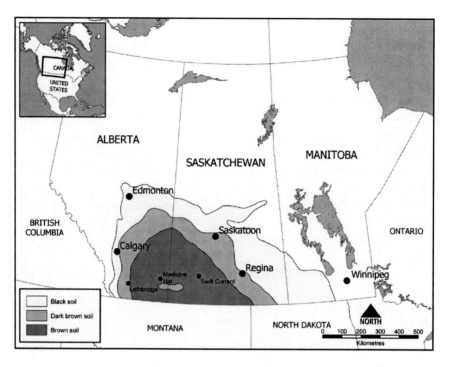

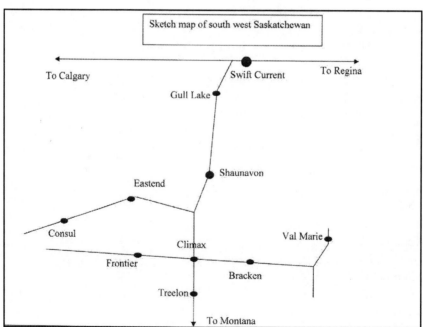

Sketch map of south west Saskatchewan

Chapter 1

SASKATCHEWAN CANADA

November 1959

A violent hammering reverberated through the timber-framed cottage of our prairie home. Startled by this aggressive intrusion in the midst of our evening meal, I bounded from my chair and rushed over to the side entrance. Hurriedly I turned on the outside light illuminating the drive and back porch trying to catch a glimpse of who might be attempting to break the door in.

Suddenly, there it was again; a fierce, rhythmic banging at the side entrance, which opened directly from the kitchen onto the drive, demanding a response. Peering out of the partially frosted door window, I could just make out a solitary Stetson-hatted figure. With increasing unease I opened the insulated doors, the first inwards and unlocking the catch on the outer door allowed it to swing out, reluctantly permitting the waiting arctic blast to rush in.

Outside, above the door, hung a low wattage light bulb, where its protective cover gyrated in the chill evening breeze. The lamp sparkled and shimmered as its light caught the cascading night frost, revealing in its ashen illumination a young farmer, who as I appeared respectfully removed his heavily stained hat gripping it in one hand. He seemed agitated clenching and unclenching the grimy fingers clutching the felt brim in rapid jerky movements, almost dropping the hat each time. In the other hand a half smoked hand rolled cigarette glowed red, revealing the stumps of chewed blackened fingernails. Close by in the road, with cab door ajar and headlamps on full beam, a truck spewed out billowing clouds of exhaust.

Tall and scrawny, without an extra ounce covering his frame, our unexpected visitor was dressed in a loose fitting buckskin jacket, plaid shirt and grubby jeans. He appeared tense and ill at ease as he blurted out, in his North American drawl.

"I need the doctor, and it's real urgent. Are you the doctor?"

"Yes, I'm Dr Powell. What can I do for you?" I asked rather too abruptly, irritated at the manner in which our meal had been disturbed by this youthful visitor who stood there, seemingly immune to the cold November night. Uncomfortable gusting icy air continued to rush into our living space, as he remained shyly on the threshold, for what seemed an interminable time. Doubtlessly he was about to convey some kind of message, but when?

"How can I help you?" I enquired once more, perhaps a little too hastily, hoping to encourage him and thereby stem the inrush of winter's chill.

"The matron at Frontier Hospital said I should go fetch the doctor from Climax straight away."

It was shortly before 7.30 pm in this southernmost region of a sparsely populated rural Saskatchewan. The telephone service stopped for 14 hours each day at 6 pm, after which communications could only be delivered in person, unless one could rouse a peevish elderly telephone operator, assuming she was still home, to perform a special favour by returning to her telephone office and its antiquated manual switchboard.

"Have you any idea what might be the problem?" I enquired trying to coax some further information from this slow prating messenger, before we all froze to death.

"She said to tell you Dr Kindrachuck's away for the week, an' there's a woman in labour with a dropped cord, an' to tell you to come straight away." Then, as an afterthought, he blurted out.

"She said tell him to come real quick! It's very urgent, and those were her exact words."

I thought. 'Small wonder in bygone age's kings had been known to cut off a messenger's head. It wasn't the bad news; it was simply the frustration in extracting the courier's information'.

Frontier had a well-equipped modest ten-bed cottage hospital, staffed mainly by British nurses and was a smaller neighbouring village almost nine miles west of Climax, where I'd been the town's doctor since arriving three months earlier in August. All Saskatchewan's diminutive prairie townships in this region had been established in the years just preceding the First World War, with waves of European and American immigrants, searching for a better life.

"Do you know if anybody's called Tom Fennessy?" I enquired, seeking news of my colleague who was the doctor 35 miles to the east in Val-Marie, the closest community with a hospital in that direction, which had been established and was still maintained by a convent with nuns in holy orders.

"No idea doc," he replied with that same soft, lifeless drawl.

"Alright; go back and tell matron I'll be along straight away. Ask her to have the operating room ready and some blood cross matched, just in case a section's necessary. Got that?"

The messenger nodded, and without uttering another word, replaced his hat and turned on the heels of his brown leather cowboy boots. Crunching on the underlying ice he strode rapidly to his silhouetted pick up truck, clambered in, slammed the door and with a roaring burst of exhaust accompanied by a rattle of tyres on gravel, drove off at speed, leaving a billowing cloud of exhaust and dust. Hastily I closed both doors. June, who'd overheard this conversation, announced that she'd like to accompany me, rather than remain alone for hours on end, not knowing what might be happening. I readily agreed, as I grabbed my new goose down parka jacket, with its fur collar and matching hat from the clothes rack and explained I'd start the car to get it warmed up, while she could join me in a couple of minutes when everything was ready.

The route to Frontier was along a typical Canadian grit road, running from east to west; straight, dusty and very rough. More than forty years earlier soil had been dragged from either side of the prairie grassland and packed to create an unpaved highway, comfortably wide enough for two vehicles and then covered with a heavy aggregate of coarse stones. These roads were built just a few inches above the surrounding prairie, while along each side was a wide ditch, which later I was to discover overflowed with snow in winter and briefly with water as it melted.

This engineering feat of thousands of miles of roadways was remarkable for the simplicity of its design. Since the highway was a fraction above the surrounding prairie, the wind constantly whipped any snow off the surface, which meant that throughout winter there was seldom any obstruction and snow ploughs were rarely seen. To keep the infrastructure serviceable, every township provided a driver for its monstrous yellow grading machine. Each regularly patrolled with its huge diagonally placed steel blade supported by enormous wheels, constantly and laboriously shifting and flattening the surface, dragging the aggregate back onto the road from the periphery where speeding car and truck tyres dumped it, creating fierce choking clouds of grey inundating dust in the process. The east-west roads each travelled as far as the eye could see, straight as an arrow to the horizon, while those running from south to north along an imaginary line of longitude were straight but described an 'S' bend every few miles to compensate for the curvature of the earth's surface.

The V8 engine of our 1952 green Oldsmobile 98, 'Rocket Model', reliably came to life with a gentle soft purr, the exhaust ejecting a small cloud of vapour as I started the ignition. I left it running to warm the engine, gearbox oil and car interior as I disconnected the electricity supply to the block heater and stowed the connecting lead safely under the hood, before closing it firmly with a resounding bang creating yet another disturbance in the peaceful night air. Having checked my fuel gauge and confirmed the presence of a car rug and emergency supplies on the rear seat, I summoned my wife to hurry, as I scraped ice off the windows.

With June safely in the seat beside me, I backed our grimy but trusted Olds out of the drive and turned on the headlamps, which were covered by saucer-shaped Perspex covers resembling giant contact lenses that protected the glass from stones thrown up by other vehicles.

'Phone less, we hurriedly drove the short distance to the 'Climax Bracken Union Hospital' where I informed the duty nurse that I was driving to Frontier to attend an emergency maternity problem; and then we headed south for the main road.

Gaining the highway, I turned west and gunned the engine, the child in me thrilling to the escalating decibels of the powerful eight-cylinder engine as it growled into life. Unleashed, our General Motors Oldsmobile leapt forward, the automatic transmission sending the rear wheels racing and screeching to mind numbingly drown out all other sounds as I pursued the disappearing cloud of dust produced minutes earlier by a farm truck now more than a couple of miles ahead. As we accelerated we produced an identical choking grimy grey smoke screen billowing in our wake, while the staccato sound of pebbles and stones striking the underside of our vehicle's fenders echoed in the car and reverberated in my head. This was the exhilarating speech inhibiting sound of travel when speeding on these unpaved roadways.

It rarely rained in this semi-arid region and I gave thanks to the dry heavens that there'd been none for several weeks, for with any rainfall dirt roads became virtually impassable to all but tractors and horses. The stones and shingle, which gave excellent traction when the road was dry or covered in ice and snow, were pressed into the packed soil when wet. The wheels could then obtain no grip in what would become a veritable quagmire, where anything but the gentlest touch of accelerator or brake would cause one's vehicle to slide uncontrollably, sometimes slithering off the mud caked road into the ditch, where only a tractor could pull it back onto the highway.

Weeks earlier I'd waited at the roadside, standing in mud, unharmed apart from a battered ego, resulting from the confirmation of my inadequate motoring skills in this terrain, when a light autumnal rain fall had claimed the new doctor as its latest victim.

A farmer passing on his tractor, seeing my predicament had stopped.

"Hi doc; havin' a spot of trouble stayin' on the road?" he called banteringly, smiling at my predicament.

"Not really. Thought I'd just stop a while and take a closer look at whether the gophers (ground squirrels) were staying dry and comfortable." I replied.

"Then you won't need me to lend a hand towing you, back onto the road."

"No; I didn't say that. They seem fine, so if you could help me, I'd like to get on my way."

"Right, I'll haul you back onto the highway, if you're sure you're ready."

"Don't mean to put you to any trouble, but that would be great."

Within minutes he'd unhitched a stout rope, and had unceremoniously pulled my undamaged vehicle, back onto the road.

"What do I owe you?" I enquired.

"You don't owe me nothin' Doc; just drive more carefully 'til the road's dried out some." Then grinning, he chugged on his way with a wave of his gloved hand.

We could see the distant twinkling fairy lights of Frontier directly ahead, as in some Christmas fairy tale, appearing almost close enough to touch and yet still with some nine miles separating us. The long straight unpaved highway permitted travel at a speed that any unaccustomed city dweller would have considered suicidal on an unpaved highway, midst the accompanying reverberating thud and crash of coarse shingle and gravel on metal.

While speech was impossible when speeding along, my mind raced over all that I'd gleaned and seen in the preceding years of medical training as I reasoned why an umbilical cord might have prolapsed out of the uterus. By the end of pregnancy the baby's head would normally have been engaged to fit snugly into the pelvis for close on 4 weeks. This meant that a descent of these twined blood vessels ahead of the infant should not take place. Among the many possible causes the most likely were some type of malpresentation or a very premature labour. Providing there was a pulse in the cord I would have to try to push it back into the uterine cavity and then determine the lie of the neonate within the womb. Should I be unable to replace these thick umbilical blood vessels, the unborn baby was certain to die unless it was delivered urgently by caesarean section. I prayed fervently to any deity who might be on my mental wave length, that this might not be so, since apart from being second assistant more than nine months previously at two previous elective sections, the most minor role possible, I'd never been involved in such a major surgical procedure.

With these and other thoughts racing through my mind, I rapidly reached the quarter mile stretch of road leading north to Frontier from the main highway. With a crunch of locked wheels on gravel, I braked outside the hospital, shut off the car lights and engine and left the hand brake off, as I'd been advised. I strode into the hospital, accompanied by June, each of us terrified at the prospect of how I might cope, should a section become necessary.

Within the hospital, the matron, a middle aged Canadian nurse of Ukrainian ancestry, whom I'd met twice previously, had seen my approaching headlamps and was waiting impatiently for my arrival inside the front doorway. She wasted no time with formalities.

5

"Dr Powell, thank heavens you've arrived in time. We've a real emergency on our hands, and it looks like you'll have to deliver this one by section." As she spoke, I shed my parka and left my over boots at the entrance on a large mat set up for that purpose. I noted the assumption the moment the doctor appeared that he would somehow unlock the answer to every medical conundrum like some latter day 'Merlin the Magician' (1).

June squeezed my hand reassuringly, as I left her to read the book she held, knowing she would periodically start and run the car engine for a while, if my absence was prolonged. Matron continued to talk as she escorted me to the doctor's changing room, briefly outlining the circumstances of the case. This was a farmer's wife, who'd gone into labour one week earlier than anticipated in her first pregnancy. She'd been experiencing contractions every ten minutes since the late afternoon when her waters had broken and she had been admitted soon after 6.45 pm.

The duty nurse, a British midwife, examined her within minutes of admission and discovering a pulsating, prolapsed umbilical cord, had alerted the matron to this potentially lethal problem. Frontier's doctor Kindrachuck, had earlier left for a week's vacation and had designated Dr. Fennessy from Val Marie, as his locum. The telephone service had stopped some minutes earlier and since Val Marie was close to 45 miles to the east of Frontier, she had elected to call me, thereby saving more than sixty vital minutes, possibly the difference between life and death.

Matron followed me into the changing room talking excitedly, as I hurriedly changed. Once in the hospital's green scrub suit I was introduced to the duty midwife in the delivery room where ignoring further formalities, I rapidly washed my hands in warm water. The midwife informed me the umbilical artery in the prolapsed cord was still pulsating and the foetal heartbeat was strong, but with every contraction the cord's blood supply was being cut off. Evidence of foetal distress had been observed, with meconium staining (the first outpouring of the bowel of a new born child) of the draining amniotic fluid and a seriously diminishing foetal heart rate with each contraction.

Placing my hands on the patient's abdomen I attempted to determine the lie of the infant, and listened for its heartbeat. Next, donning sterile gloves, I confirmed that the patient's cervix was almost fully dilated and the foetal part that I could palpate was not the head, but a leg. This was a breech presentation with the mother well advanced in her labour. I endeavoured to replace the pulsating umbilical cord within the womb, but without success. Time was now the enemy and it was likely to be crucial for this baby.

Summoning an air ambulance was out of the question. It was more than 30 miles by road to the nearest working telephone in Shaunavon to call the ambulance base in Regina, 250 miles distant. This meant a six hour delay before the patient might arrive at a major hospital. Without prompt action, there would be a tragic outcome and the baby's life would be eclipsed before it had been delivered.

Concealing my heightened alarm, I announced to all within hearing that there was no time to lose. The only way to save this baby was with an immediate caesarean, for which the mother's written consent was required. Fortunately she hadn't eaten for some hours, reducing the anaesthetist's problems. I wrote up the pre-anaesthetic medication realising the shots to be called were all mine and the prospect scared me.

As the theatre was being made ready, Matron escorted me, almost at a run to the waiting room where she introduced me to the anxious expectant father. As swiftly as I was able I outlined the nature of the crisis, since talking somehow kept my mind off the looming ordeal.

"A breech presentation means that instead of the head coming first through the birth canal, the baby's bottom or leg is the presenting part. With the cord dropping down, we have no alternative but to operate since as the delivery progresses the cord, will be squashed as the baby passes along the birth canal, completely cutting off its supply of oxygen. Without oxygen the baby will most certainly die and were this not to occur, it would be severely brain damaged. The only way of averting this disaster is with an immediate section."

"No offence meant doc, but you look kinda young; would you mind if we had a second opinion?"

"You've every right to a second opinion if you can find one right now. There's evidence of foetal distress with each contraction and at the rate your wife's labour's progressing any delay will be fatal. The longer we stand here talking, the greater the likelihood that we'll simply be too late. Our only option is to operate straight away."

As I turned away, the husband interrupted me.

"If that's the only alternative then I guess there's no choice. You jest go right ahead. Have you done many of these operations before doc?" He enquired apprehensively.

"Quite a few." I lied, convincingly playing a gamesmanship I dared not reveal to patient, or staff. "Matron's called me to perform this operation because she knows of my obstetric training and the sooner we get started the better." Fortunately matron agreed on cue in the finest nursing tradition.

"So if you'll excuse us, we've no time to lose. Before the evening's out I promise you'll have a healthy baby and everything will be just fine. All you've to do is try to relax and start thinking about names for your baby." I breezily instructed, with a self-assurance I certainly didn't feel.

I returned to check the patient's progress. Preparations were going ahead rapidly in the operating room and as the theatre sister was enquiring about glove size, instruments and sutures that I would require, it dawned on me that I hadn't seen the anaesthetist.

"Anybody know if Tom Fennessy's arrived yet?" I enquired, desperately hoping that I'd be able to persuade him to swap roles and perform the surgery, allowing me to give the anaesthetic, since he'd been in practice far longer than me and was doubtlessly significantly more experienced. Anyway he was Dr. Kindrachuck's designated locum.

"We've been in such a rush, nobody's had time to drive over to Val Marie, to fetch him." replied the matron.

"Then who's giving the anaesthetic?" I enquired, baffled.

"I don't know. I suppose you'll just have to show one of us what to do." She replied.

My level of apprehension rose sharply. I admitted to matron my only anaesthetic experience was as a student in A&E, with ethyl chloride dropped onto a thin surgical dressing, accompanied after a brief interlude, by ether on gauze layered onto a metal frame facemask, followed by a nitrous oxide and oxygen mixture, once the patient was fully anaesthetised.

We decided she would have to act as anaesthetist and I would explain as rapidly as possible what she would be required to do and give her further instruction as the operation proceeded. I hurriedly described how she would administer the anaesthetic, protecting the patient's eyes, and organised the simple apparatus of gauze, mask and airway. The theatre sister was to assist me and we delegated one of the midwives to receive and care for the baby once it had been delivered.

Every prairie hospital maintained a list of willing potential blood donors within the community, with their blood groups. Blood could then be cross-matched with the recipient's for compatibility, by either the hospital laboratory technician, or the doctor.

"How many units of blood have been cross matched?" I nervously asked.

"We haven't had time to organise any blood donors, we've been so rushed off our feet." explained the matron in what appeared to have become a regular habit of running out of time.

I conjectured; 'There's no blood available in the likely event that a transfusion should prove necessary and no way to obtain any this evening. I'm to carry out an operation I've never performed before and without supervision.

In addition I have to oversee the anaesthetic'. The only further calamity I could envision would be a power failure, a frequent occurrence in these more remote areas. I resolved not to raise the issue of when the hospital's emergency generator had last been checked fearing matron would convey her earlier worn cliché. I'd noticed a number of flashlights in the building and sensed that at least some must surely be in working order, while I also had two in my car. Deep within, I was terrified. How was I ever going to cope? Silently I questioned myself, demanding to know what foolhardy impulse had brought me to this wilderness to play act being a latter day Albert Schweitzer (2) in this remote rural Canadian community. I daren't reveal this was my maiden abdominal surgical procedure. I'd observed many operations, usually standing close by or as a minor assistant, bored and tugging on a retractor, but watching, as opposed to performing was entirely different. This was now entering a major league for which I was completely untrained and unprepared.

I'd retained some knowledge of anatomy, but my previous surgical experience had been very limited. I'd always been a gowned second assistant, customarily in somebody's way, remotely heaving on a retractor with tired arms and occasionally privileged to cut the surgeon's suture material, invariably reprimanded for leaving the ends either too long or short, but most often ogling some of the prettier operating room nurses whose faces were veiled by masks and caps, imagining what they looked like below their entrancing eyes.

About six months earlier assisted by an experienced consultant surgeon at the Maryland General Hospital and under full supervision, I'd been permitted to remove an inflamed appendix. I doubted whether this would have provided sufficient expertise to cope with what now lay ahead. A tragic debacle seemed inevitable. I was a surgical impostor, yet I was the only doctor that this unfortunate woman and her unborn infant had and I couldn't stand idly by allowing it to die. The child deserved a chance to enter this world alive and I was determined the mother must be given the opportunity to have a baby and survive to care for her infant.

Compelled to exude an air of confident authority, which I neither had nor felt, I began by setting up a dextrose-saline drip in the patient's forearm, a simple procedure, which seldom presented me with difficulty, but now I first needed to will my hands to stop trembling. Next I managed to pass a nasal-gastric tube to aspirate the stomach contents while the patient was catheterised by one of the midwives who prepared the patient's skin for surgery.

Hurriedly I returned to the changing room, emptied what had suddenly become an irritable bladder, wishing I could be in any place but Saskatchewan.

I walked back to the operating room, feeling more like a condemned man proceeding to the gallows than a courageous surgeon. In no manner did I resemble Lister's (3) famous dictum; 'A surgeon requires the heart of a lion, the eye of an eagle and the hand of a lady.

Applying a fresh cap and facemask, I scrubbed up and dried my hands. I was then tied into my green sterile gown, and pulled on a pair of sterile latex gloves. The matron, doubtlessly as uneasy as me, had commenced, under my instruction, to administer the anaesthetic, dropping the ethyl chloride, followed by ether onto the underlying gauze. For the first time since my arrival, she'd stopped her ceaseless chatter, a relief in itself.

As we waited for the patient to inhale sufficient of the volatile vapour, the operating room sister, who now appeared to be the only composed professional in the room, set out an array of sterile surgical instruments and efficiently prepared sutures and gauze packs which later would be essential to staunch the anticipated blood loss. While the anaesthetic proceeded I rapidly applied the brown 'Betadine' antiseptic solution to the woman's protruding belly and placed the sterile drapes over her, leaving the lower abdomen exposed.

Never a courageous person, I had no surgical ambitions. My training since graduation had focussed on my need to acquire those skills I considered a good general practitioner required, concentrating on paediatrics, orthopaedics, obstetrics and general medicine. I was a GP, not a surgeon, but at this moment I needed to stop wallowing in self-doubt. I knew what was required of me and I had at least assisted with such procedures twice before, no matter how minor the role. I lightly prodded the prepared skin with the point of the scalpel. There was no response. This was it; the culmination of several years' medical training in anatomy and surgery, the summit of my brief career, and I was petrified!

Somewhere close at hand a loud self-assured voice stridently exclaimed.

"Better get started if we don't want an anaesthetised baby." I thought, 'Good heavens, was that really me?' I had adopted a new play-acting role as a Walter Mitty (4) prairie surgeon revealing a poise that would have done credit in any amateur dramatic society. Hesitantly I made the start of a shallow elliptical incision over the bikini line of the lower abdomen. The die was cast and it was essential there should be no delay. The unborn infant might expire at any moment. Speed was essential and there could be no holding back. This was now a race against time for this baby's life, which I was desperate not to lose.

As rapidly and carefully as I could, I separated the superficial muscle and warily entered the underlying peritoneal cavity. Exposing the uterus I announced to all within earshot that to save time and in an attempt to reduce blood loss I was not going to perform the conventional lower segment section but would make the older vertical incision into the uterus. Thus far it had been relatively easy, but from here onwards things were really going to heat up and within my head I could unmistakably hear the gathering storm motive from Beethoven's Pastoral Symphony.

With parched mouth and lips I searched to identify the empty urinary bladder. Careful to avoid any damage, I made a small incision in the uterus just above, which I rapidly extended upwards using scissors, with my fingers as guides, to ensure I didn't accidentally damage the infant immediately beneath as I had observed when previously assisting.

Within moments a baby's creamy white knee protruded, then a blood stained leg appeared and was thrust out. Through my mind ran the horror that I'd cut the child's leg, or worse still as I enlarged the slit upwards, followed by the appearance of a second leg, that I might inadvertently have amputated a tiny finger or toe, in my haste. Fearfully wondering whether in my rush I had damaged the infant with my cutting I continued my incision. With blood spouting from the uterine wound, there was little time to think, and certainly none to lose.

It was like being on automatic pilot, as Beethoven's Pastoral storm chords flooded through my mind. There was blood everywhere and except for its head the baby was emerging rapidly. I feverishly hastened to extract the baby, which was as slippery as an eel, and interrupted my mental concert as I called matron to have a small dose of 'ergometrine' ready to contract the womb, when I gave the word.

The baby's head finally came free with a further small gush of liquor amnii and I hurriedly laid the baby on a sterile towel on the mother's chest. I asked matron, who had remained uncharacteristically quiet, to administer the ergometrine, as I clamped and cut the umbilical cord, which had continued pulsating, before passing the baby, a girl, just as she started to emit her first mewling whimpers, to the waiting nurse. This weak distressing sound was repeated several times, and was then followed by a far shriller cry, as the nurse proceeded to clear the baby's airway with a tiny, transparent suction catheter. Deep inside I thought the short, high-pitched, atonal cries with which she announced her entry into the harsh reality of this world, the sweetest sounds I had ever heard. Fantastic; we had a live baby, but now I had to work just as rapidly to ensure there'd be a healthy mother to nurture her, before her life haemorrhaged away.

Frighteningly, blood was flooding everywhere and to staunch the loss from the gaping uterine wound I hurriedly commenced my surgical repair with a number of catgut sutures. After the first two stitches I paused in order to remove the placenta and then resumed, repairing and closing the uterus in layers. The remainder of the operation proceeded more slowly as I carefully ensured full haemostasis.

The theatre nurse confirmed the gauze swab and instrument count was correct and I requested the midwife caring for the baby to check the baby's fingers and toes, as I painstakingly repaired the last tissues that I had disturbed to gain access to the baby within the uterus. Some sixty minutes after we'd embarked upon the section I inserted my last silk suture into the patient's skin and applied a dressing. We were home and dry, with a healthy baby girl and a mother who should be fit and well enough to return home within days.

An experienced obstetrician might have found such a procedure routine and pedestrian. It left me in a temporary state of complete mental exhaustion. Initially there was no elation, simply relief, as I checked the newborn infant, including a further count of her fingers and toes. I returned to the changing room and changed back into my own clothes before joining the matron and assisting nurses in her office. Reviving cups of hot coffee and chocolate chip cookies were passed round but unfortunately matron had regained her earlier loquaciousness as I used my time to write up my surgical notes, together with the mother's medication and treatment charts.

In the waiting room I was delighted to offer personal congratulations to the overjoyed new father, who'd earlier been informed of the birth of his daughter and who now presented me with the traditional cigar. I reassured him his daughter had suffered no ill effects from her ordeal and was perfectly healthy, while he could see his wife once she'd recovered sufficiently from the anaesthetic. Confirming that I would return in the morning to check on the patient's progress I considered it expedient never to divulge this had been my first solo abdominal operation, firmly resolving it was to be a never repeated performance, should I be given any choice in the matter.

Collecting June from the waiting room I recounted the events of the evening on our more leisurely return journey. From my angst at a matron with verbal diarrhoea, who hadn't made time to attend to the most essential requirements; my despair on learning there was no anaesthetist, nor any blood available, followed by my elation at the baby's safe arrival and the successful evening's outcome.

First thing next morning, like a mother hen hastening to check it's young, I drove over to Frontier. Apart from a skin rash, possibly related to the antibiotic I'd prescribed, I found my patient was progressing well. Eight days after her confinement, she returned home with her thriving newborn daughter, having made an uneventful recovery, but with the warning that due to the scarring of her womb any future pregnancy might necessitate a further section.

Later that week, during Dr. K's continued absence; I was summoned urgently once more to rush to Frontier to attend another mother in labour with a complication. By the time I arrived, an efficient midwife had delivered the baby, but there was the problem of a retained placenta. This was something I'd never dealt with previously. I rapidly scrubbed up and in gown and sterile gloves proceeded to extract the placenta piecemeal from the uterine cavity. Fortunately, it was less complicated than I'd anticipated. There was minimal blood loss and when the removal was complete, the uterus contracted well. The emergency over and mindful of an increased possibility of infection, I wrote the patient up for a course of antibiotics and returned home, slowing down only when meeting traffic in the opposite direction, as I attempted to avoid the frequent occurrence of a cracked windscreen from stones thrown up by passing vehicles.

Dr. K returned following his week's vacation, but before the end of the year had left Frontier for greener pastures. I'd learned the average duration of a doctor's stay in these more remote areas was no more than three years. Frontier's replacement, Dr Cohen, arrived some weeks later from Holland. He and his family had lived through the Nazi occupation of their homeland during the war years without persecution since their Jewish ancestry had disappeared many generations previously. The family surname was all that remained of a lost, unwanted inheritance.

The following Saturday evening I was called urgently to Climax hospital, to see a young man and his girlfriend. Both were badly shaken and dishevelled, spattered virtually from head to toe in caked blood and dust indicating they'd been involved in some major incident, while the man had a blood soaked towel wrapped like a turban over his head, reminiscent of a Rembrandt painting.

Their story was that they had been driving in the dark, possibly a little too fast, with headlamps on, when out of the gloom a deer suddenly appeared at the side of the road. Startled, it leapt forward crossing in front of them. They braked violently as the animal jumped once more, just as their car collided with it. The front bumper and hood of the car struck the unfortunate beast. The impact threw the creature over the vehicle where it landed on the roof, before being thrown into the road. The hood, hinged at the front of the car was partially opened and jettisoned violently backwards, forcing it to shatter the windscreen as it crashed into the interior passenger compartment where it came to rest above the front passenger seats. Both driver and passenger were propelled violently forward. The girl narrowly missed the sharp metal edge of the hood, as she was the shorter of the two. The taller driver was less fortunate. The young lady, still shaking with shock, was relatively unharmed apart from minor cuts and bruises. Her companion was less fortunate; His

13

head was thrown onto the sharp metal hood that cleanly lacerated through much of his scalp.

I examined the man's wounds and to my horror found that close on 80% of the scalp's circumference, starting at the front hairline, had been almost surgically sliced through horizontally, apart from a connecting portion at the rear. This created a giant flap attached only at the back, revealing his ghoulishly glistening pale grey skull underneath. This man's guardian angel must have been watching over him that evening, as in my opinion he was the luckiest man alive. These were the days before restraining seat belts, and had such been used it is very possible that both might have been impaled, one of the unusual accidents where the use of such belts might have resulted in far more serious injury or even death. I imagined this was the type of injury the Plains Indians inflicted when they collected scalps in this region as recently as eighty years ago. The disastrous defeat inflicted on the US cavalry at the Little Big Horn River battle of 'Custer's Last Stand' **(5)** had taken place in 1876, not 300 miles to the south in Montana, where the soldiers had been mutilated by scalping.

I liberally sprinkled sterile sulphonamide powder onto the man's skull and under local anaesthetic hastily debrided and repaired this gigantic skin flap, which was akin to an enormous graft. I then applied a large gauze pressure dressing. I admitted him for observation and six days later his sutures were removed and thanks to his youth and a wonderful vascular supply, the wound had almost completely healed. Fortunately most of the scarring was hidden by his hairline.

Months later, a young man had been carried into the hospital in a dreadful state, having fared less well in his automobile accident, yet he was without a single broken bone or laceration. Driving far too fast, a recurring problem in this region of straight roads, young men and few motor vehicles to impede progress, his car had overturned on a bend in the approach road to Consul, a village 50 miles to the west of Eastend. In the absence of any restraining seat belt he'd been thrown out sustaining no more than a few bruises, but had somehow become pinned beneath the engine's upturned radiator, which slowly dripped its scalding contents over him. Conscious and unable to pull himself free, he'd endured the agony of burns from a dripping mixture of scalding water and antifreeze on his lower face, neck and chest.

Fortunately the occupants of a following vehicle, who'd witnessed the accident, raised the alarm. They and other rescuers rushed to the scene and were able to elevate the front of the car sufficiently to drag the trapped teenager clear, but not before he'd been badly scalded. He was in severe shock when brought to the hospital where I immediately gave him an injection of morphine and set up an Iv (intravenous) dextrose saline infusion. There were no bone or crush injuries that I could detect and I arranged for his urgent transfer by air ambulance to Saskatoon, where his extensive second and third degree burns could be dealt with. He made a tediously slow recovery with the need for periodic skin grafts, in spite of which he was left with extensive and unsightly residual scarring. Road speed had resulted in terrible suffering for this unwary young motorist.

(1) Merlin the Magician; a 5thCentury Welsh mystic, who was a tutor to Camelot's King Arthur.

(2) Albert Schweitzer (1875-1965) A German theologian, organist, writer and physician, became a medical missionary and founded a hospital in Lambarene, Gabon where he operated on, and treated large numbers of natives over many years. In recognition of his humanitarian services he received many honours, amongst which in 1952 was the Nobel Peace Prize.

(3) Lord Lister 1827-1912 the eminent English surgeon who first introduced carbolic acid (phenol) to clean surgical instruments, cleanse the skin and in which to wash hands prior to surgery to curb the incidence of infection. He also asked Mr Goodyear if he could make some rubber gloves for his operating room nurse who had developed a contact dermatitis to carbolic acid.

(4) Walter Mitty. One of several short stories, 'The Secret Life of Walter Mitty', was published in 'My World and Welcome to it.' in 1940 by American author James Thurber. In 1947 it was made into a successful film starring Danny Kaye. Walter Mitty is an inadequate hen pecked married man who spends his time daydreaming and fantasising. Escaping from reality he imagines himself in super heroic roles, one of which is as a world-renowned surgeon performing fantastically complicated operations.

(5) George A Custer (1839-1876) a charismatic cavalry officer, constantly disobeying orders to the point of being considered reckless. At the battle of Gettysberg in 1863 he became at 23, the youngest general in the Union army. Promoted beyond his level of competence, he led his cavalry ineptly against 'Sitting Bull' leading a large group of 'Native Americans' in May 1876. Without fully determining the strength of his enemy and confidently believing in the invincibility of his cavalry, he divided them into 3 groups before disobeying orders not to attack. The worst defeat in US cavalry history followed when he and all his men perished at the Battle of the Little Big Horn River.

Chapter 2

LONDON 1943 - 1952

In August 1943, when a schoolboy living in war torn London, I discovered I hadn't made the grade. I'd botched the national 'Eleven Plus' examination, my only opportunity to secure a grammar school place and from there, a university education. Just past my eleventh birthday, the system had judged me a dullard and failure, with all academic paths thereon permanently closed. No mitigation was accepted. To whom was I to explain, in those war years, so disruptive of family life that I simply wasn't ready for examinations at that time? Doubtlessly there were many children in a similar situation, but this didn't change my predicament.

My younger brother Michael was in an even more parlous state. At least I could read and write when at ten years of age I'd returned home after being evacuated, whereas he, two years younger, through no fault of his, could do neither. That my father hadn't dealt with these problems more vigorously, when he discovered them, remains a mystery.

From September 1939 my education stagnated for six months without adequate schooling and as an evacuee from March 1940 until the autumn of 1942, this state of affairs continued, in a remote village primary school. There, in a class of children supervised by one benevolently kind, but inept teacher, who, having accepted her impossible brief, had a predictable lack of success, my education languished further. The school was an imposing single room stone building with a towering high ceiling, roofed externally with slate surmounted by a bell tower. The winter's cold was barely blunted by a large open coal fire, while the toilets outside were unheated. Most days the class exceeded 50 children with ages ranging from 5 to 10 years and once enrolled, I became the unwitting victim of an elusive attempt at mass wartime education.

Days on end were passed in writing practice, as I copied the script from prewritten cards. Numeracy involved addition, subtraction and reciting tables by rote and nothing more. I never entered a library and was neither given, or encouraged to read a storybook, prose, or poetry and received nothing that could remotely pass for an acceptable education, until I returned to parental supervision in London aged almost eleven. I was the recipient of food, warmth and little else, with an absence of parental direction and guidance throughout that time.

Disconnected snippets of recollection go back to when I was aged three, although recall of events in progression, date from when I was seven. In 1939 the most dramatic of these related to my youngest brother Michael. He had a cold, which had worsened. Dr. Doran, a compassionate local GP, who on his visits, invariably rewarded us with a bright new halfpenny, inspected the thick yellow discharge from his left ear and diagnosed that my brother's constant crying, was due to a mastoid bone infection, which needed an urgent operation. Accompanied by floods of tears from my mother, Michael suddenly disappeared to nearby Great Ormond Street Children's Hospital. Weeks later he returned following surgery, minus the hearing in one ear, which intermittently discharged. Two days later, with siblings and grandmother gathered round a huge cake in the shape of a number five, we celebrated his birthday.

Another vivid memory at this time relates to regular visits for treatment at the Eastman Dental Clinic in Gray's Inn Road, following which my mother would be required to see the 'Lady Almoner'. She would question mother in her office with a peremptory means test to determine the fee that should be paid for my weekly treatment. I believe this was 6d, and an appropriate stamp would be glued to my record card to demonstrate that with each visit the assessed fee had been paid.

My introduction to World War II unconsciously began when I became aware of my father leaving home early each morning for days at a time. Together with other volunteers, he'd been meeting trainloads of young German Jewish refugee children at nearby Liverpool Street Station. That Sunday in late spring, seated with his five children round the lunch table, he patiently explained how these unfortunate youngsters had arrived in England, in order to escape Nazi persecution. Alone, in a foreign land unaccompanied by parents, urgent arrangements had been made to meet them and find each a suitable home. Only later did I understand the term Nazi, and the tragic significance of the tyranny from which these unhappy children had fled.

Many decades later, I quizzed mother about the event, asking why she hadn't offered a home to any of the relatives my parents had living in France and Poland, almost all of whom lost their lives in the 'Holocaust'. Her reply summed up the situation leaving little room for debate.

"Darling, I was a working mother with five young children of my own. The Germans were supposedly civilized people and we never dreamt in our wildest imagination what barbarous deeds they intended. It was completely inconceivable."

With the outbreak of war on September 3rd 1939 my parents rushed to improvise black out curtains from any dark fabric available. These were hung on rails over the bedroom and living room windows, to be tightly closed every night. My father instructed that they were to be drawn at dusk and must not be opened on any account until the morning. He also painted half the vertical side of every electric light bulb that faced a window black in order to reduce the light emission that might inadvertently shine through a window. We were instructed how to recognise the air raid alert siren with its distinctive slow warbling sound, indicating an imminent air raid and the urgent need to seek shelter, followed later by one single note, to designate 'all clear'.

Gas masks were issued at school. We were each provided with a practical demonstration of how to don and use these frightful and uncomfortable dark grey rubber contrivances. The masks were supplied in brown cardboard boxes, which measured about six inches cubed and we were expected to carry this mask in its container over our shoulder supported by a short length of string, whenever we left home in case of a gas attack. My father's younger brother Harry, a handbag manufacturer, suddenly found himself inundated with work to provide leather and fabric box covers to house these masks, together with smarter and more comfortable leather straps to replace the lengths of string issued for carrying them.

In the days following the declaration of war, a massive and brilliantly organised, transport operation was implemented, to evacuate school children, distancing them from major city centres, to avoid possible casualties from aerial bombardment. Within days, trains and coaches had transported hundreds of thousands of school children, my siblings and I included, away from our parents in the centre of London, to be billeted with unknown foster parents, in safe outlying rural areas.

My older brothers Peter and Maurice were evacuated to Ely in Cambridgeshire, while with my sister Gloria and youngest brother Michael I was evacuated to Black Horse Grove in Cambridgeshire. We remained there for approximately one week, crying ourselves to sleep each night. A childless middle-aged railway-crossing keeper and his wife whose home lay a few yards from the railway track were our foster parents. The single story three-room cottage, with no acknowledgment of any modern amenity was small and simple, with a living room kitchen and two bedrooms. In the kitchen, beneath a window, was a brown stoneware sink with a long black handled water pump providing cold water for cooking and washing, a coal burning stove for cooking and a solitary oil lamp hanging from the ceiling for light. There was no electricity, no gas, no radio and no telephone. There was no bath, or bathroom, while a small garden shed housed a soil toilet where pieces of torn newsprint were used as toilet paper. The road and rail crossing was not busy and we were permitted to help open and close the hinged railway gates. After a few days I was allowed, to my delight, to perform this task without supervision. The single room schoolhouse was a considerable walking distance to which we trudged each day with increasing reluctance, feeling miserable and home sick.

Our parents came to visit at the weekend and were horrified to see us performing tasks as unsupervised railway guards, working and controlling the level crossing gates. No matter how sparse the rail and road traffic, this was not an assignment for young children, and regardless of the war they promptly took us home.

I remained in London until the following March, just prior to the miraculous naval evacuation of the BEF (British Expeditionary Forces) from Dunkirk. During a portion of this time I attended the Robert Montefiore School weekday mornings and in the afternoons played in St. Luke's churchyard in Ironmonger Row and frequented the streets round our home witnessing, in wonderment the varied preparations for war. I would watch as sand was delivered by the truckload and heaped on pavements where home-guard volunteers, air raid wardens (ARP) and soldiers would together shovel it into Hessian sacks, which would then be sealed and placed as a wall round the door openings and ground floor windows of banks, post offices and important buildings. Close to home, in Old Street, several single storey concrete flat roofed, windowless brick buildings were rapidly constructed on the pavement, which at that point was particularly wide, which were designed to provide shelter in an air raid, for anything other than a direct hit. Visits to Hyde Park revealed several large military trucks, each with its giant reel of steel cable attached to which, floating high in the sky above were the bobbing glistening silver leviathan 'Barrage Balloons', to protect London from low flying enemy aircraft. Elsewhere in the park men were digging trenches.

Windows of shops, public transport vehicles and some homes were criss-crossed with lengths of thick brown sticky tape to prevent flying glass injuries in the event of a bomb explosion, while motor vehicles had black slatted covers placed over headlamps. Police and volunteer A.R.P. (air raid precaution) wardens wore black steel helmets with white capital letters printed on the front denoting the wearer's occupation, while all, regardless of age or rank, carried the cardboard box within which reposed a personal gas mask. Talk between father and his friends after the start of the war knowingly concluded with;

"It'll all be over before Christmas, you'll see." After that first subdued festive season had passed, with the arrival of 1940, during the months known as the 'phoney war', these same voices optimistically predicted, "The war'll soon be over."

In March, with the arrival of my father's French cousin, Sylvain Podguzer at our home, there was a general air of excitement. A slim balding furrier, in his late thirties, he'd been smuggled out of France with my father's help.

In early 1940, in spite of the war, my father had been to Paris on one of his frequent business visits with his sales representative. Not unlike the 'Scarlet Pimpernel' (1), he had managed, using his representative's ticket, to assist him and another cousin, to board what was to be one of the last cross channel passenger ferries sailing from France to England, until the war's end. I recall our childish excitement as Sylvain related seeing a flight of German twin engine war planes flying low over Paris which had been declared an 'open city', and dropping leaflets instead of bombs on the terrified inhabitants.

In late March 1940, six months after returning home, I was evacuated a second time; my sister and youngest brother did not join me. On this occasion I accompanied my 12-year-old brother Maurice, when he was evacuated with his school, the JFS, (Jews Free School) (2). One of possibly a hundred school children, we walked in line, in pairs through central London with beige luggage labels bearing name and address attached by string to coat lapels, not unlike outsize self-propelled mobile postal packages. In the pocket of my over-long navy blue rain-coat, for new clothes were always purchased several sizes too large so that one could grow into them, although most clothes were hand-me-downs from older siblings or cousins, was pinned a carefully folded stamped addressed envelope that I had been given by my mother. Her parting instructions were to print my new address carefully on the rear and to mail it home the next day. We each bore the obligatory dark grey rubber gas mask carried in its box over one shoulder by an attached length of cord and in tiny hands many carried a small duffle bag or package, with immediate necessities packed by anxious mums and dads.

We had no idea where we were being taken, as foot weary and bedraggled we arrived at a railway station that ultimately linked us with Paddington Station. Escorted by a few teachers, with our destination completely unknown, we marched onto the platform and were provided with a package of sandwiches by grey uniformed ladies as we boarded a passenger train with a haversack of clothes. Tired, apprehensive and yet at times elated by this adventure, we set out upon our journey into the unknown. As our flight, continued hour after hour, taking us further from home, speculation and rumour mounted as to our final destination.

The journey was interminably long. The train stopped about twice where groups of children from other schools disembarked and we were served water and cold drinks, which were passed into the train from the platform, by lady volunteers since we were not permitted to alight. After many hours, we crossed the unmarked boundary from Devon into Cornwall and finally arrived at Penzance rail terminus, a journey in excess of 250 miles. It was early evening and through carriage windows we had caught sight of a majestic but distant, St. Michael's Mount and the closer sands of Marazion Bay. Periodically there

20

were glimpses of the tumultuous grey-green sea and morale soared as we imagined some seaside holiday resort as an exciting temporary home.

Unkempt and far too weary to be frightened, flagging spirits soared as we realized excitedly that we were in a seaside town. All chatted excitedly with the recall of earlier seaside visits, playing on sandy beaches, an ice cream cone in hand, with expectations of similar treats in store. Disappointingly we were directed onto several coaches waiting in the station forecourt and realised as we were whisked away into the dusk, this was not our destination. With fragile hopes unfulfilled, moods plummeted to match the approach of deepening twilight as our transport conveyed us on a winding coastal road through Newlyn, with its fishing fleet, the black registration numbers prefaced by the letters PZ painted on both sides of every bow, at overnight anchor in the harbour, all the village lights blacked out. The buses rolled still further onwards as we dozed fitfully, only the driver's frequent gear changes breaking the monotony until we must surely run out of purple road and land on which to travel. Passing the isolated Penlee Point lifeboat station, we reached the small picturesque fishing village of Mousehole, where all was concealed by darkness in the blackout. There, we were unceremoniously deposited outside the village hall.

Utterly fatigued, we climbed out of the coach to be herded into the forbidding quarry stone building, a group of bewildered and bedraggled parentless lambs, some of the younger runny nosed children crying, in spite of the kindly but curious adults who provided each child with a refreshing mug of hot cocoa set out on bench tables within the brightly illumined hall. Hot chocolate was a loathsome beverage to me, and I wouldn't drink mine, which with no alternative, left me thirsty and even more miserable as a small, steady stream of adults arrived. Each villager then selected one or two of these strangely accented London evacuees to take into their homes for what was to be the duration of the war. Two bespectacled grey haired ladies sat at a small oblong table by the main doorway entrance, protected within by a heavy blackout curtain, sheaths of papers on the makeshift desk, pens in hand, as they linked names of evacuees with prepared typewritten names and address of those to whom children were allocated to be billeted.

To these poor industrious fishermen, farmers and their wives, this was an act of immense charity. However to those of us who stood standing in intimidated groups it felt as though we were in some inhumane cattle market waiting to be inspected. Somebody even felt my spindly lean thigh as though determining its width and texture determining whether the weekly government allowance (**M1**) would be an adequate recompense with which to feed me. At seven years of age I was pathetically thin, standing on broomstick legs with a mop of unruly dark brown hair that hadn't seen a barber's scissors in countless months. Fretful parents had, time and again, given strict instructions over the previous days to my brother and I, that on no account were we to be separated. At this juncture we stuck together like limpets on the seashore and few foster parents seemed willing to take two boys. Consequently we were the last children in the hall. Finally a lady was persuaded to accept us. We accompanied her outside into the dark, silent street. It was cold and our adopted mother spoke with a curt authority.

"You can call me Nanny." Followed by. "Buck up you two. Look lively and follow me."

We walked a little over half a mile in the blackout along a frighteningly silent coastal road, two unkempt totally worn out walking zombies, as we accompanied her to what was to be our new home. We were shown to our bedroom, where too drained to feel hunger or thirst, we instantly fell asleep.

The following morning we descended for breakfast. As we ate our porridge Nanny explained the house rules.

"I'll brook no nonsense." She elaborated.

Her regulations included eating everything that was served on ones plate at mealtimes. If not eaten, it would be served at the next meal and so on, until it was eaten. Further, we were threatened that if we wasted food the matter would be reported to the minister for food, Lord Woolton, and a custodial sentence or being whipped with a 'cat o' nine tails', were but two of many possible punishments for infringing rules. Meals, which from my perspective had seldom been enjoyable occasions, became increasingly fraught, as I believed all these terrifying threats. Surreptitiously I learnt to conceal unwanted food in my pocket-handkerchief and pockets to be discarded at the earliest opportunity, after the meal, in the street, or down the toilet. Every morning before breakfast, we were each required to visit the toilet and any lack of bowel movement was to be reported, so that we might be given medicine to purge out the 'impurities'.

The nation was intoxicated with the need for daily bowel activity. These thoughts permeated every level of society. Adults lustily swallowed 'Bile Beans', 'Ex-lax Chocolate' and any purgative to obtain a regular motion. In addition the more affluent indulged in regular colonic irrigations and enemata, while children were not to be ignored and must be conditioned into this national bowel fetish with a regular weekly dose of 'syrup of figs', together with a spoonful of malt and cod liver oil, administered at school. Had the German High Command appreciated this national Achilles heel, they might have brought the country to its knees, without firing a shot and ended the war by cutting off the supply of laxatives for a month.

Baths would be available once a week, which was normal, but in view of the war only six inches of tepid water was permitted and we would have to share the bath, one after the other. Bad language was forbidden. On one occasion when aged 8, I had my mouth washed out with soap and water and admonished never to use that disgusting 'F' word. I had no idea what the word meant, but after such draconian measures to expunge it from my vocabulary, I made it a priority to discover its meaning. It was a great revelation to discover how many of the older boys, all swearing me to secrecy, were prepared to explain the term in luridly inaccurate pre-adolescent detail.

It was difficult to imagine how so large a number of evacuees were accommodated in such a small village. Within a matter of days a trickle returned home and this drift back to London continued so that by the time of my return late in 1942 there were very few remaining in the village.

In August 1940 the 'Battle of Britain' began. Each day, seated with the adults we listened intently to the small radio for the 6 o'clock news bulletins, forbidden to make any noise that might impede the sounds of the clear enunciation of the newscaster reaching the listener's ears. The initial onslaught was fought over airfield installations and in dogfights between British single engine Hurricane and Spitfire fighters and German bombers and fighter planes in the skies above the south coast. On September 7th 1940 the anticipated German bombing raids on London commenced. By the end of September the Nazi Luftwaffe plane losses were sufficiently heavy that raids from then onwards took place, predominantly at night. These intensive nocturnal bombing raids on London continued relentlessly, night after night, for two months and then sporadically thereafter until ceasing temporarily in May 1941 as the Nazi war juggernaut turned eastwards to attack first Greece and Yugoslvia and then in August, the Soviet Union. I recall feeling perplexed that some months earlier the public were being encouraged to provide funds for the beleaguered but heroic Finns to fight the Red Army, while now the public was being asked to contribute money for the Red Army to fight the Finns who were allied to the Germans. During the period of heaviest bombing raids, my mother, grandmother and other female family members with young children rented two small houses in Newlyn, returning to London once the severest air raid threats had passed.

Two days after our arrival in Mousehole, Nanny took me to Lardner's barbershop (M2), in a small parade of tiny shops facing the tidal harbour, where my hair was removed. Using clippers, he unceremoniously clipped and hacked off all but the shortest stubble leaving me to resemble a grossly malnourished undersized juvenile military conscript, with protruding ears. Some weeks later in spite of this tonsorial escapade, I still encountered the ubiquitous scourge of the head louse, and a prolonged course of treatment, in company with many others in my class proved essential. My mother, had she witnessed my haircut, or known of this later infestation, would have been mortified and must surely have died of shame to think of one of her offspring having 'a dirty head of hair'. At least my scalp wasn't painted with the deep violet dye the district nurse applied liberally to most of the head and face of one of the young evacuees who had the crusted stigmata of impetigo that he nervously and constantly picked.

I remained in Cornwall for more than two years, which from a child's point of view were happy, riotously undisciplined times, playing on rocky beaches, midst pools of sea water, catching fish with bent pins on the end of home made fishing lines, watching sea anemones and crustacean feed, where formal education was barely a consideration. Each summer, for weeks at a time we were instructed to avoid areas of the village because of annual outbreaks of diphtheria and polio.

In the autumn of 1942 having returned to the reality of life in London to rejoin parents and family, I was enrolled in the De Bohun Primary School in Southgate. Here accompanied by my father I met Mr. Searle, the headmaster to whom dad's parting words, deliberately spoken in my presence, were;

"You may only punish my son for any wrong doing on the understanding you first inform me. I can then guarantee whatever you give him, I'll double the tariff when he arrives home." My father wasn't jesting, and with this admonition uppermost in my thoughts, I believe I may have been considered a tolerably well-behaved schoolboy most of the time.

At the end of my first term examinations in December I came fourth from bottom, out of a wartime class of 53 children. 49 symbolised my lucky number for a time; seven squared, as well as the invisible latitude meridian separating Canada from the USA which I discovered years later, when I crossed it regularly by car over one of the roughest dirt roads imaginable. At some time past, my parents must have looked forward to the possibility that I might have shown some academic promise, but my lacklustre performance clearly revealed this was not the case. I later realised their expectations of my potential were not to be dimmed so readily.

In May 1943 I was scheduled to sit the written examination that all 11 year olds seeking a grammar school education were required to take and pass. On that important morning of the 'eleven plus', I was to ride my recently acquired second hand bicycle the 15 minutes journey from home to Minchenden Grammar School in Southgate, which was where I was to report at 9 am alongside the other hopefuls to take this vital written test.

I had allowed myself an ample 30 minutes for the mile and a half journey, and had cycled almost half way on that pleasantly warm sunny morning, when disaster struck. The bicycle chain came off the rear wheel driving cogs and my cycle rapidly came to a halt. Had I left the cycle and walked, I would have arrived on time. This trouble had occurred before and apart from the resulting oily fingers presented no insurmountable difficulty. On this occasion the disengaged chain wedged itself firmly between the wheel cogs and the frame to which the rear wheel was attached. In my panic, no matter how hard I tugged and pulled, I couldn't budge it since I had no tools to provide any leverage.

A passing cyclist noticed my difficulty and generously stopped to assist. He carried a screwdriver in his cycle tool kit and within a couple of minutes my cycle chain had been reengaged to its metallic cogged protuberances. It was shortly after 9am and I was late. Remounting my cycle and pedalling furiously, I seemed to fly along the road, in my attempt to make up for lost time. Fingers, hands and various parts of my jacket cuffs and short grey trousers bore the black oily evidence of my encounter with the well-lubricated chain. I wiped the perspiration from my brow and never gave consideration to the trails of finger marks, which indelibly betrayed my earlier predicament.

Arriving flustered and late at the examination venue, I saw the last of the children who were to participate in the marathon filing into classrooms, where invigilators were in readiness. In no way could I join them and instead found my way to the school washroom where with soapy cold water, I vainly attempted to clean and remove the sticky oil that stubbornly encrusted fingers and hands. If only there had been a scrubbing brush with a little hot water. It felt a little like the famous ride in George Herbert's poem 'For the sake of a nail the shoe was lost'. I spent what seemed an eternity trying unsuccessfully, to remove, the unsightly black tacky oil that clung to every part of me that had contacted the chain. Since there was no mirror, my face remained unwashed. In a feverish rush I found my allotted classroom. Timidly knocking, I entered and midst snickers from the clean, neatly engrossed participants completing their test papers, I hesitantly reported, to the invigilator and requested permission to join the class.

Three months later an envelope arrived from the examining board addressed to my parents. It announced in a stereotyped letter, an inability to provide a grammar school place for the applicant Arnold Powell, whose examination performance had not achieved the required level of competence. In company with many thousands of other failed eleven year olds, I was consigned to an ignominious secondary modern school education for three years, to fulfil the requirements of the most recent education act, before being discarded at 14 onto the blue collar job market.

My father however thwarted this agenda. While the words attributed to Cecil Rhodes (3) might still have rung true:

"To be born English is to win first prize in the lottery of life." I had one enormous advantage of which Rhodes was unaware; the privilege of Jewish parents who cared. My father steadfastly resolved that his children, had they any semblance of ability, should receive those scholastic benefits, that his financially challenged immigrant parents had been unable to provide.

* * *

Changing from the unscathed wartime safety of Cornwall I rapidly familiarised myself with the conditions, which then prevailed in London. There were occasional air raids and whole areas of devastation were to be seen where buildings had been bombed and flattened, leaving large fenced off derelict basements supporting a plethora of weeds and in the summer a profusion of small colourful wild flowers. Locally there were a few houses that had been bombed and were abandoned ruins. These properties were not fenced off and provided wonderfully exciting and dangerous areas for older children's games of exploration and destruction.

Travelling on the underground, every platform was lined with metal bunks, three tiers high, where people slept at night during the worst of the night air raids, carrying their bedding with them. In spite of inadequate washing facilities and the persistent noise of tube trains, absent at night for no more than five hours at any time, these refuges of safety had proven popular during the heavier night raids in central London. Sadly one of these natural shelters produced one of the worst civilian disasters of the war in Bethnal Green (4).

I invariably cycled to school. Every Monday morning we had to take milk money (M3), which entitled each child to a daily allowance of one third of a pint of milk, while some children purchased a double daily quantity. The milk was distributed and drunk from the bottle during the morning break. School dinners, which cost 5d pence (2p), were mandatory. We were also encouraged to buy National Savings Certificates to 'Help Win the War'. These cost 15 shillings (75p.) each and could be acquired by buying six pence (2½p.) saving stamps, which were stuck in a small savings book. Once thirty of these stamps had been purchased they could be exchanged for the prized savings certificate. We were encouraged to save in order that England could buy one more Hurricane fighter, which each cost £5,000, with which to defeat the Germans.

Whenever the air raid warning sounded in school time, pupils and staff had to cease their activities, straight away. All had to proceed in a practiced, rapid and orderly manner, without pushing talking or shouting, out of the school building to the long, partially subterranean air raid shelters, which had been constructed hastily in the playing field closest to the school. These shelters were of a thick, dark grey, bare concrete, externally roofed over with grass and protruded 5 feet above the rest of the field, like a series of giant worm casts, designed to give protection from bomb blast. We approached the shelter from one end descending a few steps, then had to make a right angle turn to enter the shelter which was long and narrow, with slatted wooden benches lining each wall leaving a central walk way about 7 feet high, from the roof of which hung the bare light bulbs which provided the shelter with a minimal amount of light. Nobody was permitted to leave until the all clear had sounded. Any prior attempt to collect a coat from the cloakroom, or any other detour was strictly forbidden, which could make life rather uncomfortable, since there was no heat and no facilities for refreshment, or toilet. Most of us became quite adept at recognising the various aeroplane engine sounds and could in this way detect a German plane as opposed to the friendly allied varieties.

One night in the spring of 1943 the air raid warnings had sounded just minutes earlier, when with the frightening drone of enemy planes overhead a stick of incendiary bombs suddenly struck the street in which our house nestled. One passed through the bedroom I shared with my brothers striking the edge of a bed, exploding and burning on the wooden floor in the lounge below. At the time, my eldest brother, home on leave, managed to hurl the burning fragments out into the garden, using a spade. One bomb severed the water main and a further two struck the garage. At daybreak the ARP arrived and together we spotted the remains of a further 5 incendiaries in the garden, which hadn't exploded and numerous pieces of jagged metal from anti-aircraft shells.

At the time of my arrival in Cockfosters there appeared in the service roads a number of long, low-slung, multi-wheeled, camouflaged military vehicles. These were immense exhaust spewing, diesel powered tank carriers that belonged to a Canadian Tank company. Occasionally they were loaded with camouflaged tanks with large 5 pointed white stars painted on the sides. Over the months these vehicles increased in number and at times were covered by camouflage netting until early in 1944 when they and their crews mysteriously disappeared.

Occasionally I was called upon to help with the shopping since almost every essential food commodity could be obtained only by standing in a queue. Worst of all was to shop in Sainsbury, where one had to queue at one counter for butter then at another with its patiently waiting line of housewives for cheese, a separate counter for eggs and boxes of dried eggs, and yet another for sugar etc. all in one shop. On these forays I was provided with money and the appropriate ration books without which no rationed item could be purchased, with mother's oft-repeated admonition not to lose them.

On the morning of my parent's 21st wedding anniversary, June 6th 1944, the unusual roar of a large number of low level planes flying overhead awakened me. Rushing to the bedroom window and looking up into a clear sky, an awe-inspiring sight was revealed. What I had believed from the engine noises to be a group of low flying planes was in fact something entirely different. High overhead was the largest aerial armada I had ever witnessed. Formations of Planes were flying eastwards. There were remarkably huge groups of four engine Lancaster and flying fortress bombers and twin engine Dakotas, many towing large gliders. I stood staring skyward in amazement through an open bedroom window at wave after wave of hundreds upon hundreds of allied planes flying eastwards, a breath taking and inspiring sight that I have never forgotten.

Later in the morning we saw many of these flights returning minus the gliders. The 1 p.m. news broadcast announced the D-Day landings in Normandy. Other large flights of planes had been seen and were yet to be seen, but none were as formidable as those witnessed that day. Later we understood the reason the tanks, crews and tank-carriers had vanished from the service roads some weeks earlier.

While following the progress of the battles in Normandy a new and frightening phenomenon appeared in the form of the V-1 flying bomb. The V-1, 'doodlebug' was an ugly squat, black, short winged, low flying pilotless plane. It was launched from concrete bunkers along the coast of Northern France and heralded the newest German terror technology. The high rear mounted rocket engine, coughing guttural sound and flame, was marginally less terrifying than the abrupt absence of sound, which followed, as the engine precipitously cut out, leaving the plane to dive steeply earthwards. There followed a sickeningly brief, stomach-knotting silence, and moments later came the sound of a loud, earth shaking explosion, rattling windows and doors in their frames for miles around, as the 1,000 lb. V-1 bomb indiscriminately struck a civilian target and simultaneously fear into the hearts of those in the vicinity who were not killed and maimed. Repeated air raid sirens disrupting the day's routine were once more a daily occurrence and the closest of these bombs landed a little over a quarter of a mile away from where I lived, late one evening, in Cat Hill.

In August, Paris was liberated. The Russians were advancing rapidly in the east and jubilant talk, of an early end to the war had resurfaced when in the autumn of 1944, standing in one of central London's streets I heard a distant loud bang followed by a rumbling, whooshing reverberation, not unlike the noise one hears as a train approaches rapidly in an underground railway station. There had been no air raid warning and I thought no more about it. Similar explosions were heard over the next few days, always followed by the same approaching reverberating, rushing sound. Two weeks elapsed before the public were informed that a German supersonic rocket bomb, the

V-2, was causing the mysterious explosions. There was no defence available and the only thing the allied armies could do was to capture the sites from which these devices were being launched and to retaliate with enormous mass air raids upon major German towns and cities, which were devastated in firestorms, the worst being the raid on Dresden.

Decades later these raids were described by some, as disproportionate responses. The German people democratically elected, and enthusiastically supported a leader who cared not one iota about raining death and destruction indiscriminately upon defenceless civilians and centres of population, over many years when the Nazi's were winning, from the Spanish Civil War onwards. I believe that those who initiate war as an alternative to negotiation should expect little sympathy when counting the horrendous cost that warfare visits upon them. Winston Churchill rebuked a critic of area bombing.

"Remember this. Let 'em have it. Never maltreat the enemy by halves."

The Christmas period at the end of 1944 was particularly cold and frosty. Visibility was extremely poor with mist and fog and the majority of allied planes were grounded for more than two weeks. The allied military, fighting in Western Europe, suffered a temporary set back known as 'The Battle Of The Bulge', as German forces taking advantage of the absence of allied air power, mounted what was to be their last major counterattack. Once the weather improved, the formidable British and American warplanes were airborne again. As good visibility returned the vast allied air superiority halted and then reversed the German advance, to be followed with a continuing rout of the Nazi war machine. Then in April, I recall vividly the shock as we learned of FDR's (President Roosevelt) death in his fourth term of office from a CVA (cerebro-vascular accident, or stroke).

The Germans surrendered unconditionally in May. VE day (Victory in Europe) had arrived. Accompanied by my younger brother Michael we went by tube to the centre of London, to congregate in London's main thoroughfares joining hundreds of thousands of others with similar sentiments. It was exceptionally difficult to walk anywhere, as pavements and roads were jammed with people, completely halting the movement of all vehicular traffic above ground. The crowds were enormous. I had never seen or imagined such huge numbers of people crowded anywhere. In Aldwych, outside Somerset House, Churchill appeared at a large open double window to wave to the crowd, where we stood and gave his famous, palm outermost middle and index finger "V" sign.

Two or three days later a street party for children was spontaneously organised in our road. Chairs and tables were hastily gathered from nearby homes and every local child was invited to a tea party, organised by groups of women to eat jellies, cakes, chocolate and some of the hoarded delicacies that many of us had never previously seen. These tea parties were replicated throughout every community in the country. In every village and town, streets became rivers of colour, where bunting and flags of every hue, shape and size, were hung from lampposts and across the gables of houses and windows, to provide a welcome festive appearance. The blackout was at an end, but rationing continued, with increasing severity, as did the war against Japan.

Cinemas projected news films revealing the entry of allied liberators into Nazi concentration camps. These movies were horrific and appallingly exposed the indescribable inhumane treatment by the Germans of Jewish and other prisoners. The few emaciated surviving inmates bore witness, if any were needed, of the Nazi's heartless barbarity towards their fellow man.

With the European campaign ended, there was a general election. Winston Churchill's coalition wartime government came to an end and was replaced by a labour government under Clement Attlee, the period of gratitude for Churchill's national leadership proving to be of extremely brief duration.

*   *   *

Aged 14, in the summer of 1946, at the finish of my secondary school education, when those failed 11 plus students in my school year commenced what for the majority was to be a lifetime of servile menial work, my father did more than any parent to change the course of events in my education and future. By dint of perseverance and persuasion he found, a headmaster at a local grammar school willing to use me in an experiment that had recently commenced in a few other colleges, to determine whether a failed late entrant could compete successfully with incumbent brighter grammar school students. He secured a place for me in the co-educational third year, in which there were four streams. I was to enter the second or 'B stream' to complete a five-year grammar school syllabus in three years. The headmaster William Auger, who two years previously had been promoted from chemistry master to principal at Southgate County Grammar School, was prepared to permit me to compete in this experiment, as a late entrant.

The first time I met Willie Auger, he must have been a little over sixty years of age. A tall stocky grey man, almost bald, he had a pleasantly cheerful disposition in spite of the fact that he could barely walk. He used two walking sticks on which he leaned heavily to assist him as he slowly progressed on his way, taking minuscule steps, a few inches at a time. He lived next door to the school in Fox Lane and I believe he had severe arthritis, or some similar hip condition. He appeared to be unable to flex either hip joint, since when ascending stairs he had to walk backwards, supporting his weight on the hand rail and always sat on a high stool when relieving his legs of his body's weight.

He was a courageous man, who retired from the school in 1950, a year before I completed my sixth form school studies and to whom, with my father, I owe an immense debt of gratitude.

There were an almost inexhaustible number of important events that I witnessed in the immediate post war period. A number of the most significant seemed to coalesce during 1947 and 1948, which might well be my perception, as I entered my teens. The war had ended abruptly on 14 August 1945 with the aerial destruction by atomic bomb some days earlier of two Japanese cities; first Hiroshima followed one week later by Nagasaki. The newsreels showing the destructive power and the resulting huge mushroom cloud were too horrendous for words.

Following the immediate post war euphoria, the Labour government of Clement Attlee was beset with problems from every quarter. The most notable events that come to mind were the severe shortages and diminished ration allocations in 1946 and 1947. These culminated in one of the severest winters in 1947 made worse by frequent power cuts, due in part to the ineptitude of Emmanuel Shinwell the Labour minister of fuel, who seemed too busily engrossed in nationalising the coal industry than making adequate provision of fuel stocks for power stations and domestic use.

In addition there were the international problems, most notably in the Middle East, India, Ceylon and Malaya, where former colonies and dependencies strove for independence. The Queen's uncle, Lord Louis Mountbatten, later assassinated with a grandson, by the IRA in 1979, was appointed Viceroy of India in order to oversee its partition and independence, where in January 1948 Mahatma Ghandi, a barrister and one of the most charismatic and saintly figures of the age was assassinated by a gunman.

Foreign Secretary Ernest Bevin deserved the opprobrium heaped upon him, by forcing holocaust survivors attempting to reach succour in Palestine to be imprisoned in Cyprus and then to be returned to German prison camps. Finally he mismanaged British stewardship of Palestine necessitating its hand over to the UN. A United Nations partition plan for the former mandate was voted upon and agreed. In May 1948 Israel declared its independence and was promptly invaded by neighbouring Arab armies on all sides, which ignored the UN resolution. Disastrously intent on eliminating a non Muslim state, in their midst, no matter how insignificantly small compared with the vast tracts of under populated, undeveloped Arab lands, these states failed.

Churchill's 1946 prophecy, delivered in a speech in Fulton Missouri, of a curtain of iron descending over Europe was proven correct as the Soviet Union blockaded Berlin, which was then effectively supported by a memorable allied 'Berlin air-lift'.

Everything was certainly not gloom and despair at this time. A silver tongued Welsh Minister of Health, Aneurin Bevan, initiated the National Health Service in 1948 by stampeding, with persuasion and guile, the entire medical profession into embracing this momentous social reform. He publicly predicted that the projected enormous annual cost of almost £50 million pounds would in time diminish. He asserted that as the health of the nation incrementally improved, patients would utilise the service less frequently, with a corresponding cost reduction. As we repeatedly learn to our dismay, glib politicians always make it sound convincing but invariably get it wrong.

Both in 1946 and again in 1947 I travelled abroad with my parents to Italy, Switzerland and France, meeting French family members who had survived the war. I met Roger Podguzer, a cousin almost my age for the first time and heard the soulful voice of a small French chanteuse, Edith Piaf, whose unforgettable voice described as black velvet was all the rage in France. In Paris all the motor vehicles had solid tyres and were old and decrepit, often with car parts held on by lengths of string. There was no milk. The bread was grey in colour, with apricot preserve the only addition to a frugal breakfast with bitter black coffee, yet the French appeared happy in spite of their austerity and inflation and I did not witness the horrendous post war poverty in Northern Italy, with many people in rags often barefoot and hungry, begging in the streets.

London staged the first post war Olympic Games; the most outstanding competitors were Emil Zatopek a Czech long distance runner and Fanny Blankers-Koen a Dutch housewife who captured four gold medals in track events together with the hearts and admiration of all who watched. Many of my friends and I booked tickets, as frequently as could be afforded, at the London Palladium where each month a succession of top rank American entertainers appeared, amongst whom I saw Bing Crosby, Ethel Merman, Carmen Miranda, Frank Sinatra and many others. My favourite, by far, was the comedian, Danny Kaye (10), who I saw on his opening night in 1948. It was the custom that all the main acts came on after the intermission. A slim smartly dressed man in his mid 30's, with a mop of fair auburn hair, walked to the centre of the stage as the curtain rose and stood there. An embarrassed silence ensued for about half a minute when he emitted a small shriek, exclaiming

"I'm so nervous, I'm shaking like a leaf!" following which, midst howls of laughter and to the delight of the audience he performed non-stop for more than an hour. At a performance some days later, the Royal family deserted the royal box to sit in the front row of the orchestra stalls, enjoying themselves and laughing along with the audience.

* * *

Academically all went well until September 1948, the start of the third and final year of the grammar school experiment. I had competed well with the other pupils and appeared amongst the top in my class when fate, took a malevolent hand. Vacationing with my parents in Northern Italy in August of that year, mother and I had diluted our red wine with water, which had unknowingly been drawn from a well contaminated with the bacterium Salmonella Typhi.

The symptoms did not manifest themselves until almost three weeks later once we had returned to England. My mother consulted Dr. G. our local GP, whose practice was at the end of the road. Confronted with a patient with a 'pyrexia of unknown aetiology', he failed to identify the cause of her febrile illness, delaying her hospital admission until a second medical opinion had been obtained. As a consequence she almost lost her life before being admitted to the isolation unit at the Barnet General Hospital with typhoid fever.

A week earlier my brother and I had joined my mother's sister Minnie, her husband Bert and their two sons at a holiday camp in Littlehampton and knew nothing of these events as they unfolded. Minnie was mother's youngest sister whose husband Bert Ross was an estate agent employed by his eldest brother Bennett in Cricklewood. Bert had enlisted in the RAF at the start of the war and was posted as an NCO to the Far East. When he returned home he regaled us with graphic accounts of his experiences as one of the personnel who first entered a Japanese prisoner of war camp in Malaysia releasing the starved and emaciated allied prisoners of war. Some years later, as a smoker in his mid 40's, he developed Berger's disease (thrombo-angitis obliterans), which necessitated the amputation of a leg. Having adapted to his prosthesis he returned to work. About six months later when receiving his weekly pay packet his brother announced.

"Here's your money Bert. Collect your things and don't bother coming in on Monday."

While this message might have devastated a lesser man, in retrospect it turned out to be a piece of good fortune. My father stepped into the breach providing temporary employment for Minnie, while Bert was pushed into opening his own estate agency, in a small office a few doors from his brother, trading as Albert and Co. Within a year his business was sufficiently viable to employ his wife as an assistant and from then onwards he prospered in a manner, which would have been impossible in his brother's employ.

When I became unwell my aunt communicated with father, who with his brother in law, my uncle Titch Defries, immediately collected me by car and drove me to London where I was admitted to the same isolation unit as my mother. Unaware of my surroundings for many days, I later learned that I'd been admitted to the Barnet General. Desperately sick, I remained in barrier-nursed seclusion in the next room to my mother in excess of 3 months, visited only briefly by gowned doctors and nursing staff. When my medical problem was revealed to the health authority in Littlehampton, the holiday camp was closed, while at home everything was fumigated including my schoolbooks while all notes and paperwork were incinerated.

In late 1948, Chloramphenicol, a new antibiotic that revolutionised the treatment of typhoid had been licensed by the Food and Drug Administration in the USA, but was unavailable in the UK. There was no other antibiotic with which to cure this illness and no treatment other than good nursing care as the disease ran its course, hoping there might not be any complication. The major hurdle to be overcome was avoidance of a bowel perforation followed by peritonitis, which in 1861 had resulted in the death of Prince Albert, Queen Victoria's consort. Unconscious for many days, once my perceptive senses returned I was placed on a strict dietary regimen of milk every four hours and no other food for a period of ten weeks. On this diet I lost all track of time, almost all my body hair and incessantly day dreamed of little else but food.

My episodic education was suspended, as I hovered perilously midway between life and death. Never overweight, I entered hospital weighing 126 pounds and left at the end of November a skeletal 85 pounds. My attitude to food underwent a permanent change thereafter, when it became little more than something necessary to sustain life. I left hospital before my mother and was sent to live with my paternal grandmother, Zosha, in Lent Rise, a mile from Taplow in Buckinghamshire, to recuperate. My main regret during that time was to have missed the only litter that our family pet Alsation, Pax delivered and raised during my illness.

Adored by her grandchildren Zosha was a wonderfully resourceful woman and yet she was barely tolerated by my mother, because of her persistent opposition to my parent's marriage. She had objected to the marriage since my mother, a working class woman was marrying her employer's son who was almost four years her junior.

Zosha hadn't seen me since my illness and was greatly distressed by my emaciated appearance. She immediately summoned the local doctor who instructed that her malnourished grandson urgently needed feeding up and advised bacon and eggs every morning. In spite of maintaining a kosher home, she instructed Clara, her companion home help, to prepare bacon and eggs every morning, especially for my benefit using a separate frying pan, crockery and utensils to feed me as the doctor had instructed, before she came down for breakfast. Surely no greater love had any Jewish grandmother.

During those weeks, under her instruction, I slowly regained weight and learned to play all manner of board and card games such as Casino, Cribbage,

Gin Rummey, Canasta, Kalooki and Chinese checkers. She insisted we play for money and often blatantly cheated to win. At the end her winnings were always returned with an extra sixpence or shilling thrown in for good measure. A child could never have asked for a more entertaining adult companion.

My schooling resumed in January 1949 after an absence of six months, with examinations that loomed ahead in May when I was to sit the GCE examination (general certificate of education), considered the first part of a university entrance requirement. By the narrowest of margins I somehow passed and it was at this juncture that I decided to study medicine. I explained to my father that I was not prepared to continue with my studies unless I could avoid the demeaning need to ask him for pocket money each week. As a consequence he opened a bank account in my name into which he placed £26 every six months. I was provided with a chequebook and the arrangement was that I had to manage my own budget without any recourse to further funds from him. I was delighted with this arrangement, which continued until I finished medical school.

In September I entered the first year of the school sixth form to embark upon a two-year course in Chemistry, Physics, Botany and Zoology, which would give me exemption from the first MB (bachelor of medicine) examination.

The following year I wrote to almost every medical school in the country requesting application forms, completing them and awaiting a response. Every one replied they had no places to offer for the year commencing 1951 and most stated they were giving preference to students who'd completed military service. I obtained an interview at St. Mary's Hospital medical school, where the Secretary to the Dean explained.

"Considering the poor results achieved in your G.C.E. examinations I believe you would stand little chance, if any, in completing our very exacting course of medical studies. We have twenty five applicants for each available place and our preference is to offer this to a student with a proven academic record with the ability to complete course work successfully and qualify with a medical degree." His parting words were "I would advise that you seek a career with less demanding academic requirements."

In his place I should certainly have taken the same pragmatic attitude. It was most disheartening and I was too intimidated to ask that he take into consideration the accumulation of extenuating circumstances in my disrupted education. Almost every aspiring medical student was applying to every medical college in the land, exacerbating the problem of too many students chasing too few places, particularly amongst the London medical colleges. At that time there was little doubt that each medical school ran a quota. Alongside my poor examination grade and the huge competition for places, was the absence of a parent, or close relative in the medical profession. The type of school one attended was also an important consideration. Every applicant was required to provide in addition to details of nationality, academic performance, athletic and recreational interests, information concerning religion, and father's occupation, all of which could have no possible bearing upon ones suitability as a student or doctor.

A civil war erupted in Korea in 1950. The north was communist and backed by China, while the United Nations, ostensibly the USA, with some UK support fought on the side of the non- communist South. General Douglas MacArthur, the brilliant US military commander in the Pacific war spoke out repeatedly about attacking China to stop their support of North Korea. President Harry S. Truman who coined the phrases "The Buck Stops Here" and "If you can't stand the heat in the kitchen you'd best get out." warned him that US. policy was to limit the area of conflict and not to become involved in a third world war. He instructed MacArthur to cease making inflammatory speeches. Truman, midst great public consternation then dismissed this senior ranking officer, for ignoring instructions. In England in 1951, the labour party disintegrated into squabbling over the introduction of NHS charges and Clement Attlee, Prime Minister since 1945, lost his majority. An election resulted which the conservatives won with a majority of 30 seats and Winston Churchill, an old man, was returned to office as Prime Minister.

The 'Festival of Britain' had opened some weeks earlier on London's South Bank, to the west of Waterloo station, overlooking the Thames, celebrating the 1851 Great Exhibition. All that remains today is the elegant Royal Festival concert Hall. There was a cigar shaped illuminated 'Skylon' suspended vertically by cables, a shot tower, a large exhibition hall, all of which were later demolished. With family and friends we attended, but apart from the magnificent new concert hall my impression was that the whole exhibition was over-rated. It seemed an expensive ploy, on government's part, to conceal the fact that six years post-war, there were still a host of shortages, for example continued rationing and foreign currency restrictions, a wait of two years for the delivery of a new motor vehicle, which the labour government had been unable to resolve.

In May 1951, I sat my examinations and failed to achieve the required standard in Chemistry and Physics. Consequently in September 1951, I attended an intensive nine months course at the Northern Polytechnic, now the London Metropolitan University, with the object of improving my grades in the required science subjects, while reapplying to medical colleges for admission in October 1952. The difference in tuition between school and the 'Northern Poly' was remarkable. We were instructed as students in lecture theatres by lecturers rather than as school children. The most gifted of the tutors, Mr Hetherington, headed the Biology department and under his tuition we covered a two-year school syllabus in eight months. At the end of this time I resat the 1st MB examination in June 1952.

One morning in mid October 1951 my mother asked me to accompany my father on the short walk to Doctor Hyman's surgery, in Freston Gardens, where he had an appointment, before I proceeded to college. Father had become unwell during the night and as we walked, talking to each other, he seemed to experience some difficulty walking in a straight line. He took my hand and we continued to walk arm in arm. Suddenly he bumped into a car in the roadway. He explained that he hadn't noticed it. I wasn't unduly concerned as I bade him goodbye at the doctor's surgery, although these events would have later immediately set alarm bells ringing. On my return home that evening I learnt my father was gravely ill and had been hospitalised in the St Mary's Hospital 'Lindo Wing', with the diagnosis of an intra cranial space-occupying lesion.

Mr Dixon-Wright, the general surgeon, who a year earlier had performed an abdominal partial prostatectomy on him was consulted. Our household was in turmoil. My brother Maurice was to be married that weekend. Some days later, the surgeon operated with the object of attempting to identify the cause of the problem and then hoping he could somehow affect a remedy. In this manner he discovered my father's illness had thankfully not been due to a tumour, but to a 'subdural haematoma' just beneath the right side of the skull. With this blood clot removed, and the small leaking artery that had caused his difficulty cauterised, my father made a slow recovery, although he never returned to full health, seeming to have aged prematurely. It was suggested that some minor blow to the side of the head, had caused his bleeding and thereafter he was always particularly careful to avoid knocking his head. During the first week of his illness, grandmother Zosha, requested that I escort her to a house in Golders Green. There she consulted a rabbi and had my father given the new name of Chaim (Hebrew meaning 'life'), with the twin object of deceiving the angel of death who would be unable to find his renamed victim and to provide a name that epitomised the owner's new status. This was the age-old Jewish tradition of last resort, when confronting a serious health issue. My grandmother was convinced that this action had ultimately saved his life.

I reapplied to many of the provincial medical colleges for admission in October 1952 and several invited me to attend for interview. Travelling by train from London to Leeds, Liverpool, Manchester, Edinburgh, Birmingham and Sheffield I often met the same hopefuls I had met at previous interviews.

In February 1952, King George VI, a heavy smoker, died of a carcinoma of the lung and laid in state at Westminster Abbey before his state funeral. The country went into mourning and in company with the majority of adults who wore either a black diamond mourning patch sewn onto a coat sleeve, or a black armband, or some similar black token, I wore a black tie for one week. At about this time I received conditional offers of a place at Edinburgh for 1st MB and at Sheffield medical faculty to study 2nd MB medicine commencing October 1952, conditional upon passing first MB.

With the 'Clean Air Act' of 1956, millions of coals burning fires, belching black smoke into the air, were banned. Prior to that event, no description of the United Kingdom would be complete without mentioning that synonymous with 'London' was the term 'fog'. The seeds of the industrial revolution had been planted with the mining and use of coal as an energy source. It provided power for the steam engines to drive industry and warmth for every Briton's hearth and home, belching black carbon emissions into the atmosphere in the process. The result was pollution and smog, of increasing severity each year.

Until the 'Act' was implemented, a regular occurrence every autumn and winter was a foggy mist laden with carbon and sulphur particles termed 'smog' and the certainty that each year would be worse than the previous one. At the heart of this great nation and the major recipient of this pollutant was London, renowned for its enveloping sulphurous fog. At its most unpleasant it was impenetrable, when one could barely see one's own fingertips when fully extending an arm. Underground rail traffic was unaffected, but above ground life virtually ground to a halt while even some theatre performances were cancelled. Trams were able to proceed slowly. Buses moved at a snails pace as conductors often needed to walk in front guiding drivers, while in the rear, a silent cortege of dark, shadowy vehicles inched forward. On one occasion my father drove home from his Old Street work place near City Road to Cockfosters, a journey of 8 miles, at a speed approximating to one mile an hour. Headlamps and torches were of no avail, producing a reflected glare that made matters worse.

People would get lost, even though they knew the route and area well. The fog might last two or three days at a time, aggravating respiratory problems. It caused increased difficulty in breathing for some, while many bronchitics needed hospitalisation and death ensued for many hundreds each year. When the fog cleared, every surface was covered with a film of unsightly black soot particles, which required hosing down. In London, pollution from this source is now a distant memory, much the same as for my grandparents where the introduction of sewers and the banning of the discard of toxic waste into waterways remedied the earlier pollution of our great rivers. Future generations will likewise be called upon to deal with other sources of pollution as man's progress adversely effects his environment.

* * *

During the major portion of my summer holidays as I waited for my examination results, I obtained a vacation job alongside my cousin Julius Kosky, working in a photographic laboratory, developing and printing hundreds of other people's holiday snaps. In the latter part of August, the posted examination results confirmed I'd passed my 1st M.B. which permitted me to take up either of the provisionally offered university places.

Elated, I selected Sheffield, a small faculty that accepted 60 students annually and hurriedly wrote to accept the place that had been offered earlier in the year. Sheffield the heavy industrial steel and cutlery city, described as the dirty picture in a golden frame, with the statue of Vulcan significantly gracing the summit of its town hall and all but the newest buildings deeply encrusted in the soot and grime of years.

(1) The Scarlet Pimpernel, A novel written by Baroness Emmuska Orczy, later adapted as a play and a film, starring Lesley Howard. The adventure story is set during the French revolution when a secret society of English gentry, headed by the Scarlet Pimpernel, later revealed as Sir Percy, considered a fop who crosses into France, rescuing aristocrats from the guillotine and smuggling them out to England.

(2) The Jews' Free School, JFS, was founded in 1732 as a boy's secondary school in Spitalfields in London's East End. In 1822 it moved to Bell Lane and became co-educational. By 1900 it had a roster of 4,250 pupils and claimed to be the world's largest school. Post-war, the school moved to Camden Town and further relocated as a comprehensive school with 2,000 pupils in Kenton, North London.

(3) Cecil Rhodes (1853-1902) Son of an English vicar, when aged 17, joined his brother in Durban South Africa with £3,000, given him by an aunt. He used this fortune in diamond mine explorations in Kimberley, and founded the DeBeers mining syndicate, becoming exceedingly rich. He was imbued with a fierce determination to expand the British Empire in Africa, and gave his name to Rhodesia, now Zimbabwe. A bequest in 1902 established the annual Rhodes scholarships, funding 90 commonwealth and American students to study at Oxford. President Clinton is one of the more famous alumni.

(4) The Bethnal Green Tube disaster was the worst civilian tragedy of the war when 173 adults and children were crushed to death. On March 3rd 1943, with the sound of the air raid siren hundreds of people ran to the station shelter. A nearby anti-aircraft rocket battery, which had recently been installed, discharged a salvo

of rockets, with an unexpected deafening roar, causing people attempting to gain entrance to the station to panic. There was only one badly illuminated narrow staircase entrance and there were no crush barriers. A woman near the bottom of the first flight of stairs slipped and a man behind tripped over her. Within seconds the stairs were blocked with scores of fallen people. The pressure of the crowd trying to push into the shelter prevented rescuers from going to their aid. The accident was censored and not revealed until 3 years later.

(5) Danny Kaye (1913-1987) A popular and versatile American singer, comedian, actor and film star. Amongst his many films were: The Secret Life of Walter Mitty –1947; The Inspector General –1949; Hans Christen Anderson –1952; White Christmas –1954; The Court Jester –1956. His talented wife, Sylvia Fine, wrote many of the songs he made famous. In his latter years he conducted orchestral concerts for UNICEF and worked extensively for children's charities.

(M1) A government allowance of ten shillings per week (50p) was paid to each evacuee's foster parents for food and lodging.

(M2) A child's haircut cost 4 pence (1½p.) in the barbershop in Mousehole in 1940.

(M3) Milk money was 2½pence (1p.) to purchase a five day supply of a one third pint bottle of milk per day. a double daily quantity cost 5 pence (2p.) A two course School Lunch in 1943 cost 4 pence per meal, one shilling and eight pence for the week (8p.).

Chapter 3

SHEFFIELD YORKSHIRE

1952-1957

The mail arrived and midst great excitement revealed the list of books and equipment that I would need before commencing my 2nd MB course. Father enthusiastically coughed up the funds for me to purchase the obligatory half skeleton (**M4**) and all the recommended textbooks, the largest and most expensive by far, was Gray's Anatomy.

In the first week of October, I travelled to Sheffield by train (**M5**) from St. Pancras, to find accommodation and to register at the faculty of medicine office. I obtained a government grant, which covered my tuition fees and the cost of each Sheffield University Examination, but did not contribute to either my general living expenses or any external examinations.

Father agreed to pay my accommodation expenses and provided me with an increased allowance of thirty shillings a week, (£1.50p.), paid six monthly in advance, to cover every expense apart from books, clothes and annual holidays. Within a few weeks I discovered this was woefully inadequate (**M6**) but stubborn pride forbade me from renegotiating an increase. An impoverished student by any standard, I became heavily reliant upon gifts of money on birthdays and at Christmas and subsidies from my father, brothers and close relatives for fare and holiday cash. Fortunately I didn't smoke or drink alcohol. There was a tremendous amount of peer pressure to participate in both, particularly drinking, which made life more difficult since most chaps in my year often visited the pub closest to one of the hospitals for a beer.

During the registration process, which took place at the start of every academic year, the Dean of the medical faculty, Dr. McCrie, with his broad Scots accent, interviewed each student. He informed me, year after year, that my name was not of Welsh origin, as most might believe, but originated in Scotland. I felt it kinder never to disillusion him by explaining it had been selected from a London telephone directory in 1942 when my father anglicised his Polish family name of Podguszer, prior to my eldest brother's entry into military service.

There were no places available in the halls of residence and since first and second year students were not permitted to live unsupervised on their own, we were required to select accommodation from an approved list provided by the faculty. Throughout my first two years I stayed with a family in the working class suburb of Intake, at 17 Mansfield Road. Their son Michael, was attending Leeds University and they were prepared to offer lodgings to a student willing to use his bedroom, which he didn't use during term time. I journeyed by tram to inspect the room on offer. They lived in a small, 3 bedroom semidetached house and I negotiated a weekly rate of £3 for room and board, including my personal laundry. My landlord, a tailor, and his wife Mr and Mrs Mark Black were a sympathetic and industrious couple. The food proved to be excellent and included breakfast and an evening meal plus lunch at weekends. During holiday times I paid a retainer fee of 30 shillings (£1.50p) each week. The warden of lodgings approved my choice.

The disadvantages were that the room was miniscule; measuring some 60 square feet and my landlady, one of the kindest people I'd ever met had a major hearing deficit. Although she used a hearing aid, it was bulky and of poor quality, the norm at that time, and her teenage daughter Benita spoke at a volume akin to a foghorn to compensate, which was a big problem in a small house.

The rear multipurpose kitchen, served as a dining living room with access through a back door to a path at the side of the house, which was used at all times to enter and leave the home. Another door led to the front parlour, which as with the front door was seldom used. The parlour boasted a small versatile coal fire, which supplied heat to that room, kept the kitchen oven sizzling and provided domestic hot water. Double-glazing and heat in the bedrooms were unheard of luxuries and in this respect was no different to the vast majority of homes including my parents. During the winters of 1952 and 1953 while living there, it was necessary to tuck up warmly in bed with a hot water bottle at night in order to avoid freezing.

The daily journey to the main university building for lectures and practical classes entailed long waiting times for trams and buses. I decided it would be quicker and far less expensive if I were to use my bicycle for the short journey of 4 miles each way. Built in a small valley through which flows the river Don, Sheffield is surrounded by steep hills. My trip into town was plain sailing downhill, but the return journey uphill all the way was another matter. Within days I realised this steep ascending ride home with a heavy case of books presented a major problem. The solution was to buy either a motorcycle or a motor that could be attached to the bicycle. With minimal expense I purchased a 25cc. petrol oil engine that transmitted its power through a serrated steel roller that could be fixed against the rear tyre. In use it assisted me to negotiate the steepest hills and on the flat I could travel at up to 20 miles per hour. This converted my cycle into a motorised vehicle. I was required to acquire number plates and had to take a motorcycle-driving test, in spite of holding a valid car license. An economical and rapid means of travel, the hazards from tramlines were a constant danger and when it rained I was not only soaked, but at increased risk from slippery tram lines and cobble stones. Fingers and toes froze in winter and one had constantly to be alert for 'black ice', particularly at night.

On special occasions, such as the annual Medical or Cutler's Ball when dinner dress was mandatory, several students would club together to hire a car. I was the non-drinker who also had a driver's licence and invariably had the privilege of hiring and driving the vehicle. On these occasions using an old Voiklander camera, I would take flash light photographs (in black and white), of colleagues and their partners, which I could then develop and print in a dark room at the student's union, subsequently selling them with a small profit.

My father, an astute business man, must have realised at the outset that the allowance he provided was insufficient and may have used this as a device to control my extra curricular activities. Necessity being the mother of invention I stumbled upon a modest scheme, in addition to my photography, to supplement my income. Sheffield's main department store, Walsh's held a biannual sale in which all goods were marked down by 30%. This also applied to silverware. I realised that at sale time I could purchase selected silver objects and by conveying them to London could realise a profit. This not only helped fund my conjoint examination fees, but also taught me a great deal about English silver.

In 1905 Sheffield University received its charter and had one of the smallest medical faculties in the country. The medical school, established in 1828 accepted 12 students each year prior to 1939 and by 1952 had enlarged to accommodate 60, of whom 12 were women. In the first 18 months of our medical curriculum we were required to study anatomy, physiology and biochemistry, following which we would sit our 2nd MB (Bachelor of Medicine) examination in Easter 1954. Those passing would continue with a further 3 years clinical medical course, during which time examinations in each part of the 3rd MB had to be passed in pathology, bacteriology, public health, forensic, and psychiatric medicine. Following the successful completion of the 3rd MB, all would proceed to the final M.B. examinations in June 1957 in Medicine, Surgery, Paediatrics and Obstetrics and Gynaecology. Those who failed the 2nd M.B. examination would be required to resit it 6 months later. Those who failed any pre-clinical examination twice were out.

There were assessment tests at the end of each term. In addition there was an oral examination or 'viva' (viva voce, the living voice) every 10 to 14 days in anatomy covering the dissections of the previous period. Should any student fail to obtain a 50% pass mark then the viva had to be retaken. Each week there were anatomy lectures and daily dissections in the anatomy room located on the 4th floor at Western Bank, the red brick university building, plus lectures and practicals in physiology, and biochemistry. In the dissection room the students worked in pairs, two on each upper limb, while students in the year above worked on the lower limbs. At times there were 8 students working on a cadaver. Cunningham's 'Manual of Anatomy' was used to guide us in our anatomy dissections and between each viva we covered some 60 pages from this manual.

Within a matter of days I was floundering. The volume of work was prodigious. None of my new colleagues admitted to any difficulty and I had to assume I was the most inept member of the class. The secretary at St. Mary's medical college had been correct and I would fail. At the end of the first ten-day period was the viva. Each of us was questioned either by Professor Francis Davies, who was the editor of Gray's Anatomy, his deputy Dr Wheeler Haines, or one of the handful of doctors, who while studying for their primary fellowship examinations were employed as anatomy demonstrators. If one failed, not only had the viva to be taken again, but also the work for the following viva in addition to the material covered in other subjects. One simply didn't have the opportunity to read the same textbook passage over and over again.

Gradually I acquired a technique to deal with my learning difficulties. I would read at the most two pages and would then turn the book over and write a brief synopsis. I'd rapidly scan the section, checking that nothing of consequence had been omitted. I would then read two more pages and repeat the process. By the end of the study period I might have covered a dozen pages. I then wrote another brief synopsis, following which I skimmed through the pages to ensure I'd missed no salient points. After doing this for five days I would then write a short précis summarising the week's reading and scan the passages read to confirm I'd included everything of relevance. In this way I learnt to deal with our immense workload. As an athlete improves stamina and performance with regular exercise, so I discovered I could work more efficiently. Coping with my study load became noticeably easier as the weeks went by. After years of schooling, I'd found my key to successful studying. I'd received years of education but had never been taught how to study efficiently. I discovered, for the first time, a way of absorbing large sections of information by concentrating on reading only two pages at a time.

To learn required repetition and perseverance and as in any programme it became easier once this discipline was applied. Physiology I found less onerous than anatomy, due to a marvellous textbook I found on the subject written by Samson-Wright, physiology professor at the Middlesex Hospital. On the first page, he had recorded a wonderful saying from Rabbi Akiva (1). 'More than a calf yearns to suck does the cow wish to give suckle.'

While using an 'Ishi Hara colour chart', I confirmed that I was partially colour blind in red and green. I could see the harsher colours, such as used in traffic lights, but the paler shades appeared as grey, off white or beige, which helped explain many earlier difficulties. Later in my clinical course this problem, inherited from my mother, gave me trouble when looking at slides and identifying objects coloured pink. Embarrassingly in dermatology when a patient arrived with a faint macular rash, I could often detect no abnormality.

Professor Hans Krebbs, taught biochemistry. A delightful owlish figure he'd escaped from German persecution in 1936 to become first a lecturer and then head of Sheffield's biochemistry department. He obtained fame and recognition in 1954 when he was jointly awarded the 'Nobel Prize' in medicine for his work on the 'Tricarboxalic Acid Cycle' and the 'Urea Cycle'. At the time the Daily Express newspaper commented inaccurately that Dr Lipman, the other joint winner of the prize (for his work on Co-enzyme A) had stayed in Germany, while Krebbs had fled. The whole class wrote a letter to the editor in protest, pointing out that Prof. Krebbs, a Jew, had been forced out of his academic research post by the Nazis and had no alternative but to leave the land of his birth. The Express failed to correct their error or to acknowledge our class letter. A few years later Prof. Krebbs moved to Oxford and later still received a well-deserved knighthood. He never participated in any of the Jewish Society student activities, although in 1955, I approached him, when chairman, to be honorary President, which he politely declined.

The first week in November each year was 'Rag Week', enjoyed both by the students and Sheffield's citizens as money was raised for local charity. At the end of the week the culmination was a procession when the undergraduates would dress up and each university department would have a float in the procession, followed later that evening with a 'Rag Ball' at the student's union. A magazine 'The Twikker' (The Wicker is where the water runs over the weir in the Yorkshire dialect became 'T'wicker, where twatter runs o'er 'tweir) was produced and sold by the students. There was a rag ball and a raffle held over the previous weeks, with a prize of a silver plated 'Ronson' lighter for the student who sold most tickets, which I won two years in succession. With a supply of ostrich feathers from home, I dressed as 'Ras Prince Monolulu' a well-known horse race tipster who used to obtain his feathers from my father.

I didn't return to London until the Christmas vacation, although I 'phoned (M7) home every Friday evening at father's insistence, reversing the charges, a practice that continued throughout my student years. At the end of the first semester having overcome my learning difficulties of the first weeks, I passed my end of term assessments, although there was rarely time for any midweek extra curricular activity. Furthermore I discovered that most of my colleagues had experienced similar difficulties, although initially, none would admit it, making their disclosures in less guarded moments.

Joseph Stalin the leader of the USSR died from a 'stroke' in the Easter of 1953. Over the following weeks the news media disclosed that Stalin, who'd been idolised by the allies during the war, had been one of the worst tyrannical despots, instrumental in the imprisonment and murder of millions of Russian citizens. It was at this time I came down with a dreadful 'flu like cold. I spoke to Dr Mitchell, one of the anatomy demonstrators and enquired whether he knew of any remedy.

"Sure; take a glass of hot lemon tea, laced with an ounce of brandy or rum and two teaspoons of honey, and go to bed. After a couple of hours you can repeat the treatment." He advised.

"Will it cure my cold?" I enquired.

"No, but it'll make you feel a lot happier."

And that I discovered remains one of the finest remedies one can offer for colds and flu.

At the end of my first year in Sheffield, in July 1953, shortly after sweets came off ration (rationed first in 1942) I accompanied my parents to Italy, a favourite family destination for a summer holiday. My task was to assist my father with the driving during the two days journey as we motored down in his black 2½ litres Riley saloon. Our Adriatic coast destination was the village of Riccione, just north of Rimini, with its broad expanse of pale gold sandy beaches where we were to join my father's younger brother Harry and his wife Anne, affectionately called Ginsy, (rhymed with quinsy) since there was a need to differentiate between all the Annes in my father's family. Harry, who had driven out a week earlier to stay at the Grand Hotel, sent a telegram telling my father to avoid the Grand and gave the name of the Hotel des Baines, where they had found excellent accommodation and food.

My father followed this advice. The Grand Hotel, which had deteriorated, was taking coach parties and this was not their scene. In half a century the family had ascended the socio-economic ladder, from impoverished Polish immigrant to staid English middle class.

During lunch in our second week, I fleetingly observed a GB plated motor vehicle pull up in the car park that was overlooked by a shaded dining terrace. The car door opened as it drew to a halt and an attractive slender young woman lithely sprang out and bounded like a graceful gazelle with rapid steps to the inner reception desk. In faltering Italian, I overheard her ask for three vacant rooms for six people.

The next day the new arrivals, a father and four children, played cricket on the beach. Striking the tennis ball for a boundary it unintentionally struck my father on the head, while he reclined in a deck chair, reading. He was somewhat upset, but following this assault I seized the opportunity to introduce myself to the young lady who was the eldest of the children. She confided that her parents had rejected an earlier booking at the Grand Hotel for the same reasons as my father.

With this strange introduction I invited this stunning sylph out. We became holiday friends as she revealed her name and disclosed she lived in Edgware, a North London suburb a short distance from where my eldest brother had his home. Together we would walk, talk, and occasionally eat watermelon as we planned pranks to be played on other hotel guests and acquaintances. I contacted her on our return to London and still later communicated by post and continued to meet during vacations.

With the arrival of the second MB, I developed my technique for taking examinations. I dressed smartly, wearing my best jacket and in the top pocket a white handkerchief, a clean white shirt, freshly pressed trousers and polished shoes and if available, would even sport a flower in my buttonhole. I employed any psychological technique that might boost my self-confidence. Once seated at the examination table, pen in hand, I relied upon two or three pieces of music, which incessantly ran through my mind. Hurriedly recording my answers, to the questions posed I multitasked, listening to my own personal symphony concert. This was not deliberate, but somehow the first piece was usually from extracts of Beethoven's 6th 'Pastoral' Symphony, which had a wonderfully calming effect, as did his 'Emperor Concerto'. The other was from William Walton's 'March from Things To Come', a strident piece of music which when buzzing through my mind seemingly encouraged me to put a spurt on, to write more rapidly. All were psychological devices that never let me down.

At the conclusion of our professional examinations, there was never the interminable wait for results as formerly in school. Within minutes of the last student's viva ours were available, read out by the Dean from the steps within his office. I went home for the 1954 Easter vacation; relieved and overjoyed with the knowledge I'd passed my second MB and could continue with my clinical course.

In London I met June Fraiman again, the young lady who by this time had become a steady pen friend and who was about to embark upon a trip to Israel with her friend, Vivienne Rosefield. I was travelling to Paris for a few days vacation, staying with my cousin Sylvain, and arranged to meet her briefly as she passed en-route to Marseilles for her boat journey to Haifa.

In preparation for the 'Third MB', culminating in 'Final Examinations', we embarked upon the more interesting clinical part of our course, at last coming into contact with patients. In addition we commenced studies in pathology and bacteriology together with a number of other specialities such as public health, psychiatry and forensic medicine. Members of our year were divided into groups of 6, to 8 persons for their clinical studies and were attached to 'firms' under the supervision of various consultants for periods of three months. My introductory clinical appointment was under Dr. Davies.

Our group of eight stood outside the entrance to Dr Davies first floor male ward on that first day. We chatted in happy anticipation, proudly wearing clean white cotton coats, notebooks and pens in pockets, stethoscopes prominently displayed round necks, confidently looking like doctors, waiting for our consultant's arrival. The corridor window overlooked the consultant's car park, where we soon noticed his gleaming black Bentley saloon glide into its appointed slot. Within minutes Dr. Davies had arrived. He was a well dressed, robustly built man of medium height, in his mid forties, with azure blue eyes and slightly balding, who had earlier qualified as a barrister before embarking upon his medical career. He was now a consultant physician at the Royal Hospital, with two large wards under his supervision.

There was a hasty initial greeting, followed by his curt;

"Follow me and keep up."

We walked rapidly in file, hastening not to be left behind. As he marched towards his female ward he wiped an index finger along a corridor ledge, stopped abruptly and stared at it. This unexpected halt caused us to collide unwarily into each other, while Dr. Davies haughtily invited us to.

"Gather round."

Jockeying in order that we might not miss one syllable of his erudite utterance, we strained to listen. Peering at the dust on his finger he pronounced.

"Faecal! Everything everywhere is faecal! Don't you ever forget it."

With a further brisk, "Keep up; follow me," He then resumed his invigorating progression to the first of his wards. Approaching the double half glazed doors, they were majestically opened without our having the need to slacken pace, revealing the ward sister within. In her white lace hat, pristine navy blue uniform, which denoted her senior status, with black belt and ornate silver buckle, she had undoubtedly been waiting expectantly to greet his seigniorial appearance at the entrance of his ward. Slightly to the rear she was accompanied by an attractive bevy of smart light blue uniformed white-capped younger nursing minions in black stockings, behind who were a small group of distinctive student nurses and two of the medical staff. The first exchange of greeting, as we passed was from Dr. Davies.

"Good morning Sister."

"Good morning Sir." Responded the ward sister, with almost a hint of an obsequious curtsy. I felt certain that had they guns, swords, or even bed pans to hand there would have been a call.

"Present arms."

We followed onwards behind our consultant, contentedly basking in his glory, gliding past rows of immaculately made beds, within each was a fresh, neatly washed and polished patient, reflected on an equally shiny clean floor. As we passed there was little doubt that certain medical student eyes had ensnared those of blushing recipient student nurses. The consequence was that three years later, the day after we qualified, six men in our year married nurses and more followed suit.

Our first task that morning was to learn the regulation manner in which hospital beds were made. This entailed individual instruction under one of the junior nurses, after which we had to make such a bed unaided. With tuition under such pretty instructors there was a 100% failure rate amongst the men. We all failed miserably at those first attempts. Had it not been for the eagle eye of the sister there were doubtlessly some amongst us who might have spent hours, or possibly even days, returning to the same captivating smile of the instructing nurse, struggling for extra tuition in nothing more formidable than bed making. Years later from the late 1970's onwards, as the dictatorial authority of the matron and in particular the ward sister waned, hospital ward cleanliness declined.

On the second day, screened from the remainder of the ward, Dr Davies asked one of our group, John Horton, to palpate a patient's abdomen. As John placed his hand on the patient's skin, Dr Davies noticed he had grimy fingernails. "Doctor Horton, your hands are dirty." he pronounced, to the amusement of those of us not at the receiving end of this latest cynical barb.

"Well I'm very sorry sir, but I had some trouble with my motorcycle. I couldn't get it started this morning." John stammered his response.

"Kindly go and scrub your hands clean, and please ensure you leave your motorcycle outside in future."

An observant man, he spotted a urine bottle had been left on the patient's bedside locker in an amenity room. This unintentional misdemeanour would in former days have doubtlessly been a capital offence, warranting nothing less than deportation to Australia for life. He pointed at me and then indicated the urine bottle resting precariously half full on the metal bedside locker.

"You; go outside and find a nurse to remove this offensive object."

I scurried outside as commanded. Seeing a nurse, an older woman in a dark blue uniform nearby, I requested that she attend to the removal of the offending urinal.

"Young man," she replied, as she garnered her full height "If you want a nurse you will find one over there." as she pointed imperiously, to indicate a bevy of attractive uniformed white capped nurses in the distance.

"And further more, would you not come onto my ward as though you own the whole hospital!" This was my first personal encounter with the authoritarian might of the ward sister and was not to be the last with such a formidable hospital custodian.

Under Dr Davies instruction we learned to take an accurate history. His experienced eye supervised our careful examination of a patient from top to toe, the respiratory, cardiovascular, alimentary and nervous systems. Week by week we palpated, percussed and auscultated, listening for heart sounds and undergoing training for inspecting every modality. Frequently many of us feigned hearing sounds of errant heart valves. Years later most of us found the bits of paper stuck in stethoscope tubes by erstwhile colleagues to block out most of the sounds we might otherwise have heard.

Three months later at the end of our secondment we had completed our introductory clinical course. Dr Davies as he instructed had also regaled and entertained us with one clinical anecdote after another. I believe the ultimate was the one that provided us with the single most essential guide through our medical careers.

"You must always examine every patient as thoroughly as possible and record all your findings." He stated. "A failure to do so will create a medical legal minefield of your own making. Should you be too busy at the time, or in the absence of a chaperone for a female, have the patient return and record in your notes that this has been your course of action. Fully examining a patient might also provide you with a number of unexpected benefits. Let me illustrate what I mean by telling you of one of my earliest experiences."

"I was newly qualified and held a very junior national service medical officer post in the army when I was consulted by an extremely senior General on the base. He strode into my office, a supercilious, no nonsense and cantankerous old devil, with crowns and stars galore on epaulettes, a baton gripped in his hand and held firmly under his arm. He was most intimidating. I'd only been in the army a few days, when in he marched. I rose from my desk as he entered and saluted smartly.

He had some trivial skin disorder. I knew next to nothing about skins, but without letting on, I insisted.

"Sir, this might be trivial but it could presage something more serious and I must give you a thorough medical examination."

"He stated that it was quite right and commendable that I should be so thorough. He removed his shirt and as I percussed, auscultated and palpated all over, I detected he'd become a little more impressed with my thoroughness. When he thought I'd finished and started to replace his clothes I explained that it was essential to perform a rectal examination. He was reluctant to consent, but I stood my ground, firmly explaining that it was an essential requirement. Finally he agreed and I requested very politely he turn on his left side as he lay on the couch, lowering his pants and pulling up his knees. I then inserted a lubricated gloved finger to perform the examination."

"As my finger slid into the old boy's anus, you could virtually see and as I listened I thought I could even hear his officer's ranking pips popping off his red epaulettes dropping one by one onto the floor. By the time I'd completed the medical and as he dressed he wasn't the same gruff, supercilious senior officer of twenty minutes earlier. As I reassured him he was fit and well, his skin ailment had become a forgotten trivia. He became most amiable. He didn't go as far as to suggest I should address him by his first name, but he became most accommodating and gave me access to his private military plane, complete with pilot, whenever I wished during the remainder of my military service, telling me I had only to ask. And on numerous occasions I did ask and was flown wherever I wanted."

"Performing a complete medical examination and recording your findings will never let you down. While it might be considered reprehensible when you make a diagnostic error, and we all make mistakes, it will be considered totally unacceptable not to have examined a patient thoroughly. In a court of law you could be crucified professionally for such a short coming, and rightly so."

Following the introductory course, I cycled down to London on my motorised bicycle in glorious summer sunshine. Munching sandwiches I had earlier prepared, I pedalled 160 miles non-stop in a little over 8 hours. I was proud of the achievement and the negligible fuel consumption of just over 200 miles to a gallon of petrol (M8) and my average speed of 20 miles per hour. My parents insisted I take my cycle back to Sheffield by train, which I was pleased to do, since father agreed to pay the fare.

That summer of 1954 I vacationed with my brother and two friends, Ken Teacher, (later an accountant and Nat David, (an eminent sculptor), touring Scotland. We hired a car, which my eldest brother Peter was to drive, while I borrowed his Austin A40 saloon, since car hire firms charged a huge premium to people under 25 years, in addition to which they made a mileage charge. We visited the Lake District en-route, one of the prettiest rural idylls in the world. We went boating on Derwent water and as we approached the middle of the lake found ourselves in the midst of a sudden rainstorm, without benefit of shelter. We toured parts of Scotland and finished at the Edinburgh Festival. There were several highlights, amongst which was a retrospective of Cézanne's paintings, a performance of Macbeth in the Assembly Rooms and the most memorable by far, a production of A Midsummer's Night Dream, with accompanying orchestra providing Mendelssohn's music and the Saddlers Wells ballet company, featuring the illustrious ballerina Moira Shearer.

In September I commenced my second firm in the A&E (Accident and Emergency) department of the Royal Infirmary. Five weeks later I was involved in a road traffic accident. The entrance and exit to the hospital was at a busy T- junction at the foot of St Phillips Hill. Normally a cautious driver, I was cycling out of the main gate, having looked both right and left, when in front of me loomed a truck. I suddenly discovered this immovable object barred my way. At that precise moment my front wheel struck the lorry and buckled. I was thrown forward following the same trajectory as the cycle, striking the truck with my face. Fortunately the truck stopped, my nose however entered the crumple zone before I embraced the road with the cycle on top of me. Led bleeding into A&E it was confirmed my nose had suffered the same fate as the front wheel of my cycle, which lay crushed under the truck. Some days later under an anaesthetic my nose was straightened out, more or less.

Unrelated to this shattering event, the Soviet Union launched the 'Sputnick' the world's first orbiting satellite and four weeks later sent a dog into orbit. The bicycle, a write off, providentially provided sufficient insurance money with which it could be replaced, complete with motor. The hospital unsuccessfully pursued me over many months for a fee of 17 shillings and six pence (87½p.) for accident room treatment. The NHS did not cover 'Road traffic accidents'. A considerable correspondence ensued as I pointed out that I believed the charge unreasonable since that was the department in which I was working at that time. The hospital and I spent more money on postage with a futile correspondence than the value of the charge they wished to impose and to this day the fee remains outstanding.

Travelling home for the occasional weekend was a trial, since I was living on a precariously slender budget. At times I hitch hiked, at other times I gladly obtained a lift from Rolf Burchhardt, who I met through mutual friends in Sheffield. A 28-year-old industrial chemist, he managed a small factory employing a workforce of 20 people in Sheffield for a company making 'colloidal graphite', a high temperature lubricant. He was responsible for manufacture, quality control, and sales. When in London he lived with his elderly mother in Fox Lane, Palmers Green opposite my old school, Southgate County. The manufacture of colloidal graphite required quantities of soft water, which was abundant in Sheffield and unavailable in London. Consequently he lived in digs in Sheffield during his working week and travelled backwards and forwards to London in his company Ford Consul motorcar alternate weekends. He and his mother had escaped from Germany in the late 1930's. She showed me repaired items of porcelain and glass they had carried out in their luggage, which the German custom officials had deliberately manhandled, chipped, and did their utmost to break deliberately.

Rolf wanted company on the journey and it was crucial for me to find an economical means of travel. He was an excellent driver, very level headed and with an effervescent sense of humour. On sales trips to Austria or Germany, he would always use an interpreter. His purchasers would discuss business matters in front of him, never realising he could comprehend everything they said, which provided him with many advantages during the negotiation process. He would never accept my offer to pay for petrol, since it was a company expense, so I provided fruit, in particular bananas, which he adored, for the journey, which we munched as we travelled and chatted.

One particularly cold winter's afternoon I had arranged to meet him at his industrial unit prior to our London journey. Some work requiring a pneumatic drill was in progress within the cavernous interior of the factory. An unidentified problem had developed when a number of the men had become nauseated and two had collapsed. Newly arrived on the scene, it was a simple matter to diagnose the source of what they believed was a problem of food poisoning. The petrol generator, which powered the drill, should have been outside in the open, but because of the cold the workmen had a little earlier taken it into the factory unit and closed the door, which was the only source of ventilation. On my insistence the generator was turned off, the external doors and windows opened fully and both collapsed men were carried out into the fresh air, where their highly flushed skin colour indicated they were suffering from carbon monoxide poisoning. An ambulance was summoned to take them to hospital and all work ceased for the remainder of the day.

In 1956 Rolf married his fiancée, Myra Jacobs, whom he took to live in Sheffield in a house he'd built to his specification. Thereafter we tended to drift apart and once qualified I had no time to socialise. He and Myra had two sons and he became, as one could have predicted, successful in his commercial enterprises. I never met him again and unfortunately he died in his early 60's.

Following my A & E attachment the next secondment was in my Junior Medical firm with Dr. T. Gumpert at the Royal Hospital. A cherubic man of about 60, he was far too kind and indulgent towards his students. No matter how ridiculous our responses to his questions he would always acknowledge. "Yes that is possible but,..." always speaking very deliberately and enunciating every syllable. On one occasion during a ward round he sent a nurse down to the consultant's car park to fetch some documents from his Rolls Royce. She hurried back to report an empty parking space.

"Good heavens it's been stolen. Sister would you please inform the police immediately."

Some time later the constabulary spotted the vehicle and detained the driver. Fortunately she convinced the arresting officers she was Mrs. Gumpert, explaining she'd dropped her husband at the hospital and had taken the car to go shopping and he'd simply forgotten the arrangement.

As part of the course in public health and industrial medicine, visits were made to steel works and coal mining villages. The latter, with their rows of grimy terraced Victorian houses, some even back to back, always overshadowed by grotesquely bare, black, mountainous slag heaps. We dressed with miner's lamp and overalls to descend at precipitous speed in caged groups into the bowels of the earth, the cable above rotating on two enormous spoke wheels. Filled with foreboding, in dangerously poorly illumined galleries, we followed electric torches as we walked towards the pit face. In the tunnel, above our heads the guide reassuringly explained as he indicated the rows of wide wooden slats, heaped with a powder.

"Should any explosion, occur the powder will fill the tunnel with a heavy fire retardant dust. Unfortunately while inhibiting a fire it would make breathing impossible without a mask. You'd best pray there's no explosion because there are no masks supplied to visitors or miners below ground."

As we stumbled over rail lines and sleepers we reached the pit face where helmeted miners, bare topped with backs and shoulders glistening with sweat in the subdued light, skin tattooed with blue black blotches and irregular linear scars from earlier coal falls, worked in the heat and dust, having turned off the water sprays that protected lungs from dust inhalation to avoid being constantly wet.

Above ground we visited the community miner's club where recreational cigarette smoking, banned within the mines was universal. At the time none realised the combined effects of cigarette smoke and untimely pneumoconiosis more rapidly destroyed a miner's lung function, hastening the onset of chronic bronchitis and pulmonary emphysema. This resulted in men who ought to have been in the prime of life being discarded as respiratory cripples diagnosed with 'Cor-pulmonale'. When too breathless to dress, or walk a step, they filled many of Sheffield's male patient hospital wards to be examined by medical students and be given what little comfort piped oxygen might provide as slowly they asphyxiated, until the grim reaper brought final relief to them and their grieving impoverished, families.

In 1954 Richard Doll (2) an epidemiologist working for the Medical Research Council published a report, which while scarcely noticed by the general public was one of the most significant studies of its kind. He and others had closely monitored 40,000 doctors over a ten-year period and conclusively correlated the incidence of cancer of the lung, a-nd the prevalence of heart disease to the frequency with which cigarettes were smoked.

The English Steel Corporation predominated in Sheffield's heavy industrial steel works. Some humorist with no perception of work in these steel mills stated ESC represented 'easy steady and comfortable'. The red glow from sunset onwards could be seen from miles away. Within each mill the noise and heat was almost unbearably frightening to uninitiated students like myself, heightening the awesome power and drama of raging kilns and furnaces.

The A & E departments were constantly treating patients from both coal mining and steel industries; the worst of the latter occurred in 1954, when a new centrifuge process was being demonstrated to a number of important observers. Somebody failed to tighten the lid of the machine. Revolving at speed, it sprayed molten steel injuring scores of workers and observers within a huge radius before the power supply could be shut down.

As a third year student in 1955, I was eligible to live on my own. I decided to leave my lodgings with the Black's and find my own bed-sitter accommodation. Shortly before leaving, there was a tragic incident involving a young Italian immigrant couple that lived next door. As I left for college one morning I noticed a car drive up outside their home. Upon my return that evening, Mrs. Black appeared distressed and had obviously been crying. She recounted that the neighbour's only child, a baby of nine months, had become unwell during the night, sniffling as though it had a cold and refusing to take her morning feed. Few people at the time had a telephone and on his way to work the husband had called at the surgery to summon the doctor and it must have been his arrival that I'd noticed. An hour later an ambulance had driven up taking the infant to hospital; the doctor had observed a slight rash, which with associated neck stiffness had made him suspect meningitis. By mid afternoon, 'meningococcal septicaemia' had claimed yet another young victim. No more than twelve hours had elapsed between the parents noting anything amiss and their child's demise. A coterie of tearful neighbours attended the funeral some days later, as I ruminated on the urgent response needed in some childhood illnesses if a fatal outcome was to be avoided.

I had lived in my new flat no more than a few weeks when the landlord provoked my decision to move. He objected to my entertaining a young lady in my apartment after 10pm and reported me to the warden of lodgings. One was not permitted to entertain members of the opposite sex after 10 pm. My girl friend from London had visited me for the weekend to attend the annual medical ball. We had been to the cinema and it was only 9.30pm. I was ordered to escort her back to her hotel and two days later was called to an interview with the warden of lodgings, who soundly reprimanded me and stated.

"This sort of thing must not happen again."

After a further search, I found a single first floor bed sitter at 5 Filey Street near the university and close to the major city hospitals, where two other members of my year, Tony Fox and Malcolm Williams, also had lodgings. The semidetached house was owned and supervised by Mrs. Krausz, a cutler's wife who lived next door. With each change of lodgings, my father would travel to Sheffield to inspect my accommodation.

In March 1955, I journeyed down to London to attend the wedding of Aunt Anne, my father's wealthy sister. Father was the eldest of six children and

Anne, his remaining unmarried sibling, was a younger dynamic individual, with business acumen to match her elegant appearance. She was a remarkably self-assured woman, who without the benefit of a formal education had risen to prominence through the ranks of a male dominated furniture industry. The reception, held at the Dorchester Hotel was an afternoon tea. I was unaware until more than forty years later of the drama that unfolded three weeks after the wedding, which Anne's sister in law, Ginsy, gleefully recounted to me.

Anne, then aged fifty, a successful and recently retired director in H. Lazarus, a furniture-manufacturing corporation quoted on the London Stock Exchange, had met and fallen in love with Vincent Veronique. Years earlier Jack Veronique, reinventing himself as Vincent, had over the past twelve months swept her off her feet. A successful merchant in imported fabrics with premises in London's West End he was a bachelor in his mid 50's, who lived alone with an elderly housekeeper in Totteridge

After the honeymoon they returned to London where they were to live in Anne's exquisitely furnished fourth floor flat at 55 Park Lane. When they arrived Anne found numerous unpaid bills for the wedding reception and gifts that Vincent had given her during the past weeks of their courtship. Confronting her new husband, he admitted that he was insolvent and his company was verging on bankruptcy. He had deceived her concerning his financial status and the precarious state of his business. Anne was horrified. Although Vincent had a prosperous fabrics business he had somehow mismanaged his affairs and was penniless.

Anne realised that for a seemingly entrenched bachelor part of her attraction to Vincent was his perception that she was a smart and wealthy spinster. She had both attributes, but he was shortly to learn a further less endearing quality. She had the ability to swear like a trooper with a vocabulary that without recourse to the vulgar, few could equal. This, coupled with an inherited incandescent and vituperative temperament made her a formidable protagonist whom none would care to challenge more than once in serious dispute. A disagreement of incendiary proportions followed. She ranted and shrieked her opinion both of his ancestry and deception, leaving Vincent in no doubt that his marriage, if not at an end, was precariously jeopardised. Unable to counter a verbal assault of such ferocity, Vincent beat a hasty retreat to Totteridge.

That evening, Zosha, my grandmother summoned Anne's siblings to an urgent meeting in her apartment. As tempers cooled, wiser council prevailed. They were able to talk her into returning unwanted gifts and paying for the rest. They advised her to patch things up with Vincent and to see what she could do to help revitalise his business. Anne reluctantly agreed to these suggestions, appreciating that at nearly fifty-one, it wouldn't be an easy task to find a new husband, especially with the added stigma, of being a divorcee. Swallowing injured pride, she decided to forgive Vincent and to give their marriage an opportunity to succeed.

The next day, uninvited, she strode into Vincent's premises Veronique Furnishings, just off Regent Street. Employing her considerable commercial experience, she instituted efficiency and order out of what she perceived as chaos and muddle. Within a short time she succeeded in rebuilding and revitalising Vincent's fabric enterprise. It thrived and Anne ensured they purchased their shop and warehouse premises. She and Vincent speedily became good companions and in the process very affluent, while Anne became the dominant partner in what proved to be a successful marriage. They lived happy contented lives together and without children, they donated considerable portions of their wealth to charity. Their marriage lasted for 29 years until Anne's death in 1978 from cancer of the pancreas.

While visiting my French cousin Georgette in Paris in 1990 she recounted a chance meeting that she and her husband Julian had enjoyed during a vacation in Normandy in 1956. In the summer of the year following her marriage, Anne and Vincent were taking a brief holiday in Deauville when they entered a restaurant for lunch. Sitting at the next table were a French couple with whom they entered into conversation using a mixture of languages. Throughout their meal they chatted amiably.

At the conclusion of lunch while waiting for the waiter to appear with their bill, Anne took a visiting card from her handbag, bearing the name Anne Veronique with her address and handing it to their new acquaintances invited them to contact her should they visit London. The French gentleman reciprocated the invitation and as they were preparing to leave, handed Anne his card stating that if M. and Mde. Veronique ever visited LeHavre to be certain to contact them. Anne looked at the name on the card, Julian and Georgette Podguzer. In great surprise she exclaimed that had been her maiden name. A few minutes of animated conversation followed as they discovered that although they'd never met previously, their late fathers had been brothers and they were first cousins, Julian being Sylvain's youngest brother.

* * *

During each of our three monthly attachments to a 'firm', we were required to live for one month in the hospital's student residence in which we were based. When living in we were on call and were expected to attend and assist in all the various emergency procedures. We were provided with facilities for making hot drinks in the student accommodation, while meals could be taken in the hospital canteen. A laundry service was provided for personal laundry. I arranged my accommodation for one week in every three, thereby assuring that each hospital dealt with my accumulated laundry. It was on these occasions I discovered how much time my colleagues applied to studying, although none would ever admit to this necessity. While living in we were still required to travel to lectures at different hospitals and I decided that something more robust than my motorised cycle was needed. Amongst the students in my year most used public transport, three had cars and three or four men had motorcycles, all of whom seemed to walk with a limp. I decided I would purchase a 125cc. Vespa motor scooter, the type I had used previously when on vacation in Italy.

My parents were vehemently opposed to such a fraught means of travel and would provide no financial help for its purchase even though I endeavoured to convince them there was no increase in risk compared to a motorised bicycle. At the time my brother Michael was employed by an advertising company which handled the advertising account for Vespa and he was able to assist me in purchasing the machine at a discounted price of £120. Selling my motorised cycle I made my purchase and with the use of a windscreen, I gained far greater protection from the elements. As with my cycle I once used it to drive down to London, but it was a very tedious journey on such a low powered vehicle.

Following my junior medicine firm I was next allocated to my junior surgical assignment with Mr. C. J. Lytle at the Royal Infirmary, a benevolently tall portly consultant surgeon in his late 50's. Mr Redwood, his senior registrar, later became a consultant in Leicester and appeared perfectly content to let the dynamically keen junior registrar deal with all the emergency admissions. The junior registrar was also the hospital's resident surgical officer and was responsible for our instruction during our three months secondment. A super energetic young Londoner in his late 20's with a twinkle in his eye and crowned with a delightful sense of humour, he was dubbed 'our Harold'. Harold Ellis later became Professor of Surgery at the Westminster Hospital School of Medicine, where in the 1980's my son was one of his students and who published an admirable textbook of surgery. Assisting 'our Harold' in the operating room was always a pleasure, as were his tutorials. As a surgeon his reputation was enhanced by his exceptional surgical speed and meticulous care.

One evening, when a patient with an acute appendicitis was on the operating table, I was the only student present. Harold was about to operate when he enquired whether anybody had informed the other students living in 'Charcot's Joint'(3), the Royal Infirmary student residence, that there was a patient about to undergo surgery. When informed that they had been telephoned and would arrive shortly he turned to the anaesthetist enquiring.

"Are we ready? Can I proceed?" Receiving an affirmative response he said to the house surgeon. "Excellent, let's see if we can have this finished before they arrive." At an incredible speed, he removed the appendix, closed up the abdominal wound and was putting the finishing touches to the dressing when half a dozen students arrived, running in and short of breath.

"Good evening doctors; you seem to have taken so long to get here we just couldn't wait." Harold exclaimed, a broad impish grin on his face. "Next time you're summoned, there's to be none of this dawdling as though tomorrow will do. I shall always expect to hear the pitter-patter of tiny running feet!"

He was a natural instructor and I always considered it a privilege to have worked alongside him for those weeks of training. On one busy occasion in the A & E department when there was no hospital bed available, Harold had been called to see an adult male who'd sustained a head injury. There was no external evidence of injury, but the skull x-ray revealed a small linear fracture. Unbelievably, I witnessed him addressing the patient.

"Now I want you to listen to me carefully. Thank God there's nothing broken, just a tiny fracture. I want you to go home and rest for the next two weeks. If you vomit or lose consciousness you're to come straight back and see me here. Do you understand?" Heaven only knows what repercussions might have resulted from this cavalier advice in our current litigious age.

My senior surgical appointment, eighteen months later was with a bluff Yorkshire man, Mr W. Blacow Yates, an older surgeon at the Royal Hospital who was close to retirement. During one of the out patient clinics he asked one of the students, whom he'd observed day dreaming to enumerate the causes of rectal bleeding. Tongue-tied and not wishing to admit his inattention he was stuttering a response when Blacow Yates had us in fits of laughter at the students discomfiture by suggesting that the main cause might be a patient's tape worm having a haematemesis (vomiting blood). One of his favourite aphorisms was.

"There are only two types of patients. Those who admit to having piles, and the liars."

My junior firm in Obstetrics and Gynaecology was spent at the Jessops Hospital for Women in the spring of 1955. We were under Professor Scott-Russell a delightful gentleman who insisted on taking a group photograph of all the students who worked on his 'firm' and was a strong advocate of a teaspoon of honey every morning for the treatment and prevention of hyperemesis (nausea and vomiting of pregnancy). It was alleged that he ran a successful business in the country producing honey. One of the points he emphasised was the adage 'masterly inactivity' when dealing with the majority of confinement problems unrelated to blood loss or foetal distress. A major and amazing omission was that at no time did he ever consider it necessary to teach anything remotely connected with birth control, or provide any form of sex education to his undergraduates. Not that the male student body appeared to need any instruction in this latter area, the majority busily and lustily arranging their own private tuition with any number of helpful student nurses. Nurse North, who with a number of likeminded colleagues, were known to be particularly helpful and obliging. There were a number of unofficial medical student organisations such as 'The Compass Club' whose members were those men who claimed to have travelled up north.

During part of this time I was unable to attend patients on the ward since I developed a persistent sore throat. A blood test revealed that I had fallen victim to Infectious Mononucleosis, a viral infection commonly known as 'glandular fever' and was obliged to return home for two weeks until I had recovered. Every few weeks another of the students in our year came down with this temporary but debilitating illness.

By the Easter of 1955 I had known June Fraiman twenty months. Initially we had written to each other every week or two, gradually increasing to three times each week. She had visited me in Sheffield at my invitation to attend the annual medical and graduation balls and we had dated whenever I was in London, which with Rolf Burchhardt's help was once or twice a month. She was an exceptionally kind and attentive young woman with a great sense of humour and with her slender appearance and keen intellect I discovered myself increasingly ensnared by her charms. My father did his best to discourage this friendship explaining that it would distract me from my studies and repeatedly indicated.

"It will be many years after you qualify before you can afford to support a wife."

My younger brother had written to inform me that in my absence June had been seen in the company of other young men. I tackled her on this subject when we next met. She explained that while she did care for me, there had been no indication on my part to suggest that we should consider our relationship to be 'serious', although we had been 'going out' with each other for some considerable time. Demonstrating such a lack of commitment I therefore had no proprietary rights as to whom she could date or choose as her companions during the weeks I was in Sheffield. She indicated she would be prepared to change her attitude should I want to formalise our relationship.

Having stated that I would prefer her not to date other young men during my absence, I enquired how she expected me to formalise our relationship, apart from assuring her of my affection and fidelity.

"You could announce our engagement." she replied.

I hastily countered. "You know perfectly well an engagement is out of the question. I've explained my parents would object and my father might in all probability stop my allowance."

"Well in that case there's nothing more to be said on the subject and I shall go out with whom I choose whenever I please." I attempted to assuage her by explaining that she was taking an unreasonable approach since she had to understand my predicament.

"Unreasonable? Do you seriously expect me to hang around for more than two years until you qualify, living with the fond expectation that you might then ask me to marry you?" She asked with incredulity.

"You know how much I care for you. Take me at my word. Be patient and wait for me to qualify."

"I'm not prepared to explain to my parents, or friends that I'm staying home like some old maid, night after night for months on end, simply because Arnold Powell, without making a public commitment to be my fiancé, simply asks me to wait for him."

"It's impossible to announce our engagement at this time. My parents would veto the whole thing. Perhaps we could become engaged in a year or two, but for now it's completely out of the question."

"Apart from your parent's opposition, would you wish to become engaged to me?"

"Yes, certainly, of course I would."

"Well if you're so worried about your parent's objections to an engagement, why not marry me?"

"Are you seriously suggesting a secret marriage without our parents knowledge, or consent, just as an alternative to becoming engaged?" I enquired, stunned by the suggestion.

"Yes, if you really love me, why ever not?"

"How can we possibly marry without our parents' knowledge?" I asked somewhat sceptically.

She laughed in disbelief. "It's perfectly simple. You can put up the marriage banns in Sheffield and three weeks later we can marry in a registry office without family or friends knowing."

"What about the witnesses? We need two witnesses."

"There's no difficulty there. Just leave it to me. I've a friend at work who's just moved to Sheffield with her husband and I'm certain they'd agree, and would keep our secret."

"It sounds easy enough, but would you wish to marry me on that basis?"

"If that's your proposal, the answer's yes."

Overjoyed with our decision, June arranged with her work colleague Liz and her husband Don Moyes to be our witnesses and the date for our marriage was set for 2 pm. on Friday July 1st. 1955 at the Sheffield Central Registry office. I organised the purchase of a (M9) marriage licence and posted the banns.

Investing many weeks of my meagre allowance, I purchased an imitation diamond eternity ring as a wedding ring for my intended bride, at the stupendous cost of £18. The day of our clandestine marriage I met June when she arrived that morning by train from London and overcoming any trepidation we briefly appeared for our civil ceremony at the appointed time together with the obligatory witnesses.

Nervously I escorted my graceful enchantress up the steps into the registrar's office, wearing my navy blue college blazer and striped medical tie for the occasion. June appeared very calm, slim and beautiful, dressed in an elegantly simple beige suit, with a single orchid corsage pinned to the collar, which I'd earlier presented to her for the occasion. Regrettably no photograph was ever taken to record this covert event.

Twenty minutes later, at the conclusion of the civil ceremony, we walked to the nearby restaurant in Walsh's, department store, where we celebrated the occasion with a much-needed cup of tea and resolved our secret should never be divulged. Foolishly I left my bride temporarily to attend a 4pm. paediatric lecture, which was a total waste of time, since my mind was in a whirl and my thoughts solely on my bride and my new responsibilities.

That evening we celebrated by attending the annual graduation ball at the student's union with Liz and Don. June had explained to her parents her reason for visiting me in Sheffield was to attend this ball. Fortunately there was no recurrence of the previous year when June had fainted in the midst of the union while I was making a phone call and some over-enthusiastic undergraduate emptied a jug of cold water over her head and shoulders to bring her round.

We retired to 'Charcot's Joint' the student residence of the Royal Infirmary Hospital where I was living that week and had arranged for June to stay. We spent the night in single beds in separate bedrooms. This, for the next two and a half years, was a marriage in name only. We reluctantly agreed, that safety depended upon the abstinence of conjugal rights. There was no 'pill' or reliable contraception and a pregnancy would have been a disaster at this stage. To day, attitudes are so different that it's difficult to comprehend the profound change in attitudes towards marriage and birth out of wedlock, that have swept through the western world in so brief a time span. Prior to the 1960's, in the pre 'pill' era, pregnancy before marriage was considered a scandal and an illegitimate birth an onerous stigma and lifetime burden.

Upon retirement I pursued my hobby of genealogy. In 1999 I discovered that June's parents in 1931 and also my parents in 1922 had each married in a registry office some months prior to a formal religious wedding ceremony. Both couples had married in secret to circumvent parental objections, in much the same manner as we had used this device.

In mid 1955 I informed my parents that I was travelling to Italy for a two-week summer vacation with June spending one week in Rome and one week in Naples and Capri. They were horrified. My father objected strenuously.

"What sort of parents would allow their unmarried daughter to vacation by herself with a young man?" June's parents raised no objections.

We travelled by train from Victoria to Dover, then across the channel by ferry and again by train to Paris, where we needed to change trains for Rome. Recovering from a recent pneumothorax, I was reluctant to risk carrying a heavy suitcase. We agreed to place our clearly labelled cases in the train's luggage compartment, for collection in Rome. In Paris we arrived at the Gare du Norde and were required to change railway stations to catch the onward train south to Rome. This entailed taking a taxi and dashing across Paris for our connection. By sprinting we boarded the next train with only a minute to spare and it therefore came as no surprise to find at Rome Termini that our cases hadn't arrived.

We decided to stay in Ostia as a more economical way of seeing Rome and took the local train to the coastal resort, where we found bed and breakfast accommodation in a small apartment. We left our remaining overnight baggage there and returned to Rome to see the opera 'Mephistopheles' at the outdoor 'Carricala Baths Theatre'. The opera started late and we had to leave before the end to catch the last train.

On our return to Ostia, close to midnight, we found our lodging closed. We established the apartment owner was absent and we'd been locked out. We had no baggage and no accommodation. Our chances of finding a hotel at that time of night looked grim. While debating our predicament a group of young Italians walked by and we decided to ask them whether they knew of any hotel near by. We explained our dilemma in Italian, which I spoke passably well at the time and to our amazement one of the couples insisted we return with them to their nearby apartment where we could stay the night. We gladly accepted their offer and ended up staying five nights as their guests, sleeping on their living room floor.

Next day we reclaimed our overnight baggage from our earlier lodging and proceeded to Rome's Art Deco Termini railway station. There was no sign of our luggage and we were told to return the next day. The following day was no different. We searched for an agent and requested assistance in locating our missing cases. Within forty-eight hours they had discovered our baggage in the left property department in the Genoa Railway Station, but the railway would not forward it and we were required to collect it in person. The next day we bade our Italian hosts farewell and instead of proceeding south to Naples as intended, we set off for Genoa on the overnight train in order to reduce the loss of daylight time we could use in sightseeing. Unwilling to sleep sitting up, June decided on a device she had previously used. She would sleep in the overhead luggage rack and as an additional safety precaution tied herself in with a belt. In the middle of the night the ticket collector came round to check tickets.

I gave him mine and since he failed to look into the luggage rack, mine was the only ticket clipped. On arrival at Genoa station we found our cases. The railway authorities would not however release them until we paid the charge for four days storage. We argued and stormed, but to no avail. We paid the fee under duress and obtained our property, only to discover the labels with the Rome Termini destination had been crossed out and erased. I proceeded to the stationmaster's office to have him verify June's ticket had not been used on the journey Rome to Genoa. This he obligingly did.

"Any more?" he asked. I gave him my ticket and without looking he likewise verified the ticket had not been used. We were now in a position to resume our interrupted vacation and to reclaim some of our expenses from the railway, with the portions of our unused tickets.

We decided there was insufficient time to travel to Naples and so boarded the next train heading south to Viareggio, where we obtained accommodation at the Excelsior, a hotel I knew from previous holidays spent with my parents. A week later we returned to London and I resumed my medical studies. Later, by presenting the stationmaster's document confirming we'd not used the Rome Genoa portion of our tickets I obtained a rebate of £16, which helped defray the agent's fee for locating our cases and the storage costs at Genoa.

The summer of 1955 saw a visit by the Queen and Prince Philip in celebration of the 50th anniversary of the University receiving its royal charter from her great grandfather Edward VII. The visit was preceded by the construction in the main university building of a special washroom and toilet for the visit together with a sheltered dais in the quadrangle, where we were able to hear and see the Queen make her celebratory speech.

In the autumn, my senior maternity clerking was at Sheffield's Northern Hospital. The first week coincided with one of June's visits to Sheffield and I proudly invited her to attend as an observer, clad in green cap, mask and gown, when I delivered one of my first babies.

Attached to a flying squad I would go out by ambulance accompanying a midwife to homes where maternity patients were experiencing problems and soon became firmly convinced that an ambulance and flying squad was never the best way to deal with a maternity emergency. I felt that every delivery should take place in a hospital where facilities are readily at hand to deal with the unexpected, following which the mother could return home as soon as she wished.

In my fourth year I met Dr C Royd, a public health consultant who was part of the selection team who appointed new consultants to the Sheffield Hospital Regional Board. We played chess periodically and on one occasion he explained that he'd had a very stressful day.

"You know Powell, I've just come from a meeting to appoint a new consultant surgeon. We had more than one hundred applicants and we had to shortlist these highly qualified surgical applicants down to six men we could call for interview. It was an impossible task, but we had to do it.

Our first criterion was age. All those over 36 were too old while under 36, too young. We next looked at the fellowship qualification and excluded anybody who didn't have a London Fellowship. Next it was experience. If they'd stayed in one place too long they hadn't enough experience and if they'd changed too often they were also excluded. Finally we had reduced the numbers down to about twenty candidates, any one of who could have occupied any chair of surgery. With further arbitrary paring we achieved a list of six candidates for interview. We interviewed all of them. All were splendid men and the chap we appointed was a former Sheffield graduate whose father was in practice in the city."

This conversation profoundly affected my decision to enter general practice. Government indifference to conditions of employment and a failure to create more consultant posts caused moral in the ranks of the junior medical graduates to plummet through the 1950's and 60's. This resulted in a torrent of highly trained medical professionals immigrating mainly to North America and Australia, termed by the press 'the brain drain', which the UK could ill afford. Later practicing in the US and Canada I was able to observe at first hand numbers of highly skilled English doctors as well as nurses contentedly staffing North American hospitals. The love of home and country could never adequately compensate these dedicated medics when faced with their lack of opportunity to advance to consultant and senior nursing status.

During clinical ward rounds and tutorials, consultants often regaled us with medical anecdotes. One particularly interesting story came from Dr.Tommy Lodge, a radiological consultant who described how his former chief had told him that when, shortly after he had established the new speciality of radiology in Sheffield he'd been summoned in 1908 to Chatsworth House. There, with the earliest portable equipment, he and his assistant were to attend a royal personage who had sustained a chest injury.

Two gentlemen at either end of a long stoutly built refectory table were playing a game of 'ping-pong'. However instead of a table tennis ball they had an attractive young lady lying on the table, which they would then elevate at one end, causing her to slide down to the other end, then the other gentleman would raise his end midst howls of laughter and cause the young lady to cavort back down to the other end, without sliding off. Unfortunately on this occasion as she slid down the table her heel had accidentally struck one of the participants in the chest, producing a painful bruise with the suspicion that he might have sustained one or more fractured ribs. An x-ray confirmed a fractured rib. The young lady was Lily Langtry and the royal gentleman involved, was none other than her friend Edward VII.

Since I loathed studying in an empty room by myself I invariably chose to study at the central library in Sheffield. Whenever I returned to my bed-sitter my first action would be to switch on the radio, to provide some background sound. Likewise when in London I would travel by tube to Russell Square to study at the library in Senate House.

Much of 1956 and the first part of 1957 was taken up with studying and revising for forthcoming 3rd MB and Conjoint examinations, in addition to the usual routine of lectures, ward rounds and participating in assigned tasks when on attachment to a particular clinical firm. One of the last of these clinical attachments was in paediatrics, under Prof. Ronald Illingworth, the bespectacled author of a medical textbook entitled 'The Normal Child'. He spoke with a slight lisp, mispronouncing his r's like w's, so that when seeking a response from a child when he asked. "What wars?" and receiving no response, would announce in exasperation. "A lion wars (roars) of course." He ran an excellent paediatric department, but was a terrifyingly strict disciplinarian, who it was rumoured had written his famed textbook following an examination in which he'd claimed a normal child had a non existent abnormality. His Monday morning ward round with his staff who were all petrified to varying degrees by his presence was described as a prayer meeting, when all clinical misdemeanours had to be confessed. The paediatric out patient clinic, in the basement of the hospital, with windows on a level with the trams running up hill outside, made history taking and clinical examination extremely difficult and more so in summer with the windows open.

Final year medical students were encouraged to undertake locum house officer hospital appointments of one or two week's duration when these became available. I undertook two such appointments. In September 1956 I volunteered for a locum house post at the Sheffield Children's Hospital, Thornbury Annexe, in Fulwood Road, during the holiday absence of the paediatric houseman. The weekly salary, minus deductions for food and accommodation was £1. The locum was required to live in, although college lectures could be attended when time permitted.

Upon arrival at the annexe, a converted mansion of the former Sheffield home of Lady Mappin of Mappin and Webb the silversmiths, one could hardly fail to be impressed when driving up the gently curved sweeping gradient of the driveway past manicured shrubberies, extensive lawns and landscaped garden all of which completely hid the mansion from the main road. I parked my motor scooter and reported to the head porter. A delightful spacious bedroom at the top of the house, on the second floor had been allocated for my use, with its panoramic views of mature specimen trees in the wooded garden at the rear of the building. Every morning one of the domestic staff would awaken me at 6 a.m. with a knock on the bedroom door before entering with a cup of tea and biscuits.

The ward sister, a typically dominant alpha female in her dark blue uniform, had been expecting me. With great disdain she rapidly outlined my duties. She explained the hierarchy within the unit, leaving little doubt that while I might perform some essential functions, like the bumblebee in a hive, she was the queen and I was at the lowermost rung of the staff ladder and should know my place.

My young patients were in various stages of treatment for tuberculosis. Each morning I was required to perform lumbar punctures on a number of the children with spinal TB, and on others, every three days. This essential procedure involved injecting strictly measured intrathecal quantities of streptomycin, dependant upon the child's weight, into the spinal canal. An unpleasant experience requiring the youngster to remain motionless until completed, with a nurse always delegated to assist me by holding the child perfectly still during these delicate sterile procedures. Some of the children, who had been severely and irreparably brain damaged, exhibited opisthotonos, the unsightly backward contraction and arching of neck and back muscles. These young patients were considered beyond help from the intrathecal streptomycin and were given no further antibiotics.

On my second day I noticed a small, plain, untreated wooden coffin being removed from the building by a man who carried it out into a waiting vehicle. I asked the ward sister what had happened. She told me the undertaker was removing the tiny body for internment of one of her charges, who had passed away. Reassuringly she explained that it was one of the young children who had been in a severe vegetative state from cerebral tuberculosis who had died during the night, a frequent occurrence and a blessing for the child and its family. I accepted her explanation since it didn't occur to me to question who had examined the child to confirm death, or who would sign the death certificate.

Throughout the days that followed this process was repeated on two further occasions. The undertaker, would appear in the early hours of the morning to remove, in a small sarcophagus, a second and then a third body of those youngsters with opisthotonos who had died during the night. On my last day of duty, overcome by curiosity, I questioned one of the nurses as she assisted me during one of several lumbar puncture procedures. I asked if she knew why so many of my young patients, three in the past week, seemed to have died during the night without my being summoned to see them, as a consequence of a deterioration in their condition, or to confirm that death had taken place.

Initially, she appeared evasive. As I persisted, evasion was replaced by feigned surprise at my apparent naivety. She extracted my solemn promise that I would never divulge to anyone what she was about to reveal. In hushed conspiratorial tones she confirmed, as I was aware, that these children were irreparably brain damaged. Swearing me to further secrecy she described how sister covertly administered insulin in the evening to help each of them on their heavenly journey. She explained that sister had warned her and any other of her staff, who had inadvertently observed her clandestine injections, of the direst retribution if a word of this ever leaked out. The 'queen bee', unlike her counterpart in the hive that created life, was busily terminating the seriously disabled in her care.

As a student wishing to complete my medical training, I dared not become an involved whistle blower. However, I was never able to understand who, amongst the paediatric medical staff, had signed the medical certificates without examining these young patients and why the consultant, his registrars, or the houseman for whom I was standing in, never enquired into the frightening frequency of these otherwise unexplained nocturnal deaths! The vacuous silence in one of the finest paediatric department's in the country, with its plaintive unanswered cry for justice proved intolerable, yet disturbingly, no one ever chose to listen or respond.

A number of medical students in each year took the professional London Conjoint Board examination. There were several obstacles to be overcome when taking these alternative examinations. Conjoint examinations never coincided with the examination subjects in Sheffield, which meant studying was out of synchronisation. This element had its compensation since writing answers and attending viva's under exam conditions gave additional practice and a tremendous boost to morale when attended by success.

Other problems were of my own making and arose from my resolve not to involve my parents, in order to avoid the tiresome inquisitions, which opened with "How did you get on?" This led to a further financial crisis. I had to pay a £50 fee for each examination together with my fare money to London. Further more, each time I sat the examination in Queen's Square I needed to explain my disappearance for the day by informing my parents that I was attending the Senate House Library adjacent to Russell Square to study. My father would frequently offer to give me a ride in his car and on one occasion stopped to make a call en-route which made me twenty minutes late for a two and a half hour pathology paper. Fortunately, apart from a brief panic attack, there were no other repercussions.

In the summer of 1956 I plucked up sufficient courage to tell my parents that I wished to become engaged. There was the predictable parental opposition, but they finally capitulated and my father undertook to purchase a modest diamond engagement ring on my behalf and gave June her preferred choice of design. The announcement date coincided with June's parents' silver wedding anniversary at the end of August. They had enquired where we would like the celebration to take place and two weeks later on the second Sunday in September on a warm late summer's day a marquee was erected in the rear garden of their home, where we had a celebratory family tea party.

(1) Rabbi Akiva (circa 15-135 CE) Akiba ben Joseph whose father was a proselyte, became a great teacher in Israel. A contemporary of Rabbi Tarfon, with an immense student following, he advocated the tradition of the oral law, the Mishnah, and Talmudic disputation. As a young man he met and married Rebecca in secret. Her wealthy father, hearing this, drove her out of his house and disinherited her, only to rescind this decision many years later as Akiva's fame spread. When an old man, he encouraged Bar Kochba in his revolt against Roman occupation, which failed disastrously. He was executed by the Romans who flayed him to death and then sadistically burnt his body at the stake, as a burnt offering, on the Day of Atonement. He was stated to have been 120.

(2) Richard Doll (1912-2005) was a giant amongst epidemiologists. His prolific work at the Medical Research Council was later recognised with a knighthood. In 1954, he published the first study to correlate the incidence of lung cancer and also of heart disease with the number of cigarettes smoked. Subsequently he warned that, besides smoking, exposure to nickel, asbestos, tar producing gases and radioactivity were major causes of cancer. In 1955, he published a landmark report warning of high cancer rates in asbestos workers. In 1967 Doll warned that an 'immense' number of substances were known to cause cancer, and that prevention of cancer was a better strategy than cure. His later research confirmed Aspirin in small doses gave protection against heart disease.

(3) Charcot (1825-1893) a French neurologist who taught at the Salpetriere Hospital in Paris. He was the first to describe an arthropathy (destruction) of the knee joint due to sensory impairment, giving his name to the condition 'Charcot's Joint'.

(M4) A half skeleton in wooden box cost £15, A Gray's Anatomy, £25.

(M5) Rail fare 3rd class return St Pancras to Sheffield was 49 shillings and six pence (£2.48p).

(M6) In 1952 a cup of tea or coffee in the University refectory and student union cost 3 d. (just over 1p.) A meal cost from one shilling and six pence to two shillings (7½p to 10p). Eggs could be purchased at about 4 shilling a dozen (20p.) A man's average wage was £7:5s. (£7.25p) and women received considerably less for the same job. Confectionary rationing continued after the war until 1954.

(M7) the charge for a long distance 'phone call between London and Sheffield was one shilling and six pence for a minimum 3 minute call 7.5p. Charges were based on distance and duration of call. Very few homes had telephones and there were no mobile phones. First class mail was 2½d. (1p).

(M8) In 1954 the cost of one gallon of petrol was four shillings and sixpence (22½ p). My earliest memory of this fuel was in 1939 when the price was 9d. and 11d. (less than 5p) a gallon.

(M9) A marriage licence cost fifteen shillings (75p.).

Chapter 4

MEXBOROUGH YORKSHIRE

1957

Friday June 21st was one of those stiflingly hot airless English summer afternoons. The small anteroom to Dean J. G. McCrie's office in Western Bank, opposite the red brick Sheffield University building was packed to bursting, yet still more students crowded in as we assembled for the results.

By 3pm I was one of the sixty of the year of 1957 who crammed into the office. We clustered in, virtually standing on each other's toes, waiting at the foot of the steps leading to a first floor office for the results of the final examination to be read out. There was insufficient room for everybody and the glazed door opening onto an inner forecourt was kept open, where later arrivals were compelled to stand, all desperately straining to listen for their name being read out.

The routine was that the secretary would appear promptly at 3 pm. She would read out each student's name in alphabetical order followed by the examination result, after which she would place a typewritten list on the notice board. The tension mounted as we waited for the Dean's administrative assistant, Beryl Jordan, to appear. The tight squeeze and the heat of the afternoon hardly mattered, as we nervously laughed at every bantered comment and joke.

Final vivas had taken place over the previous few days, the last that very morning at noon and now we waited on tenterhooks for the results. With every passing minute, the apprehension perceptibly increased along with the temperature in the inadequately ventilated room.

Those who qualified could immediately use the title 'doctor' and would be permitted to commence an obligatory one-year pre-registration (**P**) house officer course of employment in an approved hospital, which included 6 months medicine and 6 months surgery. Those who failed would have to resit the final examinations in six months time, ineligible to apply for a house post until they passed which resulted in 6 months forced unemployment. Coupled with this was the rule that Sheffield undergraduates were permitted to sit professional examinations no more than twice. As a consequence, a proportion of the students in each year periodically journeyed to London to sit the professionally recognized 'London Conjoint Board' examinations, held by the Royal College of Physicians and Surgeons every 3 months and I'd been amongst this group. A further faculty rule precluded any undergraduate qualifying through the conjoint board until they had sat the Sheffield final examinations.

At precisely 3 pm, the dean's assistant appeared with type written sheets rustling in her hand. There was a hushed silence as she announced.

"I shall read the results of the Final Bachelor of Medicine and Bachelor of Surgery examinations in alphabetical order, following which the list will be placed on the notice board."

Keeping us in suspense those agonizing seconds more she continued.

"Early next week, all students will receive written notification of these results, in the mail, together with two tickets for each graduating student's relatives to attend the university degree convocation which will take place on July the 6th. The chancellor will then distribute degree certificates and recipients will be required to hire the appropriate cap and gown for the occasion, details of which will be enclosed with the admission tickets. Now these are the results:"

"Nathanial Akabi-Davis;" followed by a brief pause; "Passed. Irving Aubrey;" - pause, "failed." There were apprehensive gasps, as all suddenly felt more vulnerable to hear the name of a failed classmate. The result was not unexpected, since a few weeks before, Irving, the oldest member of the year, in his 50's had earlier been taken ill during a lecture and had been hospitalised with a heart attack. The names droned on under Beryl's emotionless voice, sounding more like a newscaster reading the Saturday afternoon soccer match results.

"Maureen Lovett;" - pause, "passed. Siana McNab; - failed." Poor Siana, who always found time for a kind word for all. So far four would have to resit their finals and still the litany continued.

"John Palmer; - Passed. Arnold Powell;" I strained to listen as time stood unbearably still far beyond the tenth of a second pause before she continued in the same detached tone.

"Passed. Arthur Richards; - passed. Maurice Roberts; - passed." (The colleagues with whom I'd worked on my anatomy dissections in the second and third years) And remorselessly the list continued, while strewn in its wake were battered deflated egos amongst a few and euphoric happiness amongst the majority who'd passed. Then followed the names of the coveted prize winning students, Alan Yates, John Palmer, Roger Bradshaw and Mike Harfst, and their prizes, all destined to receive the coveted choice of jobs in any of the professorial units.

"The name of the student selected to travel to Albany, New York State for one year, as part of the newly arranged 'Exchange Visitor's Programme', John Horton." The bright affable trombone playing student, with whom I'd worked on many occasions. I envied his opportunity to travel to the US, but to my immense relief, all that really mattered was that I'd passed.

As we scrambled to leave the office there were congratulations offered and received and to the few who failed there were consoling words.

"What rotten luck, you're sure to pass next time." as we extended commiserations to those putting on a nonchalant show of bravery to conceal immense disappointment, which included Malcolm Williams, the good-natured Welsh double base-playing musician and Londoner Tony Fox, who both shared my digs. There were half a dozen of our newly qualified numbers, who within the next few days, were to be married, like the water polo playing Alan Yates, the year's top student and the serious bespectacled Pete Brasher, since in those years undergraduates rarely married.

Over 80% of our class had passed and I was amongst them. In an elated daze I rushed out to find a call box in the nearby students union to phone June and then my parents, without revealing I'd first called June. My third call was to Dr I Brody, one of Sheffield's leading consultant physicians. Softly spoken and of slight build, he was physician at the Royal Infirmary Hospital Sheffield and at the Montague Hospital Mexborough, 20 miles from Sheffield, midway between Rotherham and Doncaster. With friendly sparkling brown eyes, surrounded by a grey 'arcus senilis', he was an excellent teacher who smoked constantly when not attending patients.

I spoke to his secretary, submitting my name for employment as his house physician. Prior to taking up a hospital post, all newly qualified doctors had to formally submit applications for provisional registration to the General Medical Council and to join the Medical Defence Union to insure against possible litigation. A full registration was granted the following July 1958, with the arrival of a certificate confirming satisfactory completion of twelve months supervised house officer hospital employment in medicine and surgery.

Elatedly, I journeyed to London to see June, parents, family and friends. As I travelled south by train, my thoughts returned to the psychological challenge I'd accepted in 1950 during my St. Mary's hospital interview when the secretary opined that I stood no chance of completing a medical course and should seek something less demanding. It had taken seven years to prove him wrong.

The days that followed were of an exhilarating happiness. I called on June's father, in his unpretentiously small inner office at 9, Percy Street, just off Tottenham Court Road. As I entered, he rose from his desk smiled and extended his hand in congratulations. Thanking him, I explained the reason for my visit.

"Mr. Fraiman, June and I have known each other for close on four years and now that I'm qualified, I'd like your consent to our marriage." With the widest beam imaginable, he gave his enthusiastic approval, shaking me heartily by the hand once more.

"When would you like to get married son?" Without hesitation I responded.

"As soon as possible."

"Did you have any date in mind?"

"What about the end of August?"

"Not so fast young man, these things take a little time to arrange. We'll have to find a suitable venue for the ceremony and reception; then there's the caterer, the florist, dressmakers, printers, invitations and a host of other arrangements. First let me call Dora with the good news and then I'm taking you out for lunch." He immediately telephoned June's mother to tell her of my request and then took me for a celebratory meal with his partner Ronnie Marks, to the Elysée, a smart French restaurant close by. Prior to lunch he insisted, on escorting me to Jay's his Charlotte Street tailor, to have me measured for a bespoke lightweight suit as he generously chuckled.

"That's more befitting a newly qualified doctor."

I told my parents of my meeting with Fred Fraiman that evening and of his consent to my marriage to June. Father's response was in stark contrast as he promptly poured cold water on the idea.

"Young man; have you completely taken leave of your senses? I've been glad to support you up to this time, but you can't seriously expect me to maintain you financially once you're married."

"Dad, I'll always be grateful for your help in putting me through medical school, but I don't expect, or need your financial support any longer. Next month I'll be earning my own salary and June will continue working. Within a couple of years our finances will have improved…." My father interrupted.

"Don't talk such utter rubbish. You've nowhere to live, no money to set up a home for your wife and we're certainly not providing married quarters here. Just tell me how in heaven's name can you afford to support a wife on the pittance the NHS calls a salary? For the next two years you'll be earning less than your mother pays the cleaning woman. It's all very well thinking your wife can work, but what's going to happen when children arrive? To marry on the threshold of your professional career would be foolhardy. There should be no talk of a wedding until you're in a position to provide a home for your wife. You should wait at least two or three years before considering marriage."

18 July 2007

Dear Paul,

I have just published through Author House, an autobiography 'Raging Against Time', available through <Amazon .com>, which covers my first 10 years in medical practice. I intend that the entire proceeds from the sale and distribution of this book will go to Prostate Research Campaign UK.

Should you enjoy it, please send, mentioning the book title, a donation to:

Prostate Research Campaign UK. 10 Northfields Prospect, Putney Bridge Road London SW18 1PE

Have a good vacation.

Yours sincerely,

Arnold Powell

"If we're to wait until you think I can afford to get married, we might need to wait forever. We're going to marry and somehow we'll get by."

"Arnold, you're talking and behaving like an impetuous adolescent."

"Dad, there's nothing impulsive about wanting to marry June. I've known her four years."

"Then all the more reason she should be prepared to wait, to enable you to get on your feet."

"This has nothing to do with June, it's me. I'm the one who isn't prepared to wait. I'm the one who's twenty five and wants to marry some one very special."

"Arnold, you've always been a stubborn, headstrong boy and in spite of a college education you've not changed. I've nothing more to say, but this. If contrary to my advice, you go ahead with marriage at this time, don't come crying to me for accommodation or financial help."

"With or without your consent we're going to marry, so you'd better get used to the idea."

"If that's your attitude don't expect your mother or me to be at your wedding young man. You're behaving like an obstinate young fool and one day you'll wake up to the realities of this world and the need to make a living before you think of marriage."

My father's assessment was correct. I was young and impetuous but he failed to understand that in my university years I'd exchanged obduracy for resolution. I was determined to wed June and make a success of my career and my marriage, in spite of parental opposition, in the same manner he and my mother had succeeded in theirs, without the agreement of his parents.

As Fred commenced his search for an appropriate venue and made arrangements for the wedding, I felt that in time I could overcome my father's objections and win him over. My next mission was to obtain exemption from my two years obligatory military service in order that once I'd obtained full registration I could plan to better utilize the time that I might have spent in uniform, by working and travelling in North America.

I attended my obligatory physical examination in Sheffield the week after qualifying, knowing that with my history of recurrent chest problems I would be exempted on health grounds. At the conclusion of the physical, the medical officer came over and sombrely explained he had no alternative but to reject me for military service. Cynically I replied.

"What a terrible shame!" To which his surprising response was,

"If you're really that keen I'll see what I can do to help you."

I promptly thanked him for his offer and assured him I couldn't ask him to do anything irregular on my behalf and that I would find some way to live with this disappointment. By which time, fully dressed, I walked briskly out of the medical office without a backwards glance.

Entitled to two graduation ceremony tickets, I needed three. Fortunately Maureen Lovett helped resolve my dilemma. Her mother, a widow, only needed one ticket and she generously provided me with one of hers. Following the formal degree convocation I returned to London and then, borrowing father's Rover saloon, motored up to Sheffield to move my effects from my Filey Street digs, to my adequate, but spartan room in the Montague Hospital in Mexborough.

My duties were to commence two days later. When I arrived I walked into the hospital and gave the duty porter my name, explaining that I was the new house physician and enquiring where I might park in order to unload my vehicle before returning to London. He immediately telephoned the ward and summoned the duty nurse who came hurrying down breathlessly announcing that there was a male patient who was just about to expire and the locum houseman couldn't be located. Would I please follow her, examine the patient and then speak to the family.

I followed her as she hurriedly strode to the ward, asking innumerable questions in order to learn details of the patient's medical condition. She explained he'd been admitted two weeks earlier, the last of many admissions in the previous year, suffering from terminal liver cirrhosis, brought about by years of excessive drinking. She escorted me to a screened off portion of the ward near the door where a group of distraught, sorrowing, relatives crowded round a bed in which lay the first patient I was to examine as a doctor. He laid there, an emaciated, a jaundiced amber middle-aged man in blue striped pyjamas, propped up on contrasting white pillows struggling to take a few terminal gasps of air. I requested the nurse to ask the relatives to vacate the patient's bedside and escort them to the adjacent waiting room, so that I might have space in which to examine the gentleman.

No sooner had they moved out of the screened area, and before I could lift the hospital stethoscope, the patient gave a terminal gasp, and expired. A few moments later the nurse breathlessly reappeared carrying the patient's notes. She could clearly see that death had just occurred and now requested that I see the relatives to break the news to them.

"Why can't you speak to the family?" I asked.

"You're the doctor and it's your job not the nurse's." She replied.

"What am I to tell them?" I pleaded, as I desperately sought guidance. "I've never dealt with a bereaved family on my own before?"

"Don't worry. I'll introduce you as the house physician and give you moral support."

"But I'm not the doctor here until I start work on Tuesday." I protested. "I don't know the family and I didn't know the deceased for more than two seconds. I just came over to move my effects in. Whatever should I say to them?"

"It's really very simple." She instructed. "Invite them to sit down. Tell them you've some sad news and explain that the patient just passed away in spite of all that you and modern medical science could do for him. Explain how sorry you are that nothing further had been humanly possible to prolong his life and that he died peacefully. Indicate that if they could wait a further few minutes you'll do your best to let them have the medical certificate to take to the registrar in the morning."

Hardly daring to deviate, I did exactly as instructed. To my relief they accepted my pronouncements, as I concluded with condolences on behalf of the staff and myself. To my amazement they expressed their deep gratitude for all I'd done. Relieved I then embellished my instructions, savouring my new role as I explained how much we would all miss such a popular patient and before I could continue further, the nurse intervened sensing that I was deviating too far from my prepared script, requesting me to accompany her to sister's office to write out the death certificate. As the nurse and I walked away, I thanked her for her assistance in helping me perform my first qualified medical task and explained that I was returning to London once I'd unloaded my effects. Smiling, she invited me to return for a cup of coffee before setting out on my return journey.

"I think I owe you that much, for stepping into the breach like that and I can tell you a little about the hospital routine and some of the patients you'll be seeing on the male ward."

I returned father's car and the following morning caught the train from King's Cross to Sheffield, where I collected my Vespa motor scooter from my digs for the last time. Skirting the ever-hazardous Sheffield tram lines I drove at a leisurely pace to Mexborough and the Montague Hospital, where I was to commence my duties the next day, July 9th at 8 am.

The nursing sister tutor had died some days earlier and was to be cremated on Thursday. I was assigned to represent the medical staff at the funeral in Sheffield since I was responsible for the medical care of all resident staff, even though I'd never known the woman. Thursday was my half-day and it was considered this was the most useful way for me to utilise my time.

In addition to me there were three other doctors resident in the hospital. The surgical registrar, who was the most senior, his surgical house officer and the post registration obstetric and gynaecology houseman, Dr Mike Leigh, the next most senior living in staff member, who by coincidence had been my predecessor as house physician.

I was on call 24 hours a day apart from Thursday afternoons, which was a half day from 2 to 10 pm. I was also granted leave of absence of one weekend in four from 6 pm Friday until 10pm Sunday. During these off duty periods Dr Leigh covered my duties, while I covered his duties in turn, on his days off. As Dr Brody's houseman I was in charge of the hospital's 28-bedded male and female medical wards. Every week I was required to attend a ward round with Dr Brody and his registrar and a separate round with the registrar and to attend two outpatient clinics, one held by Dr Brody, and his registrar, for new patients, and another, a follow up clinic, by myself. Following breakfast at 7 am I conducted ward rounds and was responsible for the day-to-day medical needs of patients, supervising investigations and treatment, arranging for admissions, discharges and follow up, keeping medical notes and records, and writing patients repeat medications.

In addition I was responsible for all the children in the 15 bed paediatric ward, under Dr. Harvey the consultant paediatrician, assisting him in his weekly out patient clinic and attending the weekly ward round. Another duty was attending the medical needs of all resident hospital staff, while I was also required, to assist Dr Hathersley, an ophthalmic consultant from the USA, in her out patient clinic each Friday afternoon. This work load was doubtlessly considered inadequate, since between 6 pm. and 8am I was responsible for all nocturnal A&E (accident and emergency) attendances for any patient considered by the duty nurse to be an adult or paediatric medical problem.

Apart from their weekly clinic and ward round, my consultants each made it abundantly clear that they would deal with any other problem by telephone. There was no predicament or emergency which could not be resolved on the 'phone, or by a Consultant's brief weekly presence, or in Dr Brody's case, the additional weekly attendance of his registrar. There was no formal tuition or instruction. Perhaps this oversight was intentional, since there was no time in which to attend formal classes.

There was a spacious dining room, which was also used by the visiting consultants and also served as a lounge. Unfortunately the call system relied entirely upon the telephone. The first place anyone looked for a doctor was in the dining room where the phone constantly rang, disturbing everyone. It was a terrible system, which gave the doctors little uninterrupted free time, when using the communal area, and seldom could a meal be eaten without interruption. There was no medical library, study or quiet room. House officers devised a rota for leaving the hospital in the evenings and covering each other, when time allowed, providing we didn't travel beyond Mexborough and remained in telephone contact. The most popular evening destination was the Ferry Boat Inn, some 200 yards from the hospital, where we could be speedily reached by phone. I was befriended by Dr. Otto Flemming, a local G.P. who occasionally invited me to his home, which was a short distance from the hospital, for coffee. His wife Dorothy made the most wonderful Viennese coffee, tutored by her husband a former Austrian Jewish refugee.

I held the view that most patients, demanding hypnotic medication had become habituated to their need following a stay in hospital. Unwittingly nurses and doctors responsible for their night-time care had turned them into hypnotic 'addicts' by providing sleeping tablets on which, after a few days, they had become dependent. I resolved this would never happen to my patients. This resolve lasted almost five hours during my first night on duty. The night staff commenced their duties at 8 pm. and within a few minutes the opening salvo of an identical barrage of phone calls began, the only variation being the patient's name and the nurse making the call. Following a hectic first day as I settled into my chair, the phone rang. In fact judging by the brevity of the pauses between each call, it was likely the nurses were standing in line waiting to speak to me. It appeared that unknowingly I now headed the Mexborough popularity charts.

"Dr Powell, this is night sister. One of your patients, Mrs. Jones says she can't sleep and there's no hypnotic written up for her."

"Yes sister that's perfectly correct. Why not let her have a hot drink of milk, Horlicks, or some similar beverage and I'm sure she'll get to sleep."

"Very well doctor, but just in case she can't nod off, could you write something up for her?"

"No I'm certain she'll get all the sleep she needs without resorting to medication."

"If you were to write something up as p.r.n. (as needed), it would save my needing to disturb you again."

"No sister, it's really no trouble and I'm certain that we'll be saving the health service a small fortune."

Young and enthusiastic I knew that if I wrote up a hypnotic as p.r.n. each patient would be given a sleeping tablet as routine and I was determined that this practice should not continue while I was the doctor in charge. Within moments of replacing the 'phone, it rang again. This time another dulcet toned female voice reported that Mr Smith couldn't sleep and an almost identical conversation ensued. By the time 1 pm. arrived with no opportunity of rest, or sleep, I realised were this to continue, I'd be unable to function next morning. As 2 am approached and the incoming calls continued, I rejoined the real world. In dressing gown and slippers thinking 'to hell with the NHS medication budget' I strode onto the wards, which were my responsibility. I sat at the desk in each and with the night sister's assistance wrote up p.r.n. sleeping medication for every patient. I had unconditionally surrendered, in spite of earlier resolves. Beaming, each night sister in turn assured me these medications would only be dispensed if absolutely necessary. The next morning, following my rounds I churlishly checked the medications that had been dispensed that night and discovered every patient had received a hypnotic!

During the third month of my house job I exchanged my motor scooter for a small car. It was a sad but necessary parting in view of my anticipated marriage. The new car was a two door Austin A35 black saloon (M10), capable of carrying four adults. Everything, apart from the wheels, brakes and front window wipers, was an extra. As an economy I omitted the optional car heater and radio. Not possessing anything near the full purchase price of the car I leased it over a three-year period from the 'Medical Finance Corporation'. Nine months later, prior to immigrating to the USA, when I needed to sell the car, this corporation insisted I reimburse the interest for the full three years, a usurious sum in excess of 30% of the total cost of the vehicle. This salutary lesson taught me never lease or buy anything on hire purchase. Apart from the purchase of my home, I resolved that if I couldn't afford something I would manage without and save until I had the full purchase price.

Friday evening, the 29th November, I travelled down to London, for my weekend off duty and a two-week vacation. Rolf Burchhardt and his wife picked me up at the hospital and we set off for London down the A1, which at the time had three lanes. Some fifty miles into our journey, Rolf overtook a car, which in turn chose to overtake the vehicle in front without signalling. The result was no more serious than a dented car wing thanks to Rolf's skilful evasive action. A motorcyclist travelling in the opposite direction was the only casualty. He was so engrossed at surveying our accident, on the opposite side of the road that both he and his motorcycle nose-dived into a ditch. A cursory torchlight examination revealed that the fellow had sustained a fractured ankle.

On December 1st. 1957, I married June at the beautiful New West End Synagogue in London's St. Petersburg's Place. The ceremony was followed by a splendid dinner and ball at the Mayfair Hotel. Apart from my father's mother and some of his French cousins, none of his siblings, or their children was present. Whether they'd been invited and refused the invitation I didn't know, but the ill will that frequently erupted between his siblings was difficult to fathom and was evident at my wedding.

We stayed at the Mayfair overnight and the following evening set off for our honeymoon, which was generously financed by my parents in law as their wedding gift. Our immediate destination was Gibraltar where we arrived in the small hours of Tuesday morning. We checked into 'The Rock Hotel' and it seemed that no sooner had we closed our eyes than workmen at the break of dawn began hammering in the next bedroom. We complained, and with profuse managerial apologies the noise stopped. However ten minutes later it restarted with renewed ferocity. The hotel's response to our further complaint was the offer of a complimentary drink at the bar. Following breakfast we went for a stroll, arm in arm, in Gibraltar's main street and asked a gentleman for directions to a store we were trying to locate. He instructed us to retrace our steps to a shop we had earlier been looking into, some 200 yards back and to turn right at the next intersection.

"How did you know we were looking in that shop window? Have you been following us?"

"Yes you've been under surveillance, since leaving your hotel." He readily admitted.

"Why on earth are you following us? Have we done something wrong?" I enquired.

"No you've not contravened any law or regulation. Let me explain. This is a British naval base, of great strategic importance and non-uniformed security police follow all new arrivals."

"Then why are you revealing this fact to us now?" I asked.

"Well, I don't think it'll be necessary to follow you any longer. It looks pretty obvious to me what you two are doing here." With that he offered us his congratulations and rapidly strode away, disappearing from view in the distance.

Later that day, aboard an old twin engine Dakota plane that had seen its finest years during the 1939-1945 war and had somehow escaped being scrapped, we flew the short distance to Tangiers, as we better understood the old expression 'to fly on a wing and a prayer'. There we relaxed and spent an exciting four days exploring the myriad alleyways and shops in the Cassbah of the Grand and Little Socco, before taking the boat to Algeciras, a small port in southern Spain and then motoring by bus to the fishing village of Torremolenos. We changed hotels twice and observed American property speculators avidly purchasing beachfront land, before returning to Gibraltar and then back to London after one further week's idyll, since I was due back at work promptly at 8 am on Monday December 16th.

We endeavoured to set up home in Mexborough, but since I was constantly on duty, I was required to sleep in the accommodation provided by the hospital where there were no married quarters. June was compelled to take bed-sitter lodgings at 14 Cemetery Road, opposite the Montague Hospital, where her landlady was reluctant to accept any rent once she learned the circumstance that as newly weds we were compelled to live apart since I worked as a doctor at the local hospital. Strictly enforced hospital rules forbade medical staff from having members of the opposite sex as visitors in their bedrooms, regardless of whether we were married, as was specifically pointed out to me by the hospital secretary. During this time June obtained temporary employment in a local department store as a sales assistant and in this manner we lived and worked as man and wife until our move back to London in January 1958.

I was the only doctor on duty on Christmas day and it was traditionally the houseman's task to carve the turkey for the patients and staff on the wards. Following this pleasant custom I returned to the doctors' dining room for my solitary lunch, where I found my meal of dried up sausage and mashed potatoes sitting on the hot plate, with no food provided for the evening. Later I made a formal complaint concerning the inadequate provision of food for duty medical staff on the 25th when the administrative personnel returned to work. The hospital secretary unsympathetically replied.

"You could have eaten with the patients on the ward had you chosen." I informed him that in my opinion The National Health Service, had many deficiencies, not least of which was its treatment of overworked and under provisioned married medical staff. His attitudes and the NHS whom he represented were, in a nutshell.

"You can take it or leave it, just as you please."

This was an end to the matter, so far as the NHS was concerned, but exactly 35 years later, in 1992, in response to her telephone appeal, I visited my daughter, Melanie, a house-surgeon at the Watford General Hospital on Christmas day, with a huge parcel of food for her and her colleagues. No provision, not even a dried sausage and mashed potatoes, or a sandwich, had been made for either the mid day or evening meals for any of the duty junior medical staff. Within the NHS conditions of employment involving the most vulnerable junior medical staff hadn't improved in the intervening years, and was still foundering in the rut of a Neanderthal mentality.

We motored to London for the day on December 26th for the wedding of our friends Michael and Myrna Brest. Having no car heater we carried a rug and two hot water bottles to help us stay warm. Every hour we would stop at some workman's café for coffee. We would then produce our hot water bottles and politely ask if we could have them filled with hot water. We were never refused.

I saw an advertisement for a 'New Year's Eve Dinner and Dance' in a country house restaurant near Doncaster. I drove there only to find the price of admission was the equivalent of a week's salary, £5 each ticket. It was sold out and there was a waiting list. Just as I turned to leave somebody returned two tickets. In a moment of elated irresponsible euphoria I purchased them, wrecking our finances for months ahead. That evening, in formal dress we drove through the bitter cold, to Doncaster and the country hotel, armed with hot water bottles where we arrived to find the place deserted. A glass of champagne and a few canapés were served as a small orchestra played from a minstrel's gallery in a small hall. As time went by, I felt we'd been cheated, having spent a prodigious sum of money we could ill afford. As the evening progressed we chatted with some of the guests who'd trickled in, who gave glowing testimonies of previous year's celebrations and of the buffet prepared in an adjacent heated tent. Shortly before midnight we were ushered into the dining room where we participated in a magnificent buffet and what turned out to be a great New Year's Eve party.

Amongst the many patients I cared for was a thoughtful bachelor in his mid-sixties. He was admitted with chest pains, which I initially diagnosed as angina pectoris due to coronary artery disease. Investigation soon revealed his symptoms were the result of severe anaemia due to leukaemia. He was transfused and rapidly improved. He confided that he'd recently retired, never having taken a holiday. Throughout his working life he'd saved, planning on retirement to take a 'once in a lifetime' round the world cruise and he'd recently been looking at travel agency brochures with that in mind.

"And now this; I'll never have that holiday." He exclaimed. "Doctor, don't be like me. Don't you wait to retire; just you take those holidays whenever you can."

Some days later when he was well enough to be discharged, I was able to reassure him that while there was no cure for his problem we could give him revitalising transfusions periodically that could keep him going almost indefinitely. He thanked me for my care and disclosed he felt better than he'd felt for months, but not up to cruising round the world. Within weeks, his anaemia returned and he was readmitted to receive a further blood transfusion. This cycle of events continued over a number of months before he finally succumbed to a cerebral haemorrhage. I was greatly saddened to learn of his death, particularly since he never managed to take that one major vacation. I resolved to follow his advice, come what may and to take my vacations, no matter how brief the time available.

Mid-morning, I received a phone call from a local GP telling me he was referring a 2-year-old child with a minor breathing problem for assessment. Nearly two hours later I was summoned urgently to the A&E department. There, in a cubicle I found a mother in her late twenties holding her two-year-old son. She explained that they'd just arrived by bus and had been told by her GP, whom she had seen with the child earlier that morning, to take him up to the children's department at the Montague Hospital for assessment.

The child was in extreme respiratory distress and I hastened to admit him. The little boy with blue lips, fingers and extremities, was severely cyanosed.

His rib margins were indrawn, as was the area at the base of the neck, with each laboured inspiration. The poor little fellow could barely breathe. He was hastily placed in an oxygen tent with a humidifier. Fearing he was about to succumb from respiratory obstruction and since we had no ENT consultant, I contacted the on call consultant anaesthetist who I knew was in the hospital at the time, asking that he see the child with a view to performing an emergency tracheotomy. He correctly admonished me, stating the request should only come to him through Dr Harvey the paediatric consultant. I pleaded with him to attend, since he was on hand and there was no paediatric registrar.

"It might take some time to locate the paediatric consultant who only attends once a week, and it's likely this child will die within a matter of minutes." He sensed the urgency verging on panic in my voice and arrived immediately. The emergency procedure was carried out straight away. Breathing more freely with the tracheotomy tube in place the child was transferred to the Sheffield Children's Hospital, and fortunately survived.

Incensed and stirred by outrage at the referring GP and sadness at what had been inflicted upon the child and his mother, I telephoned the doctor and gave him a piece of my mind. How dare he send a moribund child to hospital by bus? He claimed that when he'd seen the little boy in his surgery he'd been alert and playing. However I didn't believe him. Experience in later years taught me that such a sequence of events, particularly in young children, could and did happen. I was learning the importance of dealing as urgently as possible with childhood medical problems, and the frequent need to circumvent red tape. Later in practice, a number of children who came into my care and who might have succumbed survived as a result of the lessons learned from this traumatic episode. I learnt how swiftly children who appear well one moment can sicken and precipitously deteriorate. Later I wished I could have apologized to that poor GP.

'The moving finger writes; and, having writ moves on: Nor all your piety nor wit shall lure it back to cancel half a line, nor all your tears wash out a word of it'. (Omar Khayam)

At about the same time a gravely ill young woman of 17 was admitted with breathing difficulties. Accompanied by her worried parents she complained of sharp chest pains on breathing in, together with a productive cough, which had been present for just two days. An x-ray confirmed a diagnosis of bilateral basal pneumonia. I established an intravenous glucose saline drip and had a sputum sample sent for bacterial culture and sensitivity. I prescribed treatment with large doses of intra muscular penicillin and arranged that she would be nursed in an oxygen tent. I telephoned my consultant, reported my clinical and radiological findings, and detailed the treatment I'd instigated. I suggested that he should see her since she appeared extremely ill. He assured me I was doing all the correct things and his registrar would see her when he visited Mexborough in two days time.

Her condition continued to deteriorate. Two days later when the registrar examined her during his rounds, the gravely ill patient was showing no evidence of benefit from the massive doses of penicillin she'd received. I requested permission to give her a cocktail of antibiotics to stem the deterioration. I was sternly rebuked and informed I must await the return of the bacterial sensitivities, since any other line of treatment would be inappropriate medical practice. However he did make one concession and gave me permission to add Erythromycin to the Penicillin while awaiting the laboratory report. Later that night, this sweet young person died. I had to inform the grieving parents, telling them this had occurred in spite of the best medical treatment available.

The culture sensitivities arrived next morning confirming the bacteria to be resistant to Penicillin and Erythromycin but sensitive to Tetracycline. I'd lost a patient and two grieving parents their only daughter, but best medical practice had been served. A more rapid response time from the bacteriology department, even a preliminary indication of the sensitivity of these virulent pathogens, which had produced her premature nemesis, might possibly have saved her life. A visit from the consultant, who never saw her or his permission to throw every conceivable antibiotic then available into the fight might well have altered the course of events.

That night I sobbed and raged. I wept for the grieving parents, the tragedy of their daughter who never saw an 18th birthday and most of all out of sheer frustration that by adhering to all the rules, I experienced the ignominy of losing a young patient whom I wished, above all else, I might have saved. Why hadn't I thought of obtaining an interim sensitivity report and why had my consultant or registrar not advised this? A preliminary report could have been given after 24 hours without the necessity of waiting for three days. I resolved that never again would I wait calmly for a laboratory result to appear, when a timely communication might prove to be life saving. I was learning, but at a horrendous price.

In mid October a man in his late 30's was admitted to my medical ward with haematemesis (vomiting blood). Had he been a older he would have been admitted to a surgical ward, but age was the chief determinant. He was severely anaemic and was transfused with several units of his less common AB positive blood group over the following days of his conservative medical treatment. Contrary to expectation he continued bleeding and I was suddenly informed, when at breakfast that there was no more AB blood supply available. I told the resident surgical registrar, who was seated next to me about my dilemma and asked him to see the patient for me with a view to transferring him to his surgical ward. I stated that in the absence of further blood supplies and without prompt surgical intervention he would die with his continuing blood loss. The registrar informed me the request for a transfer had to come through my consultant to his surgical consultant. Since my consultant was not due in the hospital for several days I managed to persuade the registrar to see the patient unofficially. He agreed that surgical intervention was indicated, but he could do nothing until my consultant spoke to his surgical consultant requesting a transfer to his ward. I managed to contact Dr Brody, who arranged to speak to the consultant surgeon.

In a critical condition, the patient was transferred and the following day underwent emergency surgery, where he was found to have a previously undiagnosed malignant stomach growth. He survived the operation, but died some week's later, never returning home. I was at fault. I had experienced the frustrating formality of red tape by attempting to circumvent the system by speaking with the resident surgical registrar whom I saw daily, rather than my consultant. While not affecting the final outcome of the patient's illness, it might well have done, had the condition been more acute. In spite of the paucity of consultant supervision, Mexborough provided some wonderful training with the many medical problems and emergencies that regularly assailed me, but there would have been a considerable benefit, had the medical and paediatric consultants appeared more frequently instead of placing a reliance to supervise from the end of a 'phone line.

During November there was a minor influenza epidemic. With a high fever and aching from top to toe I dragged myself out of bed for three successive days, performed my duties with ward rounds and clinics, wearing a surgical mask, before returning to bed for the remainder of each day.

One other patient I recall vividly from this time was a former collier, who'd undergone an above knee amputation due to years of poorly controlled diabetes. He'd been transferred from the surgical ward for stabilisation before returning home. A widower in his mid 50's, he lived in a council house, which he shared with several of his adult children. When sufficiently recovered and his diabetes stabilised, he was to be discharged home. I arranged for follow up assistance from social services, wrote a discharge summary to his GP and organised that he be transported home by ambulance. My farewell words of encouragement were to keep to his diet and to give up smoking.

To my amazement, he reappeared on my ward later that day. He'd arrived home by ambulance, where his children had refused to open the front door to allow a one legged man to return home. Some days later when in dire need of a bed he was transferred to a council home for the elderly. He was almost 55. An example of one of the many sad variants of Shakespeare's plot of 'King Lear', that I have witnessed over the years.

(P) Pre-registration posts were introduced in 1953, prior to which full registration was given to the new graduate who could then immediately practice medicine as a GP.

The 'houseman's' 1957 salary scale was £425 per annum for the first six months rising to £475 a year for the second, paid monthly in arrears, with no overtime payments and a two-week holiday entitlement each six months. Lodging and food were included in the hospital. There were no minimum hours of work and no off duty entitlements for rest days or weekends. A strange anomaly in a Church of England society based on the bible, which specifically stated 'Six days shall thou labour and do all thy work but the seventh day'....etc.

Chapter 5

BARNET HERTS

Bidding farewell to childhood I permanently donned long trousers in the severe winter months at the start of 1947 apart from when in Boy Scout uniform. It was also when I gave up riding my cycle to school because of the prevailing arctic conditions that made roads icy and treacherous for weeks on end. It was the severest winter in decades and was later followed by punishing spring floods. During the Easter holidays that followed, when a 14 year old grammar school student, I boarded the number 29 double deck bus, which ran from Potters Bar to Victoria station. Waving my student bus pass at the conductor I dashed up the stairs to the top deck as any boisterous schoolboy might do, when I was struck as though I'd been pole axed, yet the bus was virtually empty and there was no visible assailant.

Halted dead in my track, the knife thrust in my chest was as sharp and excruciating as I imagined a bayonet plunge must feel. Unable to catch my breath, it was worse than anything I'd ever experienced and without being melodramatic I was convinced that death might be imminent. I wasn't frightened as I focussed my attention on one dreadful thought. How might I take my next breath, without incurring that horrendously searing stabbing pain, as I attempted to inhale? The pain was of such indescribable severity I was unable to move and somehow collapsed into the nearest seat where I remained for what seemed an interminable age, motionless and terrified of the need to take that next vital shallow gulp of air as the bus sped past my destination.

Any movement on my part exacerbated the knife like pain within my chest. Short of breath I rode the bus, unintentionally, to Turnpike Lane, where it turned round, and back. Finally, taking the smallest gasps of air, like a fish terminally floundering out of water, I descended the stairs as cautiously as I was able, in exceptional discomfort, barely courageous enough to move. Every attempted gesture caused a sharp pain of such magnitude I was forced to stop, hardly daring to move or breathe.

Warily I alighted from the bus. The jolt in my chest as my foot touched the ground was agonising. Somehow I managed to shuffle home, breathlessly exhausted, terrified and in pain whenever I attempted to breathe. For some inexplicable reason I never told my parents of the event and neither they, nor my siblings ever noticed how severely incapacitated I remained for several days.

Over a period of a fortnight the pain gradually receded, as did my dyspnoea (shortness of breath) and I had almost completely recovered by the time school reconvened. Although I didn't realise it at the time I'd just experienced the sudden collapse of one of my lungs termed a spontaneous pneumothorax. The lung had abruptly deflated like a tyre's inner tube and unknowingly I'd sustained a life-threatening event requiring emergency hospital admission.

Periodically I experienced similar but marginally less painful events without knowing the cause or revealing the problem to my parents. In the Easter of 1955, when a medical student, there was a major recurrence. While driving my newly acquired, Vespa motor scooter, a sudden episode of exceptionally severe pain similar to that which I'd felt 8 years earlier, pierced knife like through one side of my chest, accompanied by severe dyspnoea. As I bumped over a pothole I felt a searing bayonet thrust within my chest with an accompanying jolt as though there was something loose within my rib cage. Greatly distressed, I immediately stopped and after a few minutes slowly drove to the student health-centre, avoiding any potholes along the way, to obtain an urgent chest x-ray.

This revealed a total collapse of one lung and was now, although previously undiagnosed, the fifth time I'd suffered a pneumothorax **(1)**. Fortunately the air inside the chest cavity was absorbed over a number of weeks permitting the lung to fully re-expand. Sir Clement Price–Thomas the eminent London thoracic surgeon was visiting Sheffield at the time on a lecture and student examination tour and the student health department arranged for me to consult him. He was one of the country's foremost thoracic surgeons and had received his knighthood in 1951 after operating on King George VI in an operating theatre specially set up in Buckingham Palace, to remove a cancerous lung growth.

He examined me, looked at my chest x-rays and recommended I should undergo a 'pleuradesis' at the earliest opportunity. This was a minor procedure where a mild irritant is applied to the surface of the lung. Over a short period of time the surface of the lung would then produce adhesions (scar tissue), which would make the lung adhere to the inner chest lining. Once this happened the lung wouldn't collapse should a further pneumothorax occur. I underwent a pleuradesis at the Royal Infirmary as a day patient where Mr. Fawcett, the consultant thoracic surgeon pumped a small quantity of sterile talcum powder into my chest cavity under a local anaesthetic.

Within a few weeks a further pneumothorax occurred and a new chest x-ray revealed an almost total collapse of the same lung. The operation had proved unsuccessful. I was admitted to the Royal Infirmary and the procedure repeated as previously under a local anaesthetic. Mr. Fawcett decided to use silver nitrate, a far stronger irritant, which he sprayed over the lung surface. The effect on the sensitive lung pleura was instant and agonising. I was immediately sedated with morphine and remained in hospital for two days to gain adequate pain control. Fortunately the procedure was a success. Although I experienced subsequent episodes of chest pain, announcing a further pneumothorax, I never had any major lung collapse on that side with the accompanying acute dyspnoea. Advised to undergo the same procedure on the other side and aware of the pain involved, I declined.

Later recounting my symptoms to my father, he recalled two or three occasions when as a young man, he had experienced dramatic episodes of severe, sharp chest pain. These events sounded similar to my own and I was left to ponder whether there might have been a congenital anomaly of a cyst on the lung surface which ruptured allowing air to escape into the chest cavity. Many years later my son as a young student likewise experienced incidents of chest pain suggestive of an unconfirmed pneumothorax.

Mr. Fawcett was a portly, thoughtful gentleman, who used gold-rimmed spectacles and closely resembled a Dickensian 'Mr Bumble'. He kept pigs in an area close to the hospital, which it was rumoured were used for developing surgical cardiac techniques. At times one would see him dressed with Wellington boots like a farm hand carrying buckets of left over food from the Royal Infirmary kitchens with which to feed his animals. He was one of the UK's pioneers of open-heart surgery. Students were never invited to assist in cardiothoracic surgery but since we'd met on several occasions I asked permission to attend and he acquiesced. I had the privilege of assisting in a very minor role at one such procedure. The patient had a severe stenosis (closure) of the mitral heart valve, which produced enlargement of the heart and symptoms of long standing heart failure, as blood was damned back into his lungs. Once anaesthetised, the patient's chest cavity was opened followed by the pericardium. A small incision was made in the heart's tiny left atrial appendage through which he quickly stuck a gloved little finger as far as he was able, into the stenosed mitral valve, tearing it open. He then withdrew his finger and rapidly repaired the small incision in the heart. A crude procedure, but the patient's condition improved dramatically, once back on the ward.

In the summer of 1973 I met Sir Clement Price Thomas for a second time. One of my patient's Mr Kay, an accountant and a heavy smoker had developed a troublesome cough. A chest x-ray revealed evidence of lung cancer. Detected early enough this might be amenable to cure, by surgical removal. Without it, he would most probably be dead in less than a year. I arranged an urgent appointment for him to consult Sir Price Thomas in his Harley Street rooms. I accompanied him at the consultation where the surgeon agreed that the mass in Mr. Kay's lung could be removed surgically and with any luck his five-year prognosis would be excellent. As the patient dressed I reminded Sir Price that he had seen me as a patient 18 years ago in Sheffield. I then asked him how often, in his opinion, should a patient have a chest x-ray.

"To be of any real preventive use when we're speaking of lung cancer I suppose the answer would have to be at least once every four, or at the outside every six months." he replied.

"I last had a chest x-ray in 1959 so I guess I'd best have another pretty soon. And what about yourself, Sir Price, when did you last have one?"

"I don't keep a track of these things, as I should. I suppose it must be all of five years or more."

"Well let's make a pact. We'll each take your advice, and get ourselves a chest X-ray."

"I think you've a point there, Dr. Powell. We'll each do that, shall we?"

Following this consultation, my patient and I chatted in the waiting room. He asked.

"Dr Powell, what in your opinion, should I do?" Unhesitatingly I replied.

"Mr. Kay, very few of these lung cancers are identified sufficiently early to be amenable to surgical removal and without surgery the five years survival rate is in the order of 4%. Price Thomas says you're one of the luckier individuals to have spotted it in time for it to be operable. If it were me I think I would take the chance. Of course there's a risk in every surgical procedure and you have to balance the risks involved in the operation and the anticipated successful outcome with a top surgeon, against the rather poor prognosis if you leave things as they are. Talk it over with your family before you make your final decision, but should you choose surgical intervention then you mustn't delay."

Mr. Kay elected to have the growth removed. He entered the London Clinic and underwent surgery the following day, when the tumour was removed successfully. All went well until ten days post-operatively. He suddenly went into severe heart failure, and died. No autopsy was performed but it was very likely he had a pulmonary embolus (2). I had recommended the most eminent thoracic surgeon of his day, yet by following my advice my patient's life had been prematurely ended and that of his family shattered, for his wife became severely depressed and never really recovered.

I took refuge in the fact that my patient was an intelligent professional man and I'd explained there was a risk to the procedure. With the surgery there was a reasonable chance of survival and without it, his life's span could probably be measured in no more than a few months of miserable existence. But I felt dreadful to have confidently advocated that he embark upon a major surgical procedure, which sadly had shortened his life.

As Brutus, in Shakespeare's Julius Caesar says.

"There is a tide in the affairs of men which taken at the flood leads on to fortune; omitted all the voyage of their life is bound in shallows and in miseries....and we must take the current when it serves."

With hindsight a portion of my remorse, was due to my failure to insist that better precautions needed to have been taken to avoid the post-operative complication of a DVT (deep vein thrombosis), and pulmonary embolus. At the time I was a young doctor and it would have been presumptuous to seek assurances from so illustrious a senior consultant that more adequate postoperative procedures be instituted. Following a successful hernia repair my paternal grandfather had died in 1926 aged 52, following a pulmonary embolus, nearly 60 years earlier. How little had surgical risk changed in the intervening years, where following a successful operation the patient died? I never again lost a patient to a largely preventable postoperative embolus.

What of Sir Price Thomas? We'd both agreed to have chest x-rays. Mine was clear. His revealed an inoperable tumour and within six months I was reading the poor fellow's obituary. Some years later Mr. David Blunkett minister of health in Tony Blair's labour government opened the 'Price Thomas Thoracic Unit' a specialist surgical unit to his memory, in Sheffield, the University where Mr. Blunkett had graduated in 1972.

In the post war years up to the late 1970's the conventional wisdom was never to divulge to a patient they were terminally ill or had a cancer and death or its possibility was never to be mentioned other than in the most exceptional circumstances. The next of kin were to be informed, but never the patient. Gradually during the 1980's this changed. Elements of this attitude still linger, such as in metastatic cancer, the spread of disease may be referred to as a 'hot spot' or some similar euphemistic alias.

*   *   *

In North London, the Barnet General in Wellhouse Lane was our local hospital, where in September 1948 I had been admitted with Typhoid. Strategically located between Edgware, where my fiancée lived, and my parent's home since 1941, in Cockfosters, it was there that Mr Donal Brooks the consultant orthopaedic surgeon, held an outpatient clinic on Saturday mornings. In September 1957 I wrote a brief letter from Mexborough, explaining my intention to visit him with the request that he might spare a few minutes to see me at the end of his clinic.

On my second weekend off duty I walked into the Saturday morning orthopaedic outpatient department, armed with chutzpah and the self-assurance of the young, requesting to see Mr Brooks. When he appeared,

I hastened forward to introduce myself and explained that I'd recently qualified and would like to apply for the post of orthopaedic house surgeon commencing in January 1958. Although taken aback, he questioned me explaining that while he admired my keenness, the job would have to be advertised in November and should I wish to apply at that time, then the post would certainly be mine.

Much to my surprise and pleasure he introduced me to his orthopaedic colleagues as his next houseman. His junior consultant colleague was Mr. Hocchauser, an extremely short and powerful multilingual man who had fled from Germany as a refugee to Spain and had then later escaped to England during the civil war. His senior registrar Alex Zaoussis, a handsome, knowledgeable Athenian who spoke English with an American accent and lastly his junior registrar Peter Nobes, a slightly built, well spoken, gentle soul, who had exchanged his post as an anaesthetic registrar at the Highlands Hospital to take up orthopaedics.

The moment the post was advertised in the BMJ (British Medical Journal) in November, I applied, and a few days later was overjoyed to receive a courteous response confirming my appointment without the necessity of a further interview. On the third weekend of January, we piled our few belongings into our car and left Mexborough to motor south to London, where on Monday January 20th I commenced my duties at the Barnet General Hospital.

June found and rented a comfortable first floor single bedroom flat in a house close to the hospital, off Hadley Green, at a rent of £21 a month, which after tax was my total monthly income. We maintained this apartment, our first home, for four months, until we gave it up, to help defray the cost of our transatlantic fare (M11) aboard the French liner 'Ile de France'. Once we gave up our apartment, June lived at home with her parents, where I joined her when not on duty.

Life was just as busy as in my previous post except. I was required to assist in all manner of orthopaedic surgical procedures and was more adequately supervised and instructed in my work by two excellent consultants and two registrars. The work schedule was far less stressful. There was no half-day weekly respite, but I now worked alternate weekends and had every third evening off duty. I lived in the doctor's residence, a separate building from the main hospital, where I took my meals when on duty. The busy orthopaedic out patient department was a newly constructed unit in the main hospital next to the A&E. The two separate single storey forty-eight bed wards 10, and 9, for male and female patients were in long, flat roofed prefabricated 'temporary' huts built during the first year of the war. Their great disadvantage was that patients had to be wheeled on trolleys through any inclement weather back and forth to the operating room for surgery or X-ray investigation in the main hospital. When June's mother was admitted to the Barnet General in 1996 with a fractured hip, these same temporary wards were still in use, after fifty six years, with patients on trolleys or in wheel chairs, sheltered under an umbrella in rain or snow, being wheeled back and forth for investigation and treatment 48 years after the inception of the NHS.

The A&E department was always busy. Gone were the Yorkshire colliery mining and steel mill accidents of student days, to be replaced largely by road traffic accidents mainly from the three lane 'Barnet by pass', with its single outer lanes for traffic travelling north and south, and a middle lane termed 'suicide alley' between these outer lanes for overtaking traffic, travelling in either direction. There were no speed restrictions or road barriers and cynically one might believe the road had been designed solely to keep those in the orthopaedic section of the Barnet General Hospital and its A&E department busy.

Working with Donal Brooks was always a pleasure. He walked with a slight limp and was a calm mild mannered pipe smoker, who lived in a spacious house in Totteridge with his large family and drove a 2.5 litre black Riley coupé. Amongst his many attributes he was an excellent orthopaedic teacher and surgeon. Whenever he operated, or conducted an out patient clinic he went to great lengths to teach his junior staff. When he sutured and struggled with a length of suture material that was just that little bit too short, he would invariably exclaim in frustration.

"Economy of material is always the enemy of time."

Particularly interested in hand surgery he became famous as the surgeon chosen by the Prime Minister Margaret Thatcher to operate on her Dupuytren's (3) hand contracture. He always seemed interested when I described my experiences as a student when working with Freddie Holdsworth, the mercurial, antacid chewing Sheffield Infirmary Orthopaedic surgeon who became president of the Royal College of Orthopaedic Surgeons. The consultant, who bestrode his wards when surgeons were treated as though they were God's anointed and who'd explained that his name was Frank not Freddie when he had come across me amongst a group of students, when waiting for him to appear for his ward round and unaware of his presence, were talking about him. He'd hurled a blunt orthopaedic chisel through the operating room window in exasperation, when having warned the theatre sister.

"If you ever hand this bloody blunt chisel to me one more time, I'll throw it out of the window." Another time a member of the theatre staff told us of the time he cut the theatre sister's finger that was assisting him. It was an accident but his hurried response was.

94

"You shouldn't have had your damn finger in the way." Although later he was more apologetic.

In contrast 'Hocky', the junior consultant was of very short stature with a particularly fiery temperament in the operating room when under stress, although at other times he could be extremely considerate and kind. Assisting him to operate always produced a backache, since one would need to stoop at the particularly low operating table. Peter Nobes, a gentle mild mannered bachelor in his mid thirties, always reminded me of someone who should have been a cleric or possibly a monk. He frequently appeared late on the scene with widely dilated pupils and often hinted at past problems when an anaesthetist. Some years later I was saddened to read he had taken his own life with a drug overdose. Later still I read of a consultant anaesthetist at Chase Farm Hospital, under whom Peter had trained, who'd been struck off the medical register having become addicted to sniffing ether and for inadequately supervising narcotic drugs under his control.

*   *   *

Having selected general practice for my future career I decided that following my pre-registration house posts, I would take advantage of the two years I might have spent in the armed services to travel. I would obtain further training in obstetrics and paediatrics while at the same time see something of America. I wrote to a number of hospitals in Baltimore, Maryland applying for a post as an intern commencing in July 1958.

Baltimore was our chosen destination, since June's school friend Eunice Gold had married Milton Kaplan, an attorney, who lived in that city. The Maryland General, a Methodist Hospital affiliated to the Maryland University, the oldest University Medical College in the USA and located in down town Baltimore, accepted my application without interview. Unable to start work on July 1st when the 12 month intern programme began, the hospital agreed that in view of the distance I would need to travel I could commence in the third week starting 15th July 1958. I requested and received permission to spend 6 months in Obstetrics and Gynaecology and 3 months each in Surgery and Paediatrics.

In Easter 1958 we obtained our immigration documents from the U.S. embassy, including the mandatory 'green card' which would provide us with the option of US citizenship and would also permit us to work, wherever we chose.

The only examination in my London conjoint board examination that remained to be taken to gain the degree MRCS and LRCP, was surgery. Having gained my Sheffield medical qualification I could see little point in completing my conjoint examinations, since the 'insurance' this degree was to have conferred was no longer necessary. Each part of the examination required a £50 fee, which represented nine weeks of my houseman's take home salary and had therefore remained untaken.

June persuaded me to complete my Conjoint Board examination and in April I obtained leave of absence on three specified days to take the last parts of my final written and oral surgical examinations held at London's Queen's Square. There was no allowance of time for revision in a busy orthopaedic department. There were two surgical papers and a week later a clinical examination and viva. The latter stood out vividly in my mind, since by coincidence, I was examined by Mr Dixon Wright FRCS the loquacious St. Mary's Hospital doyen amongst humorous after dinner speakers, who years earlier twice successfully operated upon my father.

The bell rang announcing my turn to enter. I nervously pushed open the door to walk into the sumptuously spacious wood panelled examination room with its high ceiling and proportionately tall windows, to be met by the examiner, who requested me to follow him. He escorted me rapidly past surgical instruments set out on rows of long tables, as though in preparation for some sumptuous feast and then stopped at the orthopaedic section. In front was a table neatly laden with bones at one end and a variety of instruments in neat rows at the other. He picked up the first of several instruments, and in rapid succession asked me to name each and specify its use. The faster I replied to his quick-fire interrogation he immediately shot back another question, probing for a weakness, while under stress, I was too nervous to slow the grilling. Next, his hand glided over a group of bones, stopping when he selected the longest, a femur. Pointing with his finger he cross examined me on the names of its various anatomical parts and then questioned me on fractures of the femur. Brusquely he enquired.

"A man arrives with a fractured neck of femur; tell me how you would reduce and deal with this fracture?"

My spirits soared as I thought this must certainly be my lucky day. That very morning I'd assisted Donal Brooks and Alex Zaoussis in the O.R. with this very operation. Such procedures had been almost daily fare over the past 3 months. Confidently I proceeded to detail how I would deal with such an injury, when he brusquely interrupted.

"Nonsense boy, you've never seen a fractured neck of femur dealt with like that."

Long ago I'd been warned that it was a fatal error to argue, or attempt to disagree with an examiner.

"Bight your tongue, if need be, but never challenge the examiner, for if you do, he will fail you." had been drilled into each medical student.

"That's the way I thought I saw it being reduced sir." I stammered, as my earlier optimism rapidly ebbed away. Dixon Wright started to tell me how he considered the fracture should be dealt with, when the bell rang to indicate my ordeal was at an end and warning the examiner some other entrant would shortly appear. I thanked him courteously and hastened from the hall, wretchedly certain that I'd failed. The following morning at the first opportunity I discussed the matter with Donal Brooks. In private he invariably addressed his registrars and houseman by first names.

"Arnold, you have to understand that in final examinations, surgeons are not permitted to examine in their specialised field, so it's always likely the examiner might be a little out of touch with more recent accepted techniques. In Fellowship examinations it's an entirely different matter."

The week following my viva I attended the examination Hall in Queen's Square, for the results of the Conjoint Examination. I was informed I had passed and was awarded two certificates, the Membership of the Royal College of Surgeons and the Licentiate of the Royal College of Physicians, permitting me to use the letters MRCS and LRCP after my name, in addition to the MB; ChB. from Sheffield. I last saw Mr Dixon Wright when I came across him, quite by accident, many years later in the St Mary's Hospital Lindo Wing. He was being nursed, as a private patient, suffering from senile dementia, an abysmal end for a surgeon with such a sharp incisive intellect. When in his 50th year of marriage he had divorced his wife, allegedly to marry his operating theatre sister.

It was a common occurrence that whenever any junior doctor made mention in the common room of the abysmal rate of pay or excessive hours of work, some senior consultant would relate how in pre NHS years, a doctor worked in hospital without a day off and without remuneration. One elderly consultant communicated his point of view.

"You should all consider yourselves damned lucky to receive any salary and stop this constant whingeing about money and hours of work!"

In reality junior doctors dared not complain officially. Although not employed by our consultants, we worked for them. Future career prospects were irrevocably dependent upon an exemplary written reference from one's consultant (4), to obtain the next medical appointment in an extremely competitive market.

There were far too many medically qualified hopefuls chasing too few posts. Members of the public appeared unaware of the remuneration and appalling hours of work. There appeared a belief that every junior doctor would shortly be rolling in money like the Rolls Royce owning consultants. These attitudes were of little help when endeavouring to pay examination fees and meet daily expenses. Senior consultants ignored the poor remuneration of their medical staff and worse still were indifferent to the excessive hours, junior doctors were required to labour, which placed patients at risk. Irrationally these same consultants glibly advised that transport workers should not be permitted to place the travelling public at risk by working shifts in excess of eight hours.

One of the patient's under my care, who had suffered a fracture of his lower leg, was a film director involved in the production of a motion picture at the Elstree Films Studio 'Inn Of The Sixth Happiness', starring Kurt Jurgens and Ingrid Bergman, my favourite film actress, ever since I'd first seen her, when she appeared in a starring role fifteen years earlier in Hemingway's 'For Whom The Bell Tolls'. He arranged for my wife and I to visit the set, which depicted a walled Chinese village at the summit of a mountain pass. The film producers had scoured London for every Chinese person available to participate in the many crowd scenes. On our visit these extras were frustratingly nowhere to be seen when needed and could only be rounded up by the director's helpers from where they were hidden in every nook and cranny busily gambling with each other.

My orthopaedic post continued, until late June. The last two weeks were taken as my vacation, by which time I had fulfilled my obligatory twelve months medical and surgical house posts and received my General Medical Council 'Certificate of Full Registration' in the mail. Both to celebrate and also as a farewell treat, June's parents took us to the Drury Lane Theatre. In New York a new Lehrner and Lowe musical, based on George Bernard Shaw's Pygmalion opened to rave reviews in 1956. My Fair Lady transferred to London's Drury Lane Theatre, with Rex Harrison as Professor Higgins, Julie Andrews as Eliza Dolittle and Stanley Holloway as Mr Dolittle, her father. On one of the hottest evenings of the year, in June 1958, June's parents took us to the performance given in the presence of the Queen and Prince Phillip. In spite of the absence of air conditioning, it was a memorable event, as Stanley Holloway, to everyone's amusement, banteringly included ad-lib lines directed at Buckingham Palace and the royal party.

Hurriedly we arranged our affairs, packed, and prepared for our journey to America. With fond farewells to family and friends we were ready to sail at the end of June. It was only in 1958 that a scheduled transatlantic flying service was reinstated, after the war, but due to the expense, together with the quantity of luggage we were taking for our prolonged stay, we chose to make our crossing by boat. Parents and family accompanied us to Waterloo railway station to see us off to Southampton on the first part of our journey. To today's casual onlooker it might have appeared as though we were departing to the moon. It seems strange to realise that post war monetary restrictions were still in place, which prohibited each person taking more than £35 out of the UK in a year, while coal was still rationed and the UK had no motorways. Transatlantic travel was still a comparative rarity and we were considered to be embarking upon a great exciting adventure to the new world.

On boarding the Ile de France in Southampton for our exciting five-day transatlantic journey to New York, we found our internal cabin full of dozens of bouquets from well wishing family and friends. It was so full of flowers that regardless of the delightful aroma there was simply no room for the passengers. I went to see the chief purser, who coincidentally knew my French cousins in LeHavre. He checked the veracity of our story, following which we were given an immediate upgrade to a far larger outside cabin with more adequate space for our floral tributes.

(1) Pneumothorax. The dangers are many, chief amongst which is a collapse of the other lung, bleeding within the lung cavity, or a 'tension' pneumothorax, causing displacement of the mediastinum. All are surgical problems requiring urgent intervention.

(2) Embolus, Greek for a stopper or plug. An embolism is the blockage of a blood vessel by an embolus travelling in the blood stream. The most frequent is a blood clot that forms in the lower limb or pelvis following a period of inactivity and which then breaks loose with often-disastrous consequences. Other emboli occur, such as in divers where air emboli cause decompression sickness and even death.

(3) Dupuytren (1777- 1835) was a French anatomist and military surgeon, who treated Napoleon for his haemorrhoids. In 1831 he was the first to describe a contracture of the hand affecting the flexor tendons in the palm amongst coach drivers, now known as 'Dupuytren's Contracture'.

(4) The NHS hospital employment structure was pyramidal with a consultant at the apex. The consultant appointed at about 36 yrs would remain at the summit of his career for about 34 years until about 70, seldom retiring earlier. Beneath him was anything from one to two senior registrars, usually on a four-year contract, depending upon the number of beds and hospital wards the consultant supervised, all of whom would have a membership or fellowship qualification and would have been in the age range of from 30 to 36 years old when commencing the appointment. At the end of that contract period had a senior registrar not found a consultant post he would have few medical options other than to enter general practice or emigrate. Beneath were Junior grade registrars with two year contracts which could be renewed two or three times, and there were usually one or two juniors to each senior. Most

in this grade would have obtained the higher qualification of a MRCP Membership of the Royal college of Physicians or the FRCS Fellowship of the Royal College of Surgeons. Below this grade were senior house officers who would seldom have acquired any higher degrees, employed on a one year contract and below them were the newly qualified housemen, with six monthly contracts which could be renewed several times. A mandatory, satisfactory, six months preceptorship in both medicine and surgery was introduced in 1953 before any newly qualified doctor could obtain full medical registration, which was increased to 2 years preceptorship, many years later. Salary remuneration depended upon these grades. There was no legal limit to the hours a doctor would be required to work and no overtime payments were given, until introduced in the mid 1980's and then scandalously at only one third the normal rate.

(M10) A 2 door Austin A35 saloon car retail price was £425. Amongst the extras were: Heater priced at £25; Car radio price £15.

(M11) In 1957 the minimum Trans Atlantic fare in a double internal cabin from Southampton to New York was £36 per. person. Transatlantic telephone calls were charged at £1 per minute with a minimum charge for 3 minutes. This applied from London to New York or Saskatchewan and vice-a –versa. One could make a long distance 'person to person' call at no additional charge, which meant, if the person one wished to speak with wasn't available, no charge was incurred. This was used to our advantage in our long distance travels by placing a 'person to person' call, to some fictitious individual. Our family would not accept the call, but knew of our safe arrival.

Chapter 6

BALTIMORE MARYLAND

July 1958 – July 1959

We crowded the ships rails on the morning of 11 July 1958 standing shoulder to shoulder amongst fellow passengers. Full of awe everyone stared excitedly across the grey calm water on the sea approaches to New York, as our liner glided sedately past the Statue of Liberty, before mooring effortlessly at one of the huge southwestern piers on Manhattan Island. As we prepared to disembark we were notified that customs regulations forbade the importation of fresh fruit, flowers or food and all our beautiful flowers would have to be abandoned in our cabin. We observed custom officials confiscating food, fruit and flowers from newly arrived passengers, to their owner's dismay, which were then callously discarded into the Hudson River. June and I each took a red carnation, and entered the USA with un-noticed flowers in buttonholes. We marvelled at the seeming affluence of the striking stevedores and longshoremen, many of whom were smoking and chomping on cigars, as they walked in an endless line round and round carrying placards picketing the ship's terminal.

The Travellers Aid group assisted us with hotel accommodation. We opted for a hotel without air conditioning since a supplement of $2 per night was levied for that luxury. Because of the quantity of our luggage we required two taxis. June proceeded to our hotel in one while I drove in another to the nearby Greyhound bus terminal where I intended to leave our baggage in the left luggage department until our journey the following afternoon to Baltimore. At the terminal I discovered I couldn't leave our cases without first purchasing and reserving my bus tickets. Apart from my taxi fare I had left June with almost all our American money and had insufficient for the bus fare. The taxi driver gallantly agreed to lend me the fare money and I later repaid him at our hotel, with a generous tip for his assistance. At day's end he found an unusual bonus. Unintentionally, my black bowler hat had been left in his cab.

New York was exactly as we'd seen it depicted in countless movies. Lively and vibrant, with innumerable brick brownstone houses and their external iron fire-escape staircases, against a backdrop in the southernmost portion of Manhattan Island of groups of magnificent, awe inspiring, sky scrapers. Oppressively hot and humid, only the major department stores were air-conditioned and we proceeded down the street walking through as many stores as possible in an effort to remain cool. Within hours on that first day I was compelled to purchase a lightweight suit from our slender resources, since my heavy clothes were completely unsuited to this remorseless climate change. Jackets were made to size but trousers, pants in new world terminology, only fitted round the waist. The lengths of the pants were made to fit a giant. The salesman measured the client's leg length and the appropriate alteration was made on the premises within thirty minutes at no extra charge.

We noticed that for some inexplicable reason, department store employees treated us with great deference. Months later we learned the basis for this respect. Junior executives wore plastic carnations in their buttonholes. Senior executives wore white carnations. The most senior executives disported fresh red carnations, and doubtlessly staff erroneously identified us as belonging to this distinguished coterie. The following afternoon, little more than a day and a half after our arrival, we left New York by Greyhound. We collected our luggage at the bus terminal, before travelling in comfort to Baltimore, a journey by road of under four hours, not counting rest stops. Our friends Milt and Eunice Kaplan, who'd been waiting for some time, greeted us at the bus station with great excitement and conveyed us to their apartment in their open Ford-coupe.

The next day I took up my new post at the Maryland General and found that I was required to spend alternate nights on call in the hospital. It had been agreed that I should be permitted to utilise my time with six months Ob-Gyn (obstetrics and gynaecology) three months general surgery and three months paediatrics. My salary was $200 a month paid in arrears and my annual holiday entitlement was two weeks. I briefly considered employment at the near by Johns Hopkins Hospital, but there was no minimum wage law in Maryland, and the intern's stipend was $25 per month. Never having mastered the technique of suppressing the desire to eat at least once a day, employment at that more prestigious faculty was out of the question.

All resident medical personnel when on duty were required to wear clean white cotton hospital uniforms. We were supplied with two sets that the hospital regularly laundered without charge, consisting of trousers, a short-sleeved shirt, which buttoned down from neck to hem on the right side, and a white jacket. Both the shirt and jacket had the doctor's name stitched in red script over the left breast pocket.

Each morning, when I hadn't stayed overnight at the hospital, I travelled into the centre of Baltimore by bus, to be on duty at 7 am. The bus service was erratic and although the journey took 20 minutes the schedule was too unpredictable to be relied upon. My contract stipulated medical staff must either live in the hospital, where there were no married quarters, or could live outside the hospital, when not on duty, providing the accommodation was no more than one block distant. June desperately tramped the oppressively hot humid streets, as she searched for secretarial work for herself and scoured the area seeking suitable accommodation, contiguous to the hospital.

My duties commenced in the Ob-Gyn department, which fortunately was fully air-conditioned and where I remained until the end of January. The obstetric department was exceedingly well supervised both by consultants and senior residents, which provided me with an excellent period of intensive training, delivering scores of babies. At one time the presence of the father witnessing the birth of his newborn had been permitted, but this had been abandoned the year prior to my arrival when during a difficult delivery the obstetrician was about to apply surgical forceps to assist the emerging foetal head, the father had drawn a handgun from his pocket, threatening to shoot anyone attempting to place forceps any where near his unborn child.

June soon located an acceptably clean, modern unfurnished apartment at 823, North Howard Street, facing the hospital, which had recently been vacated by a hospital resident. Located on the second floor above a shop, it consisted of two good-sized bedrooms, a spacious living room, kitchen and bathroom, with an external iron fire escape at the rear. It had an efficient central heating system but no air conditioning. June negotiated our rent, which was to be paid monthly in advance. Fortunately the landlord required no deposit and gave us a helpful two weeks rent-free period. Although we didn't realise it at the time he was required by local statute to redecorate the flat with each change of tenancy, which he failed to do. It didn't need painting anyway and not having to pay rent until I'd received my first paycheck was a considerable advantage. We opened a joint account at a local bank, acquiring a bathroom scale as a gift to a new customer and friends advised that it was essential to enter into modest debt with the 'phone and utilities companies, demonstrating we could reliably repay our debts, to establish a sound credit rating.

I spoke to the deputy hospital administrator telling him of our need for beds and furniture to furnish our empty apartment. Sympathetically he authorised us to select some old metal beds and surplus wooden hospital furniture that was scheduled for donation to a charitable organisation. The furniture given us by the hospital included two old metal hospital beds, unfortunately of different heights, a pair of antiquated oak dressing tables and a pair of beech arm chairs, all of which were carried to our apartment by two hospital porters for a couple of dollars. He also permitted me to purchase through the hospital, at cost, a refrigerator freezer, advancing me the money, interest free, to be repaid over three months, displaying a generosity unknown to NHS employees in Britain. A refrigerator in the hot Maryland summer was essential, while other small items of furniture we later bought as economically as possible at the charity 'goodwill furniture' shop and at local furniture store sales, as we slowly earned a little money.

Following several weeks of searching and interviews, June obtained employment as personal assistant to the home furnishings merchandising manager at Stewarts in downtown Baltimore, a major department store and part of the Lord and Taylor group and remained there for eight months before changing to work for the Baltimore Housing Authority. In each job application there was a question asking for her father's occupation, to which she would always write 'Brassiere Tycoon'. While working for Stewarts she was encouraged, as were all employees, to make a 'voluntary contribution' of a percentage of her salary to the Community Chest. This voluntary contribution to charity was commendable. Corporations and industries vied competitively to donate most with results published in trade journals showing percentage of staff contributing and the total collected in a particular time span. June enquired what her contribution should be and was left in no doubt that should any employee fail to contribute a stipulated minimum amount they would soon be looking for another job. She could ill afford this 'voluntary' largesse from her meagre salary, but there was no option.

Our first few weeks in that unbearably hot, humid Baltimore summer, with its static electricity constantly producing minor shocks, were miserable and to make life tolerable, we prioritised the purchase of an electric fan with my first pay check. In addition to the unbearably high temperatures and humidity, June, as a young doctor's wife, had to live on a pittance. She had to contend with extended periods of loneliness in a strange city when I was on duty, passing her time patching and decorating old furniture in her endeavour to create a home. In the evenings, armed with paint stripper, wire wool, and sandpaper followed by a brush and paint she did a magnificent job of home furniture decoration, while I was able to provide minimal help on my alternate evenings off duty. We were desperately short of cash during those first weeks in America and had to live on what little I earned. My salary paid at the end of each month was barely adequate for one person and when shopping, June had to replace food items at the check out counter when she found insufficient funds to pay for them.

After a few weeks, with June in full time employment, our combined salaries made life more comfortable as we were able to afford to visit the cinema, local art galleries and museums. Down town at one of the five and ten stores she purchased an inexpensive 10 by 12 foot rubber backed cotton rug and trudged home through the sweltering noon time streets, to save a taxi fare that we could ill afford, carrying it in her arms and when tired, on her shoulder, that we might have something to place on the bare floor of our living room.

In September we were introduced to a Johns Hopkins surgical resident who wished to sell his five year old 1952 'Oldsmobile 98' saloon car with 60,000 miles on the clock, since his father was giving him a Porsche. $300 was the asking price (a little over £100). Pale green and in excellent order, it had been well maintained. With automatic transmission, room for the driver with five passengers, electrically operated windows and a radio it was a luxurious bargain. The only stumbling block was that we didn't have any money. Doctor Irving Kuperman a resident gynaecological colleague from Chicago, a friend of Julie Glazer who we knew in London, generously offered and loaned us the purchase price, which we repaid at $50 a month, interest free, over 6 months. Petrol was then between 23 and 27 cents a US gallon. We were required to take a Maryland vehicle driving test, which was quite simple, providing one remembered that automatic failure followed should the applicant fail to lock all the car doors before starting the engine. With poor inner city public transport and without a car, life had been restricted to the few blocks we could walk. Once we acquired a motorcar, the only reliable means of rapid mobility in this sprawling metropolis, life became far more agreeable as we were at last able to sightsee, explore and travel further afield.

We became very friendly with Irving Kuperman, who in appearance, speech and mannerism bore a striking resemblance to the comedian Woody Allen. An eligible bachelor we couldn't resist introducing him to June's unmarried school friend Shirley Rappaport, who worked for the William Morris theatrical agency in New York. Intellectually bright, both were interested in the arts and seemed ideally suited. They dated over many months and just when we believed they were really making a match of it, the relationship collapsed.

Irving had introduced her to some of his friends at a party as his fiancée, without first consulting her. A trivial misunderstanding it somehow incensed her to such a degree she tempestuously discontinued their friendship. He travelled to New York the following weekend to apologise and patch things up. Unannounced he knocked on her apartment door, where she stubbornly and foolishly refused to see or speak to him other than to tell him to go away. Extremely upset and disappointed he returned to Baltimore and thereafter illogically refused to speak to me for having introduced him to Shirley, thereby severing two sets of friendship within the week.

We met him again almost forty years later when he visited London. A successful gynaecologist, still the double of Woody Allen, he'd settled in Little Rock Arkansas, married the mayor's daughter and was the proud father of four sons and two daughters. We chatted over old times. He claimed complete amnesia over the period when he knew Shirley. This was a blatant selective memory loss, since Shirley was the sort of gal once seen, one could never forget, and for all the correct reasons. She remained a bachelor, doubtlessly fulfilled in her chosen theatrical agency career, in Manhattan.

Jules Glazer, an accountant with a degree in psychology was a tall man, ruggedly built from Chicago. Hardly handsome, nature had more than adequately compensated him with a friendly extroverted personality, who garnered friends about him with consummate ease. His poor myopic vision meant he was ineligible for military service. He gained employment with the American PX and was transferred to Europe where he was stationed in Paris and there became friendly with one of my father's French cousins. He was transferred to London in 1951 and was provided with an introduction to my father's family, beginning a friendship that continued for more than 50 years until his death, two wives and two sons later, following cardiac by pass surgery in Phoenix Arizona.

Shortly after setting up home we purchased a small tape recording machine and recorded messages that we mailed home to June's parents. Transatlantic telephone calls (M11) were extremely expensive and this proved a more cost effective way of speaking to each other. We would invite English friends round and discuss with them our impressions of life in the USA. June's parents would then send us a tape with messages from family and friends in London. My mother wrote telling me we had cousins living in Baltimore specifically mentioning 'Lou Cheslock' and requesting I should visit him. Initially her instruction were ignored, since numbers of family and friends were constantly requesting we contact and visit all manner of distant relatives and friends living all over America to convey greetings on their behalf. A second followed by a third letter was received, as each enquired had we made contact with the Cheslock's. My mother's request could no longer be ignored and we telephoned Lou. He was delighted that we had made contact and invited us to his home at 25 Sulgrave Avenue to participate in one of their monthly cousins meetings the following weekend at their home.

This was on one of my weekend's off-duty and at the agreed time on a mid October evening we rang the doorbell. The house was in darkness, with no sound to indicate a meeting within. As we debated whether this was the wrong date, or house, a porch light went on and the door swung open.

"You must be the Powell's, it's so nice to meet you; I'm Elise Cheslock, your cousin Lou's wife. Please come on in and meet the family."

After this brief introduction we followed our hostess to a doorway, which opened to reveal a staircase leading down to a basement family room. We descended and ahead found a further entrance beyond which there were muffled sounds of conversation. As the second well insulated door opened we found a spacious living room crowded with chatting Cheslock's, who were introduced to us. Louis was a professor of music at the Peabody institute. Elise, his charming wife had some years ago been a ballet student there when she met him. Gladly accepting their generous hospitality, we frequently visited them and established a great rapport.

The first of our distant forays with our newly acquired Oldsmobile was a weekend away in Virginia to the scenic 'Skyline-Drive' in the Appalachian mountain chain of Virginia. Every Baltimorean recommended that we must see the colourful leaf display of trees in the Shenandoah Valley in the fall. Each autumn, as winter's bight creeps inexorably southwards, picturesquely verdant-forested hills and valleys change from green to hues of autumnal red and gold, before turning brown as deciduous trees shed their leaves. Nature's colourful progression southwards induced by the fall in temperature produces sights of magical colour that are a wonder of to behold.

We arranged to drive into Virginia for the weekend accompanied by Ruth Appleton another of June's Copthall Grammar School friends and her companion Don Rudin who were temporarily living in Washington DC. Hotel reservations were made for Saturday night We planned to motor a short distance along the skyline trail, a road running many hundreds of miles from Maine along the Appalachian Mountain chain, to view the marvellous colour changes.

June made arrangements by phone with Ruth to rendezvous in downtown Washington DC, at the church on the corner of 4th Avenue and H Street at 10 am. We left Baltimore with a picnic lunch to drive the 40 miles to our destination. Arriving shortly after 9.30 am we parked at the kerbside just opposite the church. We waited patiently for more than an hour, when with no sight of June's usually punctual friend, I went in search of a pay phone, to call her. She immediately answered the phone.

"Ruth, whatever's happened? Why didn't you meet us as we arranged?"

"Arnold, we stood waiting on the corner by the church for more than half an hour and when you didn't show up we thought something must have happened, so we returned here in case you phoned to say you'd had a puncture or something."

"Ruth we arrived early and didn't see you. Didn't you see us sitting in a Green Oldsmobile 98 opposite the church?"

"No, I don't recall seeing the car, but don't worry. Just stay where you are and we'll be with you in less than five minutes." She assured me.

I returned to the car, told June of the conversation and reassured, we prepared to set off within the next few minutes. During the following thirty minutes, I periodically left the car and wandering round the street corner, endeavoured to catch sight of Ruth as she approached. With the time at 11.30 am. I set off for the 'phone box and again called Ruth. She answered.

"Arnold we searched and searched and you weren't anywhere to be seen. What game are you playing?"

"Ruth, we haven't moved. We've been waiting in the car right on the corner by the church on 4th and H Street as you arranged with June, and we just haven't seen you."

"Wait a bit. What address did you say?"

"The church on the corner of 4th Avenue and H Street."

"Arnold did you say H or 8th Street?"

"Ruth, let's stop this nonsense. I said H as in Harry."

"Oh my goodness: No wonder we didn't see you. I said 8th, the number after seven, not H for Harry."

Having acknowledged our misunderstanding, I returned to the car, and drove to the corner of 4th Avenue and 8th Street, where there was a church, as Ruth and Don breathlessly hove into sight. Once inside the car, with mid-day approaching, we set off belatedly driving west and shortly before sun down booked into our hotel. Having squandered much of the day in travel we decided to retire early to make a dawn start next morning to explore the Shenandoah Valley acknowledging our earlier error in communication, which highlighted the reason aeroplane call signs are given in the format of Alpha, Bravo, Charlie rather than A, B, C.

Next morning we arose and dressed to find a heavy autumnal mist shrouding everything. We decided to have a leisurely American breakfast in the dining room, after which we felt certain the mist would have cleared. We selected a table near the entrance and ordered eggs, sunny side up, followed by blueberry pancakes, orange juice and hot coffee. American meal portions are generously huge and our breakfast was no exception.

Unhurriedly we sat taking breakfast, re-ordering as much coffee as we wished, waiting for the mist to clear when two portly middle aged gentlemen, dressed in weekend leisure attire walked in, escorting two slim, attractive young ladies, and sat in an adjacent table, where they engaged in animated conversation. From their accents it appeared the men were English, the most portly of the pair spoke with what I took to be a Lancashire accent, the ladies were American.

Some weeks earlier there'd been an intermittent rail and bus strike in the UK, to the discomfiture of the commuting British people who travelled by public transport, which was still ongoing. Heading the TGWU (Transport and General Workers Union) was their leader Frank Cousins, whose photograph frequently appeared in the British tabloid press. We realised this was he, seated at the next table, in recreational chequered shirt and red braces. We debated whether or not to challenge him and ask him why he wasn't back in the UK resolving the transport dispute, when he rose from his table and as he walked past our table I called out.

"Hello, good morning Mr. Cousins. Are you waiting for the mist to clear, like us?"

He stopped, approached, and standing at our table, the quintessential trade unionist returned our greeting and shook hands all round as he introduced himself. It came out sounding like; "Ahrm Fraynk Coozens."

He explained he was visiting Washington and his companion, the British ambassador, seated at the next table, to whom we then nodded politely and exchanged greetings, had brought him to the Shenandoah Valley for the weekend to witness the colour changes of the fall foliage.

Seldom did the Queen's personal representative and the leader of a major British trades union take the time to speak with us. Elatedly we left the dining room, greatly encouraged to have witnessed the exemplary manner in which, in their own recreational time they fostered Anglo American relationships and extended British hospitality to young Americans. From 1964 until 1966 Frank Cousins became Minister of Technology in Harold Wilson's government before giving way to Jack Jones in 1969 as TGWU leader. It was at this time we learned that the first 26 miles section of the long delayed, much-vaunted new English motorway the M1, linking London to Birmingham had opened in 1958 and then closed but 3 weeks later for surface repairs.

With visibility down to less than 100 yards, we left our hotel and proceeded slowly to the Appalachian Trail roadway. We drove several miles and stopped at each vantage point. The view was always identical. The entire valley, with its tree-lined slopes, was filled with a dense impenetrable mist. Many years were to elapse before we were able to return to view the fall foliage in this beautiful valley.

One of the few English doctors at the hospital was Ross Thompson and his wife Christine, a radiographer, who within a few months found she was expecting their first child. They had arrived with visitor's visas, which restricted the place of one's employment. The job promised her by the hospital never materialised, and with her visitor's visa she was unable to obtain employment elsewhere. Needing to survive on an intern's salary they were always desperately short of money. Fortunately we were able to travel some distance to explore the countryside in our car and Ross's off duty weekends coincided with mine, which enabled us to share our transport with them. To economise we even shared the same hotel bedrooms using twin beds. (There was no wife swapping). At the completion of our year they returned to Huddersfield where Ross like his father became a surgeon and we completely lost contact.

I had imagined I'd be working with American doctors. All the consultants were American born, but amongst the interns and residents 19 different nationalities were represented and were all men except for a solitary female resident in the pathology department, Sybil Kyne, whose husband was also a pathology resident. Amongst the interns there were some who were unable to speak or understand English. As a consequence in addition to my own allocation of patients I assisted at least two other interns with history taking and physical examinations while they in turn lightened my work load by taking bloods from my patients as well as their own. Duty commenced at 7 am and alternate days I worked a 36-hour shift, when accommodation at night was provided in designated rooms where bunks were available to snatch a few hours sleep in between cases.

Unlike the British system there was a continuity of formal postgraduate medical education. Twice every week a formal 2-hour period was set aside for all residents and interns to attend lectures, in which medical and surgical cases were presented, with case presentations prepared by residents with an emphasis on assessing diagnostic problems. This was a far better scheme than the British model, where post-graduate medical education was left to each individual, without any formal hospital programme. Every second weekend was my own from the completion of duties at 6 pm on Friday. All meals were provided without charge in the hospital dining room to uniformed staff while on Sundays when on duty, we were permitted to invite wives for lunch. In order to economise on food I always breakfasted at the hospital when on duty.

As in England, during the day there were specific A&E personnel, but at night the interns were always summoned according to the speciality they represented. The A&E department was not particularly busy apart from Friday nights and weekends. Although the hospital had a policy of not admitting 'coloured' patients (African Americans) to the private beds, a token few were admitted into the public wards, while the A&E department accepted any patient for treatment, regardless of ethnicity. On Friday nights we were inundated with problems that were largely unfamiliar to me such as occasional gunshot injuries, knife wounds and stabbings, particularly amongst the poorest Afro-Americans. Police, who not infrequently interrogated the victims in our presence, as we were dealing with their injuries, escorted most of these patients. The conversation invariably followed a familiar pattern. Some burly armed police officer would roughly enquire.

"Tell us who did this to yah?"

"It was jest a friend, thet's all, a friend." Was the plaintive reply.

There were also considerable numbers of very inebriated people, particularly men, especially on a Friday evening when 'pay checks' were too liberally squandered in local bars. The police were required to have each of these drunks examined in A&E to ensure there was no underlying medical cause for their condition before hauling them to the police precinct to be booked. I was unaware of any large-scale drug problem apart from alcohol. Down town bars were open until 4 am and it was a distressing sight to see numbers of intoxicated men in the streets, barely able to stand, on my walk to work in the predawn mornings.

In winter the temperature regularly fell as low as 5 degrees Fahrenheit. A timed thermostat monitored the central heating in our apartment, over which we had no control and which responded only to the ambient temperature in the stair well outside our front door. The timer switched off at midnight and resumed heat at 7am. This meant that in the middle of winter when I rose to dress just after 6 am to walk to the hospital, the apartment was cold. The previous tenant had warned us of this state of affairs and we followed his solution to the problem. Each night before retiring we placed a small tray of ice on the thermostat. This boosted the temperature enormously, and the apartment remained sufficiently warm in the morning when I needed to climb out of bed. The incriminating ice tray evidence was removed every morning as I left the apartment for work.

A worrisome 'peeping tom' had been seen in the vicinity of our apartment block that fall. Late one evening I received a desperate 'phone call from June.

"Arnold, please come quickly, I'm frightened." Following which the line went dead. Hurriedly I explained to the duty officer I was urgently needed at home and rushed out of the hospital. I sprinted the half block to our home, and dashed up two flights of stairs to our apartment. Fumbling with the front door key I pushed the door open. June was nowhere to be seen. The window to the fire escape was open. With mounting apprehension I breathlessly shouted her name. A muffled response came from within. Dashing to the bedroom I found her trembling cross-legged in bed. In a state bordering on hysteria she rapidly explained there had been an unexpected visitor. She had screamed and fled to barricade herself under the covers in our bedroom and phone me. I searched for the mouse she had seen in the kitchen, but there was no trace. It too had fled.

To our disquiet, apartheid was a reality in Maryland, with no integration in schools, public buildings or transport and with many facilities, from hotels to restaurants, and water drinking fountains to toilets displaying signs in varying shapes and sizes bearing the simple uncompromising message 'White Only.' The senior Ob-Gyn resident was from the Philippines. He and one of the American nurses had fallen in love and were married in Washington DC, since differing ethnic groups were not legally entitled to marry or live together under Maryland state law. The majority of the lower paid menial hospital workers were Afro American, such as cleaners, porters and kitchen staff. I often chatted with some of these acquaintances, with who I was in day-to-day contact. Imagine my distress to find, when I passed a group in the street, and waved a friendly greeting, when they, in response chose to ignore me completely. There was prejudice on both sides. The Afro Americans were not however the lowest paid staff, for the interns and junior residents had this dubious distinction.

One afternoon a 'coloured' gentleman entered the Stewart's department store restaurant, which bore a sign 'White's Only' and seated himself at a table. The personnel manager asked June to proceed without delay and deal with the matter by telling him that he must leave, failing which the police would be called to eject him. June expressed her reluctance to do this but was unceremoniously informed that if she refused this instruction her employment would be terminated at the end of the week. In a quandary, she descended the stairs slowly, rather than take the elevator, rehearsing what she might diplomatically say in this difficult situation. Entering the dining room she saw her employer's unwanted guest. Approaching the table she asked if she might sit down and join him. Seated, she spoke quietly and as she hoped, diplomatically.

"Forgive me disturbing you but I've been asked to speak to you. I feel terribly ashamed and embarrassed, but I've been instructed to point out that this is a segregated restaurant and I must request that you leave, since the staff will not serve you. Conveying this message is not something that I wished to do. For my part you're welcome to dine here or any where you choose but I've been informed that if I don't ask you to leave I'll be fired and the truth of the matter is that it took me nearly 6 weeks to find employment and I desperately need this job."

The gentleman, who was articulate and well spoken, replied that he quite understood the situation and did not want any trouble, so he would leave. He thanked my wife for her courtesy and explanation. With that he quietly stood up and with dignity walked out of the restaurant. June felt humiliated that she'd been compelled to participate in this degrading charade. As a consequence she felt this was not the sort of corporation she wished to work for with their forced benevolence and colour discrimination, although at the time she had little choice. She decided she must look for alternative employment.

In addition to racial segregation we perceived another social problem. There was the derogatory manner in which groups of poorly educated white people, termed 'white trash' were treated. They were the city equivalent of the people from 'the other side of the railway track' or the country 'hill billys'. Their relatively low socio economic status, often with large families, unbecoming dialect and strange dress usually identified them. They were considered no better than the Afro Americans, amongst whom they sometimes lived in close proximity.

On December 1st my wife and I celebrated our first wedding anniversary by making a reservation to dine at Haussner's, one of the city's better restaurants. We went there straight from changing out of our work clothes. Once seated at our table for two, we had a celebratory drink and had the opportunity to look at the walls, sumptuously bedecked with paintings and mirrors before ordering our meal. After a few minutes June stood up and announced she was going to powder her nose. A few moments after leaving our table she returned, quickly sat down and falteringly said.

"I don't think I'm going to make it." As she spoke, she fainted. Her head slumped and with eyes closed she started to slide down in her seat. The best thing would have been to have her lie flat on the floor but this was a crowded busy restaurant. As I struggled to prevent her from slipping further under the table a large buxom woman who had been dining at the next table with her companion brusquely leaned across me, crushing me out of the way as she grabbed June's wrist and announced.

"Out of my way young man, out of my way. I'm a nurse." She held June's wrist for ten seconds as I continued my struggle to keep her from sliding under the table and then releasing her arm pronounced.

"Obviously pregnant. She'll be alright."

Too surprised to tell this well meaning interloper what I thought of her and her misdiagnosis, I held on to June until she regained consciousness. Later I had her promise never to drink alcohol on an empty stomach.

Immediately after Christmas I was entitled to 3 days leave, as part of a long weekend. We had earlier contacted June's Boston cousins, the Glovin's, whom she'd never met. We travelled by car staying at a motel on Beacon Street and met as many of the family the following day as we were able. In the evening we attended one of the 'Boston Pop Concerts' conducted by Leonard Bernstein. During the intermission, while facing the stage and speaking to June who was seated at my side, I became aware of a strange sound emanating from her as she tugged at my coat sleeve. As I glanced round to ask what she wanted I became aware that June was sitting with her mouth wide open, with tears in her eyes, unable to speak. She'd dislocated her tempero-mandibular jaw joint on the left side when yawning. Fortunately I was speedily able to deal with the problem, though we felt embarrassed that it should be remedied in full public view in a theatre auditorium. Luckily we were still able to enjoy the remainder of the programme and our weekend.

On the third day we returned to Baltimore, but prior to leaving the motel we were astounded to discover the Glovin's had generously paid for our two nights accommodation. Upon my return to the hospital and totally unconnected to my temporary absence I found the maternity department in crisis. Every maternity bed was filled with an overflow in the corridors and in a contiguous surgical department, with staff working flat out. Virtually every maternity patient due to deliver during the first four weeks of January was endeavouring to be delivered by surgical induction prior to midnight of December 31st in an attempt to benefit from the considerable tax advantage given to parents for a child born in the financial year ending at that time. The tax allowance, I was told, would more than cover all the hospital maternity costs.

As the time approached for June's parents and her younger siblings Peter and Wendy to make their intended four weeks visit to the USA in April 1959, we each requested time to join them from our employers with a four week vacation or leave of absence. June applied to personnel at Stuart's, which was declined on the basis that her vacation entitlement was 2 weeks at the end of a full year's employment. As her employer was unyielding on this point June resigned in April and immediately commenced her search for another post to start in May 1958 and readily obtained employment with the Baltimore Housing Authority. Similarly I was only entitled to two weeks annual holiday. I made an appointment to see Mr Crawford, the hospital superintendent, in his office.

Seated at his desk I stood in front of him like a schoolboy and explained.

"My wife's parents will be making their first trip to the USA to visit us. They'll be staying four weeks and my wife and I wish to travel with them during that time. I'd like permission to take my vacation in April together with a further two weeks unpaid leave of absence."

Adamantly he refused permission. I explained I wanted to accompany my wife and her family and my request was not unreasonable, since they would have travelled many thousands of miles from London. Furthermore if he would grant my leave of absence, I would be prepared to work a further two weeks at the end of my contract. This I elaborated would be of considerable benefit to the hospital since knowing the procedures and speaking English I could show many of the new interns how to perform their duties. He remained unyielding and said he could not grant any extra vacation time. Uncompromisingly I stated my intention to take the extra time as unpaid leave of absence whether he agreed or not.

"Dr Powell, if you persist in that course of action you'll leave me no alternative but to fire you."

"I should be very sad if that were to happen sir, since I've enjoyed working here, but I should simply seek employment in another hospital." I replied.

"You certainly would not. I would be obliged to inform the immigration authorities of our course of action and you would be deported immediately."

"I think not Mr Crawford, sir, since I've a green card and holding an immigrant visa, I'm entitled to work wherever I choose." I announced nonchalantly, attempting to call his bluff.

"Very well Doctor. Let's not be hasty about this. I suggest you come back to see me tomorrow so that I can put the matter before the hospital board and give you their decision."

The next day I again knocked on Mr Crawford's office door. He invited me in and I stood before him at his desk again feeling like a miscreant before the head teacher.

"Doctor, I've spoken to the board and put your case to them. I'm pleased to be able to tell you they think by agreeing to stay on for an extra two weeks to show the new interns the ropes, you've hit on a splendid proposal and one which they would be happy to go along with. On that basis you may take two weeks unpaid leave of absence in addition to your two weeks vacation entitlement."

"Thank you very much sir."

"And be certain to bring the folks over to show them round and have them join us for lunch at the hospital."

We needed more beds to accommodate June's family and for that reason bought a six months old bedroom suite of furniture from Dr Vacquerano, an intern from San Salvador. He'd arrived the previous July with his wife, young daughter and sister in law, but unable to speak English, in spite of that having been a condition of employment, they decided to return home prematurely and left in March. They lived next door to us on the second floor. Once having purchased their bedroom suite, the deal was that we would all move the furniture into our apartment, leaving them the bed, which they would deliver on the morning of their departure. That evening we discovered they hadn't delivered it. Although we lived on the same floor, they were in the flat next door in a separate portion of the building. We dismantled the bed and negotiated the various parts round a narrow spiral staircase to exit from their flat. Try as we might, we were unable to manoeuvre the box spring down the staircase.

"If they got it in, then we can get it out." I muttered as we heaved and struggled, but to no avail. In desperation we called the janitor for assistance. He explained it had never entered by the staircase, but had been delivered through the window and would have to leave the same way; a problem the landlord would have responsibility to deal with. Our friends the Vacquerano's had chosen to conceal this fact.

Dr Khamoun, a delightful man, in his mid 20's, from Tunisia was another intern whose tenure was cut short. An excellent cook, with whom we'd become friendly, he had become increasingly hoarse in the New Year. A cancer of the tonsil was diagnosed as the cause of his problem. He lost weight and became extremely depressed as he underwent a course of radiotherapy in February, while colleagues assisted him by shouldering much of his work. In March I was summoned to Mr Crawford's office and upon entering, he got straight to the point without preamble.

"Dr Powell, I understand your colleague Dr Khamoun is very unwell. Do you know whether he has any health insurance?"

"I'm sorry sir I've no idea, never having discussed such matters with him. Neither my wife nor I have health insurance and since many young people don't appear to give such matters any priority it's very probable that he doesn't have health cover either." I replied, taken aback.

His next probing question shocked me further, as both unfeeling and misplaced.

"Doctor, have you any idea who would be responsible for shipping his body back to Tunisia should he succumb to his illness?"

"Mr Crawford, I'm afraid I can't answer such a question. I would have thought that the person to ask is Dr. Khamoun, which would be extremely insensitive, or failing that, one would need to communicate with the Tunisian Embassy in Washington."

"Thank you Dr Powell, I'd like to request your discretion in this matter and that you do not discuss this conversation with your colleagues."

I was never able to fathom why Mr Crawford selected me to enquire into another intern's private circumstances in such an uncharitable manner, but shortly after this brief interview Dr Khamoun disappeared. He just moved away without bidding any of his associate's good-bye. We assumed the poor fellow returned to Tunisia, to spend his few remaining weeks with his family.

During the visit of June's family we travelled by car to New York and Boston visiting family. We flew to Miami for a ten days vacation and concluded by visiting historic sites in Washington DC, Virginia and the battlefield site at Gettysburg. I then resumed my duties at the Maryland General, while June commenced work as a secretary to her boss Esther Siegel at the Baltimore Housing Authority.

On one occasion I found myself in hot water, and was nearly fired. A patient and her attending surgeon reported me for being rude and discourteous, which I emphatically denied; cynical perhaps, but never intentionally ill mannered, or rude. The circumstance related to a middle-aged woman who required a two units blood transfusion prior to undergoing surgery scheduled for the following morning.

I had set up a preliminary Iv dextrose saline drip in the patient's forearm and secured the needle in place. I explained to her that I was leaving to collect the first unit of blood from the haematology department and would be back shortly. I returned and checked the label on the plastic blood container bearing the patient's name, blood group, and hospital reference number, with the patient. Next, while preparing the blood giving set with its filter I was taken aback by the patient asking.

"Doctor, before you give me that blood, does it say that it's white blood?"

Knowing full well what she meant, but never having been asked such a question, I replied.

"The only information I have is the blood group, which matches yours, and I can see its colour is red. In fact I've never seen blood of any other colour but red, no matter who gave it."

"Well I'm sure you can't be so simple that you don't know precisely what I mean, an' if you can't tell me that it's not anything but white blood, then I'll not be wanting it."

"I'm unaware who donated the blood, whether they were white, yellow, blue or black. We all have red blood and two generous people with your blood group have each donated a pint of blood. You need two units which have been cross matched for you and I can give you no assurance as to the colour of either of the donors."

"I don't want any coloured blood in me. If you can't tell me that it's not come from coloured folk then I don't want it, an' you can take it away." She snapped belligerently.

I reported the patient's refusal to Dr Nipkow, the chief surgical resident with the reasons. Mistakenly I thought the matter would rest there. The incident was reported to the patient's indignant surgeon. Later that day I was hauled before the hospital administrator and chief of staff to explain my attitude and to apologise to the doctor and his patient for my rudeness. I had no alternative but to eat humble pie and apologise; however much it rancoured.

Following the visit of June's parents, I decided that since we'd seen so little of the USA, it would be interesting to work in another part of the country and if possible earn a little money to improve our impoverished state. Enquiry revealed my British medical qualification would enable me to practice in most Canadian provinces without the need to sit further examinations. I responded to a number of advertisements in a Canadian medical journal and found an advertisement for a small rural practice on the Canadian prairies in Climax Saskatchewan, 14 miles north of the Montana border. There was a 12-bed cottage hospital, which provided accommodation in a rent free unfurnished modern 3-bedroom house. No salary was given but the applicant was assured of an income of no less than $20,000 per annum, a princely sum compared with my $200 a month. Working in such a location would give us the opportunity of touring the mid west and finally the west coast before returning to the UK.

We went to the public library to research the area. We learned the annual precipitation was 12 inches a year. Used to the wet climate of England and the US Eastern seaboard, this seemed ideal. It didn't dawn on us until much later the terminology was precipitation and not rainfall, a significant difference. In mid May, I telephoned the hospital and arranged to take up the post on offer in the first week of August, to replace Dr. Sutherland, the doctor who'd vacated the town a month earlier to practice in Alberta. I was notified that before commencing my appointment I needed to obtain proof of my registration with the College of Physicians and Surgeons of Saskatchewan where I would also be required to pay an annual licence fee. This could be accomplished most rapidly by a visit to the college in Saskatoon with my British medical registration documents.

Having finished my ob-gyn, I next completed 3 months paediatrics in the Maryland University Hospital. This was the most intensive and valuable training one could wish to receive. Each night was passed in A&E, where the majority of children were treated intensively in a specialised paediatric department, thereby avoiding the costly necessity of admitting them to the wards, where only the more complicated cases were admitted. Young children's needs are frequently urgent and success was due to the speed of the medical response in instigating appropriate intensive treatment. This protocol worked extremely well, as every night we were inundated with sick children with respiratory, gastro intestinal, dehydration and lead poisoning problems. Very few ever needed admission.

At any one time there were more than a score of young children with respiratory difficulties being treated with humidifiers in oxygen tents and miraculously the majority were well enough to return home within twelve hours to be followed up later in an out patient clinic. The work was tiring but invaluable. Most of our patients were poor and many were Afro American. On one occasion I was involved in the care of a 12-year-old Afro American girl, who was admitted with vaginal bleeding and subsequently miscarried.

At the girl's bedside I discussed with the mother, who was in her mid 20's, placing her daughter on the newly available contraceptive pill (p). The mother declined on the grounds she had been told, and firmly believed.

"A girl has to have her first chil' before her bones set, 'cause if she don't, the birth canal'll be too tight an' she won't be able to have no babies no how." She had delivered her first child before the age of 14, as had her mother and all those she knew.

Aghast, I attempted to explain that these ideas were totally untrue. I described the process whereby the newborn baby's head moulded to adapt to the width of the birth canal, which in turn had ligaments, which permitted it to expand slightly during the confinement no matter the mother's age. She didn't appear to understand my explanation and convinced I'd made no impression, I stood to leave. As I walked dejectedly to the door she summoned me.

"Hey Doc; where yo goin' so fast? Come back here; what'd you say those pills was called?"

I'd made two converts for the birth control pill.

The prized American dream was of freedom, opportunity and wealth. Unfortunately there was also prejudice and in particular, poverty, amongst its Afro American citizens. This applied in Maryland and everywhere we travelled in America. Amongst this group, vast numbers of teen-age pregnancies often seemed to be the self-inflicted, problem. Many of the women I met had delivered two or three children in their early teens, mainly with different partners, before settling down and marrying in their 30's, when the chosen spouse was seldom the father of any of her children.

With so many children born out of wedlock to immature young mothers in single parent families, it was small wonder in this Afro American matriarchal society that there was endemic school truancy and failed education. There seemed little place or regard for the young men in these families and the consequence was one of high unemployment, with greater poverty, and a huge increase in crime.

These observations were frequently discussed amongst my medical colleagues and the general consensus was that many years of co-ordinated government planning and action would be needed to offset the dearth of education in the 'coloured' community. Deep seated attitudes needed to be changed and in the segregated school system of that era such instruction was unavailable. The problem of poverty and delinquency in 1959 amongst the Afro-American community was like an open sore, festering in an otherwise affluent society and was set to persist, unabated.

(p) In 1937 investigators demonstrated that Progesterone, a female hormone is able to halt ovulation. Mexican Indian tribeswomen had been known to drink an infusion made from yams to stop conception from which researchers were able to extract progesterone. Large-scale testing of the Pill during the mid-1950s proved successful. In 1960 the US Food and Drug Administration (FDA) approved the first oral contraceptive and by 1965, the Pill became the leading method of reversible contraception in the USA. Through the 1970's lower levels of hormone were used than were initially considered necessary to suppress ovulation, reducing the incidence of side effects. The availability and use of the 'birth pill' as a reliable, safe and inexpensive method of contraception must be considered one of the foremost defining steps in the emancipation of women in the 20th century.

Chapter 7

BALTIMORE -to- SASKATCHEWAN CANADA

July 1959

I was present on July 1st 1959 at the inaugural meeting I'd missed the previous year when the new interns and residents met with the hospital chief of staff and were introduced to the working practices at the hospital. At the conclusion of the meeting, the chief of staff eliminated any feel good factor by warning the assembled doctors that if they failed to work diligently and as directed, their contract would be terminated without hesitation and they would be deported immediately from the USA. I pondered whether I would have stayed, had I been threatened in this singularly high-handed manner on my arrival?

My internship should have finished on July 1st at the completion of my final three months in general surgery, but I continued working for a further three weeks, until Monday 20th July 1959, fulfilling my obligation to the hospital administrator, who summoned me to see him prior to my last weekend on duty.

With some concern I knocked at his office door. A voice from within called.

"Come in."

As I entered and crossed the threshold, Mr. Crawford stood up for the very first time from behind his expansive executive office desk, to greet me with a smile. He was gracious and charming. Beaming, he hastened forward to shake my hand and picking up a rolled object from his desk, unfurled it and presented me with an elaborately impressive certificate with a gold seal stating that I had satisfactorily accomplished my year's internship at the Maryland General, with the dates. Placing his arm round my shoulder, full of camaraderie, he wished me well and stated that should I later be interested in completing a residency, the hospital would be pleased to accommodate me. This was a far cry from an earlier interview, when attempting to brow beat me, he threatened to fire me and have me deported.

June and I had meticulously worked out on graph paper the dimensions of the trailer that would accommodate the furniture and belongings we'd acquired over the previous months. On the Monday morning of our departure I collected the U-Haul trailer that we had hired by the day and cautiously drove my elongated load and parked it outside our North Howard Street apartment. There we carefully packed the trailer according to the plan I had drawn, with assistance from our fair-haired, blue eyed Afro-American caretaker, (whom we'd befriended during our stay and initially thought might be of a sun bronzed Scandinavian origin, until we met his children) and two of his colleagues. Locking the trailer securely we drove to our Baltimore friends Milt and Eunice, where we stayed the night.

Having plotted our journey, which was expected to take 5 days, we made a start next morning shortly after sunup. We should have taken a more leisurely trip, but our finances were as usual, perilously low and the community where I was heading had been without a doctor for more than four months. In addition I was keen to get started on what we perceived as our new adventure. While not obvious from her appearance June was now 3 months pregnant and we decided to conceal our exciting news from family and friends for a further month until we could be more certain that most of the dangers of her first trimester pregnancy had passed.

Cautiously I drove our loaded car as we travelled northwest over a journey of some two thousand miles, our destination the town of Climax in the southern portion of the Canadian province of Saskatchewan. We motored steadily north-westwards hauling the heavy U Haul aluminium trailer, almost the length of our car, through Chicago, then on to Minneapolis St. Paul until we reached highway route 2 that traversed North Dakota and Montana, running parallel to the US border. Motoring carefully, we progressed without mishap covering almost 500 miles daily until we arrived at noon on the fifth day of our travel, Sunday July 26th at Harlem, Montana, a small town on the last paved road we were to see for several days.

We stopped briefly for a light lunch and to refuel before proceeding north along a 'dirt' highway, the like of which I had never seen before, leading to Turner and then to the US border; 14 miles beyond which lay, our destination. The border post of Treelon closed at 4.30pm and I was determined that we must pass before that time. We drove warily along this track and as we approached the village of Turner there was a tremendous bang, causing the car to swerve. Hot and tired I stopped. A rear tyre had blown out. In desperation I looked at the shredded tyre with the knowledge that miles from anywhere, I would have to unhitch the trailer to gain access to change the wheel, and then reverse the whole process in the heat of the day. As I stood looking on the formidable task at hand, a farm truck came along in a cloud of dust and screeched to a stop.

Our 'Good Samaritan' in the guise of a local young farm hand alighted and immediately offered to help. In almost the twinkling of an eye he had removed a huge jack he carried in his truck and elevated the side of our car without the need to unhitch the trailer. Within a few minutes the wheel was changed and we set off to limp slowly to Turner to replace our defunct tyre. A replacement set us back $40, which was twice the amount we would have paid in Baltimore. The tyre was changed, leaving our finances in a precariously low state as we set off once more, even more slowly and watchful, in order to safeguard our remaining tyres from the jagged outcrop of rocks on the road. The border post was some 8 miles distant to the north of Turner and we had little more than an hour before it closed.

At the Baltimore public library we'd diligently researched all that we could of the region before I'd accepted the post of town doctor. In life it isn't so much what you read that's most significant, but rather the absent information that's of greater importance, as we were shortly to discover. We read that Saskatchewan is one of three huge Canadian Prairie Provinces. To the east is Manitoba, to the west Alberta and then British Columbia and the Pacific Ocean. In the north are the huge tundra and arctic North West territories and to the south, the 49th parallel, which we were shortly to reach, separating it from the northern US states of Montana and North Dakota, an area formerly home to the Blackfoot Indian tribes. With a population of almost one million people it occupies an area of some 252,000 square miles with a land availability of 4 people to each square mile, compared to the ratio in the UK of more than one hundred times this number. The land mass is more than one and a half times the size of the United Kingdom, with its capital Regina, named in honour of queen Victoria. The main produce are wheat and oil, with Saskatchewan producing 50% of Canada's wheat crop.

In the distant past this state was part of an endless glacial expanse extending down from the arctic, following which, with earlier periods of global warming, there remained a large shallow inland sea. In more recent chronological times the shallow sea vanished, to reveal a huge plateau, now some 3,000 feet above sea level. As the last ice age receded, extensive herds of buffalo migrated northwards to roam slowly over these flat grassland areas with its sparse gently undulating hills and valleys. During the time of the plains Indians, small tribes of nomadic Indian hunters in tepee encampments followed buffalo herds that provided almost all their food and clothing needs.

With the encroachment of the earliest European settlers these great herbivores were hunted virtually to extinction, with disastrous consequences for the itinerant existence of the native inhabitants, who were reduced to a terrible penury. In addition, as the Saskatchewan Indians came into contact with European railroad workers in the 1880's, they fell victim to TB; a disease unknown to them and over several years some 10% died each year, further decimating their depleted numbers.

During the next four decades cattle were introduced to roam freely on gigantic ranches. The area was not fully opened or explored, until the Canadian Pacific Railway was completed in 1885, to link coastal British Columbia with the eastern provinces, following which, in 1905, Saskatchewan became a separate province.

A Canadian Homesteaders Act in 1895, copying earlier American legislation created an environment in which free land was given to encourage farmers to migrate into these immense areas. Three huge ranches occupied a semi arid region, the size of Wales, in the southwest portion of Saskatchewan, named Palliser's Triangle after the 19th century surveyor Palliser, and farmers commenced settling in the region from 1910 onwards. It was in this area we found ourselves in August 1959 approaching the customs border post of Treelon and where, unknowingly, the next dramatic phase of my training would shortly begin, shattering those misconceived notions where I might have considered myself as a university graduate educated, well travelled and sophisticated.

In less than half an hour we were relieved to spot the solitary flag pole flying the star spangled banner, fluttering ahead in the afternoon breeze, as we approached the US border post. We continued carefully skirting round huge stones more akin to boulders and deep plunging potholes that in open warfare could have been accepted as tank traps, to keep half a second world war Panzer division at bay. With the formality of a friendly smile the American border guard raised the road barrier and waved, as we proceeded onwards through the day's dust and heat, without seeking to inspect our passports or see the contents of our huge trailer.

We continued a further 300 yards to the Canadian post with its flagpole flying the red maple leaf flag. Here we expected to be waved through in like manner as we happily contemplated that within another thirty minutes we would have safely reached our destination where, before unpacking, we could take a long drink of cool water and rest, followed by a refreshing bath, to clear all the dust accumulated in throats, clothes and hair since leaving the paved highway three hours earlier. Our illusions were soon rudely shattered.

Parking our car in the unshaded blazing afternoon sun. I entered the customs office, which appeared to serve both as customs post and home for the customs and immigration officials, in this remote outpost of the British

Empire. June accompanied me to stretch her legs and escape the stifling heat. Initially all seemed deserted but an official in a navy blue uniform soon appeared behind the reception counter. Mutual smiles and greetings of;

"Good afternoon." were followed by the good-natured enquiry by the seemingly sociable customs officer.

"What have you got in the trailer?"

"Our household goods, we're relocating in Canada." I responded.

"That's nice. Can I see your papers please?"

"Certainly." I replied as we handed over our passports. He briefly glanced at them stamped, them with a rubber-dated stamp ' Point of entry Treelon', and handed them back. Replacing them in my pocket I was turning to leave when;

"Could you show me your immigration documents?"

"We don't have any. As you can see from our passports we're not Americans, we're British, and we don't need immigration papers."

"You're mistaken. I need to see your immigration documents before I can allow you in."

"No. I don't quite think you really understand. I know we're driving an American car, with an American registration, which is pulling an American U-Haul trailer, but we're not American at all. We're British subjects, with British passports and this is, or until recently was a part of the British Empire."

"That may be so, but I still need to see your immigration papers."

I felt that I was talking to some bureaucratic knucklehead who couldn't understand that Canada had been, until very recently, a British possession and that as British subjects we shared the same Queen as he did, the same Anglo-Saxon birthright and heritage, which gave us a natural right of entry. I felt this border custodian must be half witted not to understand so simple a concept.

"Look, we don't need any immigration papers. We're not Americans, we're B-R-I-T-I-S-H subjects, and Canada is part of the British Commonwealth." I endeavoured to explain as patiently as I was able.

"That may be perfectly true but you don't enter Canada without immigration papers no matter who you are."

"Are you certain of that?" I enquired incredulously. "Even though we're British subjects?"

"Absolutely; even if as you say, you're British, you must have your immigration papers."

He wasn't smiling and didn't seem willing to back down. Since there was no other more senior person in charge than this apparent simpleton, upon whom I could call, I decided to humour and accommodate him. My wife as was her custom gave me an unseen tap, with her foot, warning me to smile and stay calm, though she sensed and knew that I thought him a moron, and was fast losing my cool.

"Alright; if, as you say, we need immigration documents, then tell me, where do we obtain them?" I enquired with a charm and show of affability that I certainly didn't feel.

"From any Canadian consulate."

"That's fine. Could you possibly tell me where the nearest consulate can be found?"

"Certainly. There's a Canadian consulate in Chicago. There's another somewhere in California, probably San Francisco. There may even be one in New York and of course there's an embassy in Washington DC, but I'd suggest Chicago is your closest bet. You'll have to go back, get your medicals, chest x-rays and blood tests and fill in the required documentation."

"But we passed through Chicago almost four days ago." I exclaimed. "Then you'll have to turn right round and go back. You'll probably get to know the route better that way." he replied, his response clearly indicating he was enjoying our predicament.

I was aghast. This was sheer madness. I had suddenly left the US to enter cuckoo land and this was the custodian of this bird emporium who was denying our entrance. I felt we were somehow playing out a sequence from Alice's Adventures in Wonderland that I'd yet to read. Perhaps, I thought, it might have been a visit to Canada that had provided Lewis Carol with his inspiration. And bereft of manners, he had noticeably omitted the customary 'Sir.'

We were in deep, deep, trouble. The logistics were remarkably simple. To retrace our journey to Chicago and return would involve us in an eight days trek with the trailer. The car tires might not stand up to any more pounding on these rock and boulder strewn tracks that were euphemistically called unpaved highways. To obtain the medical tests he was indicating might take a further three or four days. To cap it all, we were almost out of money. Another couple of tire blowouts would leave us financially destitute and completely stranded. We didn't have sufficient funds for nearly two weeks trailer rental and hotel accommodation, let alone the other expenses for such an extended journey. In fact, we didn't have the wherewithal even to attempt to bribe our way through the border control, which fleetingly crossed my mind, although heaven knows what the penalty might be for attempting to coerce a Canadian customs official.

"Good heavens! You can't really be serious!" I exclaimed. "That'll take us the best part of two weeks and I just can't spare the time."

"I'm sorry, but those are the regulations. You should have considered the immigration requirements before you started your journey. No matter who you are, you can't come through without your immigration documents."

"But they're expecting me and I have a contract to fulfil." I endeavoured to explain.

"You'll just have to let them know there's been a technical problem that's delayed you for a couple of weeks, while you go back to Chicago and make an appointment at the Canadian consulate." he replied with coldly supercilious scorn that belied his seemingly conciliatory words.

"How can I possibly do that? They've been without a doctor in Climax for more than four months. There are sick people who need me." I pleaded, approaching the depths of despair, not knowing how, with our depleted finances, we would ever cope with this nightmare situation.

As I spoke he turned his back on me. The thought crossed my mind 'This callous uniformed brute is ignoring me. How rude and insensitive. He's not looking at me and isn't listening to a thing I'm saying.'

He then strode two paces away from the polished wood reception counter without saying another word to me, or my wife and bellowed in frenzy through the half open door through which he'd earlier entered. He could see us standing our ground and I was in no doubt that he was now summoning help from a concealed companion to have us forcibly deported back to the US. I was now of the opinion that not only was he a discourteous uniformed moron he was also a coward. It was difficult with his back towards me to hear what he was yelling? He repeated his summoning call and could it be that June was actually smiling and my ears deceiving me?

"Mary, put the kettle on for tea. It's the new doctor and his wife. They've just arrived."

With that utterance his whole demeanour instantly changed. He turned round to face us again and bounded back to the counter with a face wreathed in one enormous smile. He leaned over, grabbed my hand firmly in his, pumping it up and down as though he'd grasped the village pump handle during a drought, as he exclaimed.

"Welcome, come on in and have a cup of tea." Then turning to June "You must be Mrs Powell. Come in, come in." He enthused like a happy puppy catching sight of his new owner. He all but rolled over to have me tickle his tummy in his unrestrained enthusiasm and excitement.

"I'd like you to meet my wife and my mother in law Mrs. G. We've been desperate without a doctor for more than four months. They'll both be your patients. Why on earth didn't you tell me you were the new doctor right at the beginning? You must be hot and thirsty. Come on in, and put your feet up Mrs Powell. While you're having your tea I'll phone ahead to the hospital to let them know you'll be arriving in a few minutes."

"What about our immigration papers?" I enquired, accompanied as I spoke, by a further staccato tap from June's shoe on my bruised shin.

"Think no more about them Doctor. I'll arrange for them to be sent down from Regina and when they arrive I'll bring them round for you to complete in your own time, once you've settled in."

We completed our immigration formalities three months later in October, when John the customs officer with whom we grew very friendly brought them to our home. He turned out to be a particularly good chess and checkers player and we enjoyed many happy hours tussling as opponents.

It had been fortuitous that we'd chosen to cross the border at the customs and immigration post closest to the hospital that was our destination. We climbed back into our stiflingly hot car to drive a further 14 miles into Climax to complete our marathon journey. We soon found the hospital, where the staff had been expecting us following the earlier 'phone call from Treelon. Unfortunately Laurence, the hospital secretary was away and we were unable to obtain the key to our new home until the following morning, when with the help of the hospital maintenance man we rapidly unpacked the trailer, leaving the dust covered contents in the middle of the front room to be cleaned and positioned once we had returned the trailer and I had registered with the Medical College in Saskatoon.

Unable to unpack we booked a room with a bath at the hotel, failing to note the weird look given us by the hotel clerk. We dined at the Chinese restaurant next door, the only restaurant in town and decided to retire straight after an indifferent meal. We were not only hot and clammy, but also very tired and dusty. Our night in the local hotel provided an unimagined series of surprises. We discovered that our room did not have a bath, and there was no bath or shower facility anywhere in the building. To our further horror we realised the building lacked any plumbing facility and there was no flushing toilet. The hotel amenities were Dickensian and worse revelations were in store.

We were desperately thirsty and felt that we dare not drink the water, so we remained awake throughout much of the night sucking oranges to slake an unquenchable thirst. The next day we discovered that the town of Climax had no piped water or sewage system, no mains gas, and no television reception. In fact its only concession to the 20th century amongst its public utilities was a mains electricity supply and a manually operated antiquated telephone system that creakingly functioned ten hours each day, less one hour for lunch each noon time and was probably an original exchange designed by Alexander Graham Bell (1) that was still in use. We had unwittingly landed in a time warp from which there was to be no escape, until we had adequately replenished our funds to travel elsewhere.

We had never dreamed of asking some of the most basic and elementary questions before accepting this post. As a consequence we found ourselves in a forlornly uncomfortable situation. There could be no turning back. We were destitute. I had to work to earn some money and would need to work for some considerable time to be able to move on to a town with amenities that we could consider acceptable for 20th century comfort. We simply had to put a brave face on things and agreed that we would put on the best show possible to indicate we were enjoying life in this prairie community of 450 inhabitants that everyone called a town, but in my vocabulary was little more than a hamlet. We had inadvertently travelled half way round the world to enter a rural society, in many respects not unlike that from which my grandparents had escaped in 1896 when they fled Poland.

(1) Alexander Graham Bell, (1847-1922) born in Edinburgh, his father Alexander Melville and grandfather Alexander taught elocution and voice production. His mother (Eliza Symonds) was deaf, as was his wife, which gave Alexander a keen interest in voice and sound transmission. Both his brothers died of TB and the young Alexander migrated to Canada for health reasons. There with his cousin Chichester Bell he invented the telephone in 1876 and the following year started the Bell Telephone Company. He became a US citizen in 1882 and invented a 'photophone', using a light beam to transmit sound, the forerunner of fibre optic and laser technology. He later collaborated with Curtis in the development of hydrofoils for aeroplanes.

Chapter 8

CLIMAX SASKATCHEWAN

1959

We entered the Canadian prairies of Saskatchewan at the end of July 1959, totally unprepared for all that lay ahead. Had the funds been available I am convinced we would have turned tail and headed somewhere else; in fact anywhere else, without waiting. However we were young, broke and with no option but to stay.

Climax was a very small town with a population optimistically put at 450, which I think might have included every domestic pet including the odd budgerigar, parrot and cat. Uniquely it sat astride two major intersecting roadways in Palliser's Triangle, an ill-defined semi-arid prairie area the size of Wales in the south west of Saskatchewan. The north south dirt road proceeded southwards to the border and then to Havre in Montana, and north, to Shaunavon, Gull Lake, and connected to the paved Trans Canada Highway. The East West road led to Val Marie in the east and Frontier in the west. It was for this reason that it had a brick built RCMP (Royal Canadian Mounted Police) office, which we discovered had one, of only two flush toilets in the community.

That first morning, our initial task was to finish unpacking with assistance from the hospital maintenance man, since our hired trailer, rented by the day, had to be returned to a depot in Montana. Our furniture, covered in an impenetrable film of dust was placed haphazardly in the living room to be later cleaned and placed where needed once we had time. In the midst of our endeavours the town's mayor came to visit and welcome us. I called briefly at the hospital to introduce myself to the matron. There I explained I would be unable to practice for at least a further week since I needed to obtain my Canadian registration by journeying to Saskatoon, prior to which my first priority was to return the huge ungainly trailer, which was still firmly hitched, to the rear of our car, as this had to be returned to a U-Haul depot in the US. Those chores would involve a round trip in excess of 900 miles, over some rather rough unpaved roads.

She begged me to look at a young boy of eleven who had just arrived with injuries sustained when a tractor he'd been driving had overturned. Had he been crushed there'd have been no saving him, but phenomenally he'd been thrown clear. X-rays were taken, which revealed fractures to both forearms. Fortunately the bones were well aligned and so it was that I applied two full length plasters to his arms, flexed at the elbows, and arranged that he should remain in hospital with his arms elevated for at least 48 hours following which I would see him again on my return. I questioned how anybody could possibly let a child of 11 drive one of the mammoth tractors that were a frequent sight in this area. I was soon to learn the realities of life in a rural community together with the frequency with which farm accidents occurred, particularly to children and young adults.

My most pressing port of call, before setting out on any further expedition, was to the Bank of Montreal, the only bank in town, where I introduced myself to the manager. He greeted me warmly saying that he'd heard the new doctor had just arrived and he looked forward to assisting me in any way possible. Promptly and courteously he assisted me in opening a current account and without the obligation of any security, or guarantor, offered me an overdraft facility of $5,000, simply on the basis that I was the town's new doctor. What a marvellous change in attitude compared to his British banking counterparts. Totally amazed at this largesse I declined to burden myself with such untold riches and explained I would accept the lesser sum of $1,000 to tide us over. He insisted however that we maintain an overdraft facility of at least $2,000 in case of contingencies.

Fortified with a welcome new chequebook and cash, June and I drove past vast expanses of ripening wheat, unique in its stunted growth (no more than eighteen inches high), back to Treelon crossing the border into the US where we returned our trailer and paid for its hire. We then set off north to make our way to Saskatoon as speedily as road conditions would permit.

In Saskatoon I located the Royal College of Physicians and Surgeons and introduced myself to the registrar, to whom I'd earlier written. He confirmed he'd received details of my medical training and background, efficiently mailed at my request from England by Beryl Jordan, Dean McCrie's administrator at Sheffield's Medical faculty. I produced my various medical documents and references to facilitate my registration as a member of the college. In addition I was required to pay an enrolment fee of $250 together with an annual registration fee of $150. With all my documentation in order, registration was soon a completed formality once I'd written out a cheque to be drawn against my overdraft facility.

As part of the registration process I was given a navy blue loose-leaf ring binder. This was a financial bible from which college members were expected to work and adhere. It provided a comprehensive range of every conceivable medical and surgical procedure with a minimum schedule of fees a member of the college might bill and receive for these services. We spent the night in

Saskatoon and after breakfast started out on our 250-mile journey south to Climax. Registration and further travel expenses severely depleted our funds we were now in debt to the bank for the enormous sum of $1,000 (£320), without having earned a penny to live on.

On our return journey from Saskatoon we decided on a refreshment stop in the regional city centre of Swift Current, some 110 miles north of Climax, with its population of 10,000 people. As a matter of courtesy we decided to introduce ourselves to the major health insurance provider in the area, 'Swift Current Health Region Number One'. Unannounced we called, explained who we were, and that we would like to meet the administrator, should he have a few minutes to spare. Fortunately Mr. Robertson, a florid charming man, of Scottish birth, with a delightful Scots brogue and chuckle to match, was able to see us without an appointment. He invited us into his office and over welcome cups of hot coffee and biscuits we sat and chatted. I explained I had just obtained my Saskatchewan registration and licence and had undertaken to practice in Climax.

He gave us a brief history of the Health Region scheme and its method of operation. He explained that it had been set up some years earlier as a pilot scheme to provide health insurance cover for the poorest farming communities in southwest Saskatchewan. Every resident in the area was compulsorily covered by health insurance. Each person had a registration number that had to be given to a doctor practicing under the scheme, whenever there was a consultation. They could choose any doctor they wished, see as many different doctors as often as they might desire and the insurance would pay for every out-patient consultation, investigations, and hospitalisation, but medication only while in hospital. Surgical and maternity services were also covered, as was the emergency air ambulance service, but dental services were excluded. The insurance paid doctors a negotiated fee for service that amounted to 70% of the fee stipulated in the Royal College's fee schedule. In addition the doctor was both entitled and expected to collect a $1 deterrent fee for every office consultation and $3 for each domiciliary visit at the time of the consultation. The Insurance also funded hospitals in the community and dealt with the annual budget of each.

Later I found that no patient ever complained when paying the deterrent fee and it was entirely at the doctor's discretion to waive this should he choose. In my opinion one of the major shortcomings in general practice in the NHS has been the absence of a modest deterrent fee such as this. The scheme was a great success and in 1963 was introduced into the remainder of Saskatchewan and some years later throughout Canada. Having briefly explained the modus operandi of the health region insurance he then enquired about my present financial state.

"Initially a little precarious, to put it mildly, but I've been able to secure a loan of $1,000 from the local bank and I've arranged a further $1,000 overdraft facility should I need it." I explained. He virtually exploded as he heard this and vehemently exclaimed.

"Nonsense. Just you go and pay it back." He left his desk and striding to the door, through which we'd earlier entered, opened it, summoned his secretary and returned to his seat. As his secretary entered he instructed her.

"Make out a cheque for $2,000 in Doctor Powell's name straight away, and bring it in for me to sign."

When I protested he explained.

"I'll no' ha' ye paying interest to the bank. You just pay them their money back straight away."

"But how will I ever repay this loan?"

"Doctor Powell, just you take this as an interest free advance. I'll deduct $400 each month, starting the month after next, from your monthly Health Region Insurance income until it's been repaid."

"Mr. Robertson, that's extremely kind and generous of you, but are you certain that I can repay this loan at that rate?"

"Dr. Powell I've no doubt whatever; I'm absolutely certain you'll be able to repay this without difficulty an' I kenna have one of my doctors owing money to the bank."

Financially, things were starting to look up. The attitude towards a doctor in the new world was a great improvement from the parsimonious approach found in England.

On our return to Climax we cleaned and shifted our dust saturated possessions from where we had initially placed them a week earlier into the appropriate rooms in our new home. We had a refrigerator, but no oven or cooker. In spite of the limited choice and steep cost, we purchased one from the town's only hardware store. We felt that if we were to earn our livelihood here, we should support the local trades' people, although we learned that many people bought most of their goods through the Sears or Eaton's catalogues that provided far better value, but contributed nothing to the local economy. I then felt ready to settle down to work as a country doctor in an office (surgery) provided in the basement of the local hospital.

There were many household surprises. The only premises in the village with a flush toilet were the hospital and the home and office of Bob Parnell of the Royal Canadian Mounted Police. Our first major problem that needed to be resolved was the toilet. Every home had a deep hole somewhere close to the house, sheltered by a wooden outhouse, smaller than a garden shed with a single door and no windows termed a 'Biffy', inside which was a seat made from a short plank of wood with a bucket size circular hole in the middle supported at either end. This outhouse in some homes sported a plank with two holes for multiple use, and in schools many more.

In our recently built hospital bungalow we had two toilets. An outhouse where a pioneering citizen could scurry, at nature's call regardless of light and temperature and a conventional internal toilet that we hoped to use once it had been connected to a water supply and a waste system with a septic tank. We learned that Doctor Sutherland, my predecessor, had paid his wife $1 for each bucket load of toilet waste that she emptied into the biffy.

Spiritedly June succinctly explained her position.

"This is one wife who's not prepared to empty a soil bucket for $1 or even $100. You just tell that hospital board that if there's no flush toilet your wife's not staying."

I'd never fully appreciated June's aversion to the healthier fresh air approach to life, even though I'd known her for six years. Since I couldn't afford to increase the former doctor's rate for each bucket of waste, I felt there was an urgent need to confront the hospital board.

In my first meeting, I explained that we required a flush toilet in the hospital's house forthwith. The board members couldn't understand our attitude, or the necessity to change a custom that had stood the test of time. With my insistence they agreed to provide us with this extravagant luxury, providing I paid for its installation. This was agreed since I felt time was of the essence, although I should have taken a firmer stand in the bargaining and made them pay for everything since it was the hospital's property. Pending the arrival and fixing of the new toilet, June and I walked or drove the 200 yards to use the hospital WC whenever nature called.

There was no piped water supply and our house, like the majority of our neighbours, had a large open concrete tank in the basement, capable of containing several thousand gallons of water. Drainage pipes ran from the roof into the basement to trap what little moisture descended as rain or snow and additional water was purchased periodically from a local drayman at $5 per 500 gallons.

Fortunately I was in the house, when June ran her first bath. She placed the rubber plug in the waste, turned on both taps and left the bathroom, intending to return to adjust the temperature and depth of water. A few minutes later there was a sudden scream from the bathroom. A primeval cry; a wordless desultory call for help, pierced the air. It was repeated twice more before I reached the scene. Fearing there'd been some calamitous accident I rushed into the bathroom as the last tortured whimper tailed off. I found June, standing with her face covered by her hands, in a deluge of anguished tears. Unaware of what had happened or the cause of her obvious distress I placed an arm round her shoulders and attempting to console her as I asked.

"What's happened? Whatever's wrong?"

She stood sobbing, unable to speak. Then, deprived of speech, as though mesmerised, she turned and pointed. As my gaze turned to follow her finger I discovered I was being invited to witness the foul hot water splurging from the faucets, filling a bath tub now more than half full of some muddy steaming effluent that was doubtlessly a plagiarised version of the Macbeth witches brew.

"Arnold, I can't stand it, I can't take any more of this! Take me out of here. Take me home." She wailed.

"June you're over reacting." I comforted her trying to hold her in my arms, offering what little solace I was able.

"I'm not over reacting. I haven't had a bath for days. It's hot, dusty and I'm sticky and just look what I'm supposed to bathe in. Do you want me to have a normal infant, or a baby hippopotamus?"

"I'll find out what we need to do to obtain some clean water."

"Your father always said you shouldn't marry me and I'm beginning to see his point of view. I wish you'd taken his advice." She wailed.

"I promise I'll take care of it as soon as we get rid of this horrible concoction." I assured her as I turned off the faucets and groped in the hot murky depths. At last I found and removed the rubber bung to purge our senses of the malevolent odorous potion that filled the bath. Within moments we were standing deep in this evil hot liquid putrescence, as it gushed out and flooded the floor, to the accompaniment of another high octave cry from June's tortured spirit. Hastily groping through the murky depths of liquid remaining in the tub I attempted to locate the plughole in order to replace the bung. Once the outflow had stopped I crawled on hands and knees, with a torch, seeking the cause of this flood. It was then that I discovered the true state of affairs. The bath waste had never been connected to any outlet. We just stood in the middle of this dirty flood of slurry and laughed, wondering how the previous doctor and his family had bathed. Giggling we consoled each other as we agreed. "Whatever would our parents say if they could see us now?" and commenced the unenviable task of mopping up.

Water was such a precious commodity that the previous doctor's wife had baled it out of the tub and used it to water and nurture the few plants that struggled to somehow survive in their parched environment. I was disappointed to discover June's complete lack of interest to know haw much the previous incumbent paid his wife for that baling service.

Enquiry revealed that we had to empty a gallon of bleach into the water tank for every 500 gallons of water that was delivered in order to obtain and maintain a clear water supply. I had the bathtub connected to a proper waste at the same time as the W.C. was installed, but from then onwards whenever a bath was taken, the water was baled out in buckets to water the garden. We were beginning to understand the meaning of an annual precipitation, as opposed to rainfall.

With the installation of our new toilet we were suddenly inundated with pre-school children who had been playing in the street and who suddenly found the need to use a toilet. Finally June had to put her foot down. As each batch of children arrived she explained that the toilet was out of order. There was therefore no syphonic water display and they should return to their nearby homes or use the outhouse, 'biffy' at the back, if they felt desperately in need.

Drinking water was a separate, but more pressing issue. At ten cents a bucket, this vital commodity was purchased from the same drayman from a sealed wheeled tank that he pulled by tractor from house to house three times a week. Following our first purchase, we inspected the delivered drinking water and to our horror discovered tiny almost microscopic organisms swimming in it. Upon enquiring who was responsible for supervising the fitness of this water for drinking purposes I was told that it was the doctors responsibility.

I decided I would turn a blind eye to the drinking water situation, for the time being, since none of the local inhabitants appeared in any way unwell from drinking it. I had made enough waves concerning the installation of a toilet, connecting the bathtub, and discharging a number of fit, but incumbent patients, from hospital. I resolved however never to obtain water from that source. Instead we purchased a heavy-duty plastic waste bin capable of holding 10 gallons of water, with a large lid that could be clamped in place. I then periodically went to the local train station and filled this with water I obtained from their well, which had been filled with water brought in by train. I then carried this heavy load home in the back of our car. Alternatively I would drive to Shaunavon, where there was an excellent mains water supply and take my water from friends. Whatever the source, with each gallon of water weighing ten pounds, it was quite an assignment to haul water home, every few days, particularly in winter.

We were not enamoured with the dark colours in the rooms of our rented home and we decided that the place needed brightening up. There were no local painters or decorators. The hospital provided the paint and we learned how to paint walls, ceilings and doors. This left very little spare time in the evenings for recreation, which was to our advantage since the television reception was abysmal and far too poor to be watched. Since I was constantly on call and couldn't spare the time to scrub plaster filler or paint off my hands when I was urgently summoned to the hospital I learned to perform all my household tasks while wearing latex rubber gloves.

Purchasing household items was far more expensive than in the U.S. and often without the choices that were available south of the 49th parallel. There was only one hardware store in Climax and the majority of shopping had to be carried out by mail order using huge illustrated catalogues produced either from Simpson Sears or Eaton's Stores. One would mail in the order with a cheque and within 7 to 14 days the goods would arrive on the weekly train service. In addition to the train there was a twice-weekly bus service to and from Swift Current. We resolved to periodically travel 250 miles south to Great Falls, the closest large town in Montana, where we could make our major purchases at about one third less than the cost in Canada and at the same time enjoy a restaurant meal and the recreation of a dinner dance.

Climax sat at the crossroads of two main highways. By the side of the main east west road were three towering grain elevators alongside which was a small railway cottage and station, served by a single straight railway track running from east to west over which an immensely long CPR (Canadian Pacific Railway) train pulled by a huge diesel locomotive would call briefly once each week. European communities each have one or more churches dominating the skyline with architecturally inspired domes and spires. On the prairies the dominating features were groups of overpowering bulky painted grain elevators alongside a railway line.

From the late 1890's onwards when the region was first opened with the development of branch lines from the CPR, farmers had been encouraged to settle the land. Along each 8 miles of prairie railway track, grain elevators and a railway station were built. Round the station a store and café would appear, as would a schoolhouse, church and other facilities that any nascent community would need. It was to these elevators that each farmer hauled his wheat and other grain crops according to a strict quota and received payment per bushel for allocated quantities from the government, a system initiated to assist farmers in the 1930's during years of the depression. These payments for wheat were about one third of the price that could be obtained on the open market in the US. This led to two major anomalies. The farmland in this region was valued at less than half the value of equivalent farmland south of the 49th parallel in Montana and North Dakota, while any wheat that a farmer could smuggle across the border would be worth considerably more than in Canada. Wheat could be taken by truck, covered by tarpaulin and then further covered by three or four inches of oats, barley or other grain unaffected by this regulation, hoping to conceal the true nature of the truck's contents from Canadian custom officials.

During the era of American prohibition from Jan 1920 with the enactment of the 18th amendment to the US constitution until its repeal in December

1933, with the 21st amendment, illicit liquor became big business. Alcohol was made, and imported locally, before being smuggled in quantity across the largely unguarded border, for a time creating a lucrative cottage industry.

Climax village lay just like many other prairie communities just off the main dirt highway, with a similar small township some 8 miles to the east and west. The 12 bedded Climax Bracken Union Hospital was staffed with English and Canadian nurses. In the basement were the hospital laboratory and X-ray departments with a separate medical suite for the doctor, together with staff room, laundry and kitchens. In addition to the only hospital for many miles, the village was typical of the many prairie communities with its small school and two churches. In the main street were three or four stores, amongst which was a hardware store, a lumberyard, and a food store and tucked out of the way at the end of the main street was a locker plant for the butchering, refrigeration and storage of meat. In the post office were numbered lockers where each homesteader's mail could be collected. There was a brick built bank, a small hotel, and a solitary restaurant, while at one end of the main street were the gasoline station, garages and a dealership for one of the major tractor and farm equipment manufacturers.

There was a beer parlour where beer could be purchased and consumed on the premises by adults. Women, Indians and non-Indians placed on the 'Indian List' were legally denied access. The law forbade driving a motor vehicle with a bottle of alcohol that had been previously opened on board. Recreational facilities were provided in a community hall, where film shows and the occasional dance and communal events were held and two separate enclosed ice rinks for ice hockey and curling. Individual homes were located either side of the main street in parallel rows. The majority of communities had provision for a small airstrip on a separated portion of prairie grassland and some even had a golf course. No national daily newspapers were available, but many small communities produced a four to eight page weekly newssheet, with syndicated articles and news events.

In time, some villages thrived, while others diminished, shrinking until there was just a grain elevator and a handful of occupied timber buildings, with the occasional derelict wooden house that had long fallen into disrepair. While different ethnic groups set up many of these villages there was invariably a restaurant with a Greek or Chinese proprietor with their family and in like manner a general store whose proprietor was often Jewish. One amusing and confusing anomaly witnessed every year was with summer's arrival when each tiny township voted to accept Central Standard Time, or CST plus 1, or even plus 2. This led to many errors when making appointments, since the first question one needed to ask was "What time is it?" and then comparing that time with your own town which might differ by no more than eight miles in distance and one or even two hours in time.

Shaunavon, 28 miles distant to the north was the closest large town with a pharmacy and Swift Current the regional town centre was 110 miles to the north, which we could reach by road in a little over an hour and a half and which had a small commercial airport in addition to being served by the Trans-Canada Highway and the Trans-Canada Railway. A twice-weekly bus service connected these communities throughout the year, which carried passengers, newspapers, the mail and smaller objects that one might send as a package that would arrive more speedily than by train.

No consideration had been given to the presence of a river, water, or any other natural geographical phenomenon that was an indispensable criterion for a community's development in the era before the steam train. The sole object of the Dominion Government had been to install a railway line with a grain elevator and railway station every 8 miles apart, to encourage people to settle and populate the land. Where drinking water was absent, the train could haul it in from Shanavon, as well as lumber, building materials, and other essential supplies from further afield. This 8 miles distance was arbitrarily chosen, since it was believed that the maximum distance a farmer could travel and return, in any one day to deliver his harvested grains by horse, or ox drawn cart, was no greater than 16 miles. The advent of motorised vehicles and improved roadways dramatically changed that concept.

A further major change occurred during the years of the depression following the Wall Street stock market crash in the fall of 1929. Families had been encouraged to settle on almost every quarter section of available land when land was distributed. Men and women were enticed from all walks of life by the promise of a grant of 160 acres of virgin grassland simply for the taking, where bountiful crops of wheat and other cereals growing shoulder high could readily be produced. Some of the earliest pioneers left the area, unable to withstand the horrendous rigors and hardship of privation and almost constant isolation. Later numbers rapidly dwindled with the realisation that in this semi arid region a far larger acreage was required to support a farmer and his family. Optimally, at least one section and preferably two or more would become the accepted minimum requirement together with an understanding of the modified techniques necessary to avoid the dust bowl phenomenon of the 1930's when clouds of top soil were lost during particularly long dry periods.

Chapter 9

CLIMAX SASKATCHEWAN

August 1959

The myriad mysteries of life in a small prairie town gradually revealed themselves during our first weeks and a steep learning curve ensued, while we attempted to adapt as rapidly as possible to our new environment.

My first morning at work commenced with the matron benevolently escorting me round the hospital building. There was a small well-equipped operating and recovery room at one end of a central corridor separated from the 12 spacious single bedrooms, where I was informed that more than half were occupied by long term patients. She introduced me to staff and showed me the lower ground floor office suite where I could see and examine patients and where we had laboratory and X-ray facilities, adjacent to my office, dealt with by Rochelle, a competent young trained technician. She next assisted me in conducting a ward round, as we visited each of the hospital patients whose medical care would be my sole responsibility.

Having met all my patients I decided to examine each in turn as soon as possible to review medication and treatment. The first of these patients was Annie F; a feisty elderly lady, who was reclining in her bed. In 1910 Annie, then a young wife, with her husband Alfred and a number of Scandinavian friends had trekked slowly north-westwards from Climax Minnesota by wagon, mile after mile, over trails and virgin prairie grassland, in search of farmland that they could claim, when the Dominion government first opened the southwest corner of Saskatchewan's prairie to homesteaders. They rode in wooden wagons and at times walked over open grassland, their only guide a compass as they covered a dozen or so miles on a good day for days on end without respite covering hundreds upon hundreds of miles. Some migrants were fortunate to travel most of the way by train, but at journey's end many score of miles needed to be walked, without benefit of a road, sign post, or any kind of easily distinguished land mark, often in appalling climactic conditions.

Groups of farmers and tradespersons, of similar cultural background, peopled the majority of hamlets, formed round grain elevators established alongside railway stations. Some evolved into villages such as Val Marie, which were French. Other communities might be Scandinavian, Ukrainian,

Polish, Scots, or a mixture of national groups. Some of these outposts grew into villages and small towns, while others failed to evolve and remained, only as a sadly isolated grain elevator alongside a railway line.

Annie, with her husband and friends had decided to name the nascent community after the hometown, which they had left in Minnesota. She was a rather short, plump elderly lady, a delightful grandmotherly figure, with a kind, beaming smile and a captivating Scandinavian laugh, who had been hospitalised for many months. Particularly gregarious and friendly, she walked with difficulty using a walking cane, as a consequence of a severe shortening of one leg, the result of an earlier bone injury that had never been set properly. This however, was not her main problem.

Short of breath, particularly at night, she was suffering from poorly controlled congestive heart failure, which was the reason for her prolonged hospitalisation. Her heart, unable to cope adequately with the demands placed upon it, was unable to deal with fluid, which accumulated in her lower legs and in the base of her lungs. Treatment included the use of Southey's tubes, which I had last seen in my first clinical year as a medical student and not since, having been superseded by the use of thiazide diuretics in the mid 1950's. These short narrow tapered Southey tubes, made of sterling silver, with holes along the shaft, were inserted into the oedematous swollen lower legs of patients to drain off the fluid that accumulated in dependant parts of those suffering from heart failure. This amber serous fluid was then drained directly from the tube into a collection bowl, for later disposal, as the patient remained uncomplainingly seated and immobile for hours on end, often developing skin infections at the entry point of the tube.

Oral diuretic medication had recently been added to the physician's armamentarium, which helped the kidneys excrete this unwanted, accumulated liquid. Within a few days of starting this seemingly miraculous treatment, Annie for the first time in many months experienced successive nights of uninterrupted sleep, and had recovered sufficiently for me to advise that she would shortly be fit enough to be discharged home. She claimed that she would never be able to manage at home with her elderly husband to care for her. I reassured her that her improvement would continue indefinitely, providing she took her medication as prescribed and attended my office periodically for cardiac and electrolyte monitoring. Annie refused to accept my repeated reassurance that she was well enough to return home and was adamant that she needed to remain in hospital, as two of my predecessors had advised.

The very next day, to my surprise, I received a small deputation from her family to, whom Annie had complained. A little later that afternoon, I was summoned urgently to the hospital secretary's office, where I was taken aback to discover I had somehow upset a veritable hornet's nest in my first day in practice. Laurence, the hospital secretary informed me in no uncertain terms that he had received complaints from the patient, her family and friends and a number of the members of the hospital board. Claims were circulating wildly that I'd misdiagnosed and upset Annie F, one of the founding members of the community. He requested, on their behalf, that I reconsider my decision and, if needs be, would I please reassess the patient. This would not only be in the best interest of the hospital and patient, but in mine, since as a newcomer I should seriously consider the consequences of alienating so many of this small community within days of my arrival.

Annie had become institutionalised. She enjoyed being waited upon hand and foot, in the privacy of her spacious hospital room. She thrived on the fuss and frequent visits of family, friends, and well-wishers in contrast to the lonelier existence of an elderly woman on her own with her frail husband in her home without the sanitation advantages found in the hospital. She had, at this stage, happily accepted the trade off of her limited independence, for the provision of food, board and lodging, in addition to her relatively costly medications, which thanks to her insurance, were all completely free of charge, while in hospital.

I learned that the hospital budget was assessed annually. Payments were made according to bed utilisation. The fewer beds occupied, the smaller the allocation of funds the following year. The more beds occupied, the greater the distribution of resources. Should the bed utilisation decline below a certain level, not only would money dwindle but the hospital would ultimately lose its financial support altogether, as had happened to the nearby village of Bracken, eight miles to the East. The Climax Bracken Union Hospital derived its name from the earlier amalgamation of these cottage hospitals as the village of Bracken, without any medical facility, continued to shrink.

Should grants be substantially diminished or lost, the hospital would be closed, with profound economic and social consequences for that community. The absence of a hospital would mean that no doctor would remain in the village. Farmers and their dependants from the surrounding region would travel elsewhere for their medical needs and at those times, would frequent stores and shops in those other towns. The community that lost its medical facility, for whatever reason, would soon enter into a state of economic decline.

Finally, the doctor, according to the schedule of fees provided by the Saskatchewan College of Physicians and Surgeons, was entitled to claim a daily fee of $3 from the insurer for each day a patient remained under his medical care in hospital. It was likewise in the physician's best financial interest to keep his hospital beds as full as possible.

In overwhelming debt, I was new and had to earn my living in this practice. I could neither afford to antagonise the hospital board members or the community in their entrenched attitudes and beliefs. The outcome in the face of this opposition was very simple. To everybody's satisfaction, Annie would remain in hospital for a further two weeks and would then be reassessed. Fortunately, with some guileful persuasion, common sense prevailed by the end of the month. She appeared happy to return home, although every time I saw her for follow up visits, she invariably complained, with an impish twinkle in her eyes, of the dreadful cost of her previously free medication and blamed me for this state of affairs, in spite of the huge benefits her diuretics conferred.

By tradition doctors from neighbouring townships helped each other when an anaesthetic or surgical assistance was required. My closest medical neighbour some 9 miles to the west at Frontier was Dr. Kindrachuck, while about 35 miles to the East at Val Marie was Dr. Fennessy. Both these communities were smaller than Climax with smaller hospitals. Some 28 miles to the north was Shaunavon a town of 2,500 people where there were two medical practices. The larger, consisted of three Canadian doctors whose senior partner Dr Guttoremson was said to be a surgeon and Dr Johnson who gave anaesthetics. The other was initially a single handed practice run by Dr Norman Green, an English graduate from Leeds and who was by far and away the best doctor in the area. Later a London University College Hospital graduate Dr Alan Fletcher, an excellent fellowship surgeon from the U.K, who was unable to progress his career in England, joined him. Further to the North was Gull Lake and then eastwards on the trans-Canadian paved highway was Swift Current, a city of 10,000 people with several medical and dental practices sharing a 110 bed hospital. Whenever the service of a dentist was needed a round trip of over 220 miles to Swift Current was required, while the nearest ladies hairdresser was in Shaunavon, as was the closest pharmacist.

Prior to my arrival Dr Kindrachuck had supervised the care of the patients in the Climax Bracken hospital. Shortly after my arrival he called to introduce himself and invited me to visit his hospital at Frontier. He was very cordial and explained how the system of medical practice was conducted in this area. It had been the tradition that if a practitioner found that one or more doctors were required for anaesthetic or surgical assistance then he would summon help from the doctor in the adjacent practice and we would refer patients to neighbouring colleagues when a second opinion became necessary. Similarly if a weekend or holiday vacation were taken then the same circumstance would apply for locum cover. This tradition of mutual assistance that had evolved seemed most reassuring to somebody new to general practice. It was most encouraging to find colleagues who were prepared to co-operate in this manner. He arranged for me to meet Dr Tom Fennesy, who although much further away in Val Marie was party to the arrangement of co-operation rather than using the doctors to the north in Shaunavon. Further, he advised that I should apply to the Coroner's Office in Regina to seek an appointment as a Coroner.

On a number of occasions during those first weeks I co-operated as Dr Kindrachuck suggested and contentedly worked with both doctors in Climax and once in Frontier. I also took it upon myself to visit Shaunavon and introduced myself to the two practices in that town. Somehow my personal preference was for Dr. Norman Green, a Yorkshire practitioner in his mid thirties and his wife Barbara with whom we soon became firm friends.

Each Saturday there was a surgery list. With help from colleagues for anaesthesia and surgical assistance we dealt with tonsillectomies, hernia repairs, haemorrhoids and similar minor surgical problems. Every month there were always a small number of such cases. Anything considered more major including treatment of cancer meant a patient and their relatives journeying a distance of 250 miles each way to Regina or Saskatoon. Less significant emergency problems were dealt with as with minor surgery. Serious emergencies necessitated summoning the air ambulance, providing weather permitted, and transferring the patient to Regina, or Saskatoon.

We had been in Climax no more than a few weeks when one morning, to my surprise, I recognised Tom Fennessy in his Pontiac car travelling at great speed towards Frontier. On another occasion I chanced to see Dr K performing exactly the same antic in the opposite direction. When Dr. K took a weekend break, Dr Fennessy travelled a round trip of nearly 90 miles to cover for him, as opposed to the 18 miles I would need to have journeyed from Climax. Doubtlessly this was their arrangement since they had known each other for almost three years, but was contrary to what Dr K advocated some weeks earlier.

When next I visited Frontier Hospital to provide an anaesthetic, with Dr F; assisting Dr K; I made it my business to inspect the operating book more closely. This confirmed my suspicion. Both these doctors were advocating that I use their services, while they were busily assisting each other, excluding me, when mine was the closer and larger practice. What I had believed was altruistic co-operation was turning out to be nothing of the kind.

The last straw was when I saw an elderly lady with a large facial mole. Uncertain as to whether this might be malignant I sent her with a covering letter to Dr K. for his opinion. A week later she returned requesting me to remove the sutures. The carbon copy of my letter clearly stated that I had requested a second opinion. Dr K. brazenly explained that he thought I had asked him to remove the blemish and apologised for the misunderstanding. As a consequence I resolved to co-operate with Dr Green and to have as little to do with this closest doctor to my practice.

Following my initial ward round I discovered two long-term patients with diagnostic conundrums and attempting to solve these medical challenges made me feel like a latter day Sherlock Holmes. There was Hal Larson, a weathered bachelor farmer in his sixties, who had lost a leg some years previously as a consequence of poorly controlled diabetes. A helpful, cheerfully talkative man, in spite of his disability, he had been in hospital six months. He walked with two crutches, received twice-daily injections of insulin with a strictly monitored carbohydrate diet, and yet his diabetes remained refractory to treatment. Under my medical supervision with strict dietary control we were making no progress.

The staff and I persisted for over a month. The blood supply to his remaining leg was exceedingly precarious. I warned him that he was in great danger of having that leg amputated if we were not able to return his blood sugar to a more normal level. There had to be a reason for our failed treatment and in my opinion he was cheating. My thoughts turned to the old film 'Lost Weekend', where Ray Milland portrayed a dipsomaniac who hid his bottle of liquor in the ceiling light fitting. Where was Hal Larson hiding his forbidden chocolate, cake, or cookies? Without his knowledge, when he was in his bath, we checked his locker, for hidden foods and searched his pockets and every item of furniture in his bedroom. I all but accused him of cheating with food brought in by conniving relatives, or friends, which he flatly denied, but we made no progress no matter what new regimen was introduced.

One day at lunchtime, with time on my hands, I left my office and walked up the double flight of stairs into the main hospital corridor where meals were being served. The kitchen, food preparation and storage areas were at the farthest end on the lower ground floor, separated by a set of double doors from the other lower ground floor facilities including my office. Cooked and prepared food was plated in the kitchen for each patient, placed on a labelled tray with cutlery and paper napkin, and then 3 trays at a time were sent up to the ground floor on the 'dumb waiter', a small, manually operated, lift. The duty staff would then distribute each of the three named trays with the patient's food to the appropriate bedroom before returning to collect the next batch of three trays repeating the process until every meal had been distributed. Desserts, or cheese and crackers where appropriate, with hot post-prandial beverages were sent up some fifteen minutes later.

Having served the meal trays, all but one of the staff disappeared to the lower ground floor staff room for their own lunch. At the conclusion of the meal, the remaining duty staff member returned each patient's tray with used plates and cutlery to the dumb waiter. Some patients who were well enough, or sufficiently mobile, would return their own plates. Foremost amongst this helpful group was Hal Larson. In spite of his need to manipulate crutches he somehow managed his own plate and cutlery. Smilingly, he even relieved the busy overworked nurse of a tiresome task, while she could sit and write up the patient's notes and observations in the nursing office, by slowly assembling the crockery from other less mobile residents, taking one plate at a time to the dumb waiter.

I saw Mr Larson struggle manfully past me with his own dishes and then an empty tray and later more plates, as he slowly and courageously walked on crutches and one almost gangrenous leg down the corridor to the dumb waiter. With his back towards me, while precariously balancing, he carefully loaded each onto the dumb waiter. He would then return down the corridor and cheerfully pick up two or three more dishes stacked one upon the other from another bedroom. Having watched his third journey, I sauntered down the corridor to see how he'd managed to stack the dishes and cutlery. It was then I noticed something intriguing.

As Mr Larson, always smiling happily, passed me in the corridor, I'd noticed that some trays bore meal portions that had hardly been touched by the recipient. Yet when I looked in the dumb waiter these plates were virtually empty. I asked the matron to check my observations at the next mealtime. She confirmed our suspicions. The ever-helpful Mr Larson was hurriedly eating the leftovers on other patient's plates when stacking them at the dumb waiter and thereby more than doubling his restricted carbohydrate intake.

Over the next three days we contrived to deprive Mr Larson of his crutches at meal times. The results were most encouraging. While Mr. Larsen became increasingly agitated and morose at meal times, his blood sugar levels decreased to acceptable levels of control. Having failed to regulate his blood sugar for months on end, satisfactory blood glucose levels had at last been achieved over successive days. Mr. Larsen adamantly denied all wrongdoing. Some weeks later he developed gangrene in one of his toes and was flown for treatment in Regina. His remaining leg was amputated following which he was permanently confined to a wheelchair in a nursing home in that city.

Grace L was an emaciated farmer's wife. A chain smoker, she looked far older than her fifty years. She was a childless descendant of pioneer settlers and lived with her husband on a large farm of many sections some miles from Climax. She had been in hospital with intractable diarrhoea for many weeks and had become a permanent resident. She had undergone every conceivable investigation over the past 8 years up and down the country from as far afield as McGill to the Mayo Clinic and even briefly to Baltimore's famed Johns

Hopkins Hospital. There had even been a laparotomy in a failed attempt to determine the cause of her bowel problem and in spite of all these investigations her health continued to deteriorate. In the absence of any firm diagnosis, a label of 'Irritable Bowel Syndrome' had been given to her problem.

Her very attentive husband regularly visited, although he was known to have a lady friend on the side. I was informed by the nursing staff gossips that she would wait in his truck as he visited his wife and had been a clandestine companion for nearly ten years. The secret relationship was so patently obvious that all the community including his wife had been aware of the liaison almost from its inception.

In the absence of any positive findings I had ample time in my first weeks to take a detailed history, enquiring whether she knew or suspected anything in her diet or history that might contribute to her malady and delved into the possibility of any hereditary trait. In company with many fine gastroenterologists, I was unable to determine the cause of her irritable bowel problem. In the absence of any specific disease, I decided to treat her symptomatically without any benefit as she continued to grow weaker and more emaciated.

As I pondered the problem my thoughts went back to my student days three years earlier. In Dr Sneddon's Sheffield skin clinic we had seen an attractive Moslem teenager, with appalling excoriations and bruising on the front and sides of both thighs and upper legs. The dermatologist, a canny fellow pointed out to the assembled students in the young woman's hearing, the unusual distribution of the lesions which did not involve the rear of her legs. He stated that he would arrange for some blood tests and would see the patient the following week.

On her next outpatient visit we observed that her skin abrasions had now spread to the rear of her legs, in those areas Dr Sneddon had drawn our attention to on the previous week, which was clear of any disease. Furthermore the blood test was normal. We never saw the young woman on her next visit but Dr Sneddon later discussed these self-inflicted wounds. The patient's parents were putting pressure on her to accept an arranged marriage with somebody from Pakistan, whom she'd never met, while unknown to her parents, she had a boyfriend in Sheffield.

Could it be that Grace's problem might be a variant of the psychological problem of Dr. Sneddon's patient, a Munchausen's (1) syndrome? Might she be inducing a medical problem for her own bizarre reasons? A search of her locker when she was taking her bath soon revealed a metal box containing white phenolphthalein tablets, a laxative.

When confronted with this evidence she tearfully capitulated. She admitted taking surreptitious daily doses of this medication. This had started shortly after discovering her husband's infidelity. She perceived herself to be unloved, overweight and unwanted. Throughout the years of her marriage she had remained childless, had gained weight, and had become increasingly lethargic. The final straw was to discover that her husband had found a younger slimmer companion. She had read in some magazine that by taking phenolphthalein, which she could purchase over the counter in any pharmacy, without prescription, she would be able to lose weight. She believed that by accomplishing this she would recapture her own self-esteem and her husband's affection. She certainly gained her husband's attention, at an immense cost in medical bills and in the process jeopardising her own life.

Mrs. Jenkins, an older lady, presented with severe pain in her right upper abdomen, where an examination revealed a swelling just below the edge of her liver. Mystified I hospitalised her for observation. Over several days the swelling increased in size and tenderness. Uncertain of the cause, I advised that she needed to be transferred to Regina for further investigation, but she adamantly refused to be moved. The swelling rapidly grew in size over the following week, becoming increasingly tender and red. Fearing that this was some deep-seated malignancy about to fungate, a dressing was applied to cover the inflamed swelling that was now the diameter of a hens egg. Still the patient refused my advice that she be transferred and so treatment continued with analgesics and general nursing, while the skin overlying the centre of the swelling became a deeper angrier red.

On the ninth day following her admission, the duty nurse greeted me, her faced wreathed in a broad smile as I entered the hospital. In her hand she held a kidney basin.

"Dr Powell, guess what I've got here?" As she said this she lifted the lid to reveal a small faceted shiny brown object a little larger than a coffee bean.

Recognising it as a gallstone I enquired. "Where did this come from?"

"I found this in Mrs. Jenkins dressing when I changed it this morning."

"I don't believe it! Let's check her dressing."

I accompanied the nurse into Mrs. Jenkins bedroom, where she speedily pulled back the bedclothes and removed the patient's dressing. There in the gauze pad were two more similar stones, and in the centre of the raised red wound was a small hole, a fistula. It looked like an angry miniature volcano, and as we watched, Mrs Jenkins coughed and out popped another small gallstone. Smiling in wonderment, we watched as the patient coughed again and two more small brown stones were extruded. Like delivering miniature rabbits from a hat, this was better than a conjuror's trick as further glistening gallstones appeared.

Over the next days more than sixty of these tiny missives were delivered, after which the wound spontaneously closed and completely healed, to my immense relief. This was the first time I'd seen an inflamed gall bladder cure itself in this manner. The grateful patient returned home in the best of spirits, holding a labelled bottle containing her souvenir gallstones. She gave me credit, quite undeservedly, for her miraculous recovery. Reputations are often built on such fragile misconceptions.

One seemingly very impoverished elderly farmer consulted me in my new office. Following my examination, a number of blood tests were arranged after which he was given an appointment to review the results. At the end of the second consultation I waived my deterrent fee. Learning of this episode the matron laughingly explained that this was one of the wealthiest bachelor farmers in the area, who spent five months every year in Phoenix Arizona to avoid the Saskatchewan winter's cold.

A very sick Mrs. R. was persuaded by her husband to consult me. She had become increasingly weak and unwell over a number of weeks and reluctantly permitted me to examine her and take a sample of blood for investigation. Because of her strict religious belief as a Jehovah's Witness she declined any suggestion that she enter hospital for further medical investigation, or treatment. The blood sample together with my examination revealed that she was probably suffering from either leukaemia or a lymphoma. I communicated with Mr R who told me that his wife adamantly refused any further investigation or treatment.

As the weeks progressed she became weaker and finally became so weak that she was confined to her bed. I then received a 'phone call from Mr R, who explained that he had been able to persuade his wife to permit me to visit her. That afternoon I set out for their farmhouse. I entered the bedroom and found Mrs R a weakened shadow of her former self, lying in a darkened room, too weak to move. Through her husband she weakly agreed by nodding her agreement that she wished to be admitted to hospital to receive a blood transfusion. Since there was no ambulance service Mr. R would need to arrange with the help of neighbours to transport his wife to hospital by truck. I returned to arrange for her admission when a 'phone call was received. There was to be no admission. Within minutes of my leaving the farm Mrs R had succumbed. Sadly I revisited the farmhouse. There I confirmed the patient's demise and offering my condolences, issued the statutory certificate.

There were two events I vividly recall that first October, while working in my office. The first was a pleasant surprise visit from the Anglican Bishop of Regina who was visiting his pastoral flock in the most distant regions of his diocese. We had tea together, he in his deep red hassock, with me in my white jacket from my Baltimore uniform, during which we had a most congenial chat as I related my impressions of life in this part of Canada. At the conclusion of his visit, he asked if he might bless my wife and me, even though we were not part of his flock, to which we readily agreed.

Two days later, while seated in my office, I became aware of the light fixture attached to the plasterboard ceiling above my head rattling. Books and other objects fell off shelves, clattering noisily down, some of the latter shattering, while other items juddered and moved across the floor. Cupboard doors sprang open, some of the contents spilling onto the floor. The door to my office suddenly creaked silently ajar as though moved by a hidden hand. Other doors and window frames simply rattled, shuddered and creaked. Startled, I didn't time these events but I guessed the general erratic shaking continued unabated for the better part of a minute. In great consternation I dashed out to ask what might have caused these changes, and found that everybody in the hospital had experienced similar vibrations and none had any explanation. The next day on the radio we heard there had been a major earthquake some 350 miles to the south in the Yellowstone National Park, which in 1872 had been the world's first designated national park.

Recreational activities were somewhat limited. At weekends in the village hall there might be a film show or the occasional square dance. There was no lending library and no daily newspapers, although there was the small local weekly broadsheet. Horses were available for riding and there was always a welcome on any of the cattle ranches where one could participate in roping the young calves for branding and the young bulls for branding and castration in the summer months. October was also the start of a brief hunting season. A license had to be obtained to hunt deer and antelope. Those skilful enough to hunt with bow and arrow were permitted to commence a week earlier. The danger to these animals in the wild was as nothing compared to the stories we heard from reliable police sources concerning the incompetence of some of the huntsmen. Twice we heard tales of horses being shot from under riders by hunters thinking they were bagging some distant moose, while occasionally huntsmen were the accidental gunshot victims of other less experienced hunters.

In the winter there were regular intercommunity games of ice hockey. Many of the young men were skilful players and speed skaters. There was always the additional excitement of the hurly burly of collisions, confrontations and near open warfare as tempers rose over some perceived injustice or foul play that the referee wasn't quick enough to adjudicate on, or control. There was also the more sedate activity of 'curling' a Scottish import that in wintry environs was almost as popular as golf. Each township had its curling rink permitting those of every age and ability to participate throughout the winter. During warmer weather if one was prepared to travel a little further there was golf and for the more affluent, flying. Snowshoes may have been used in pioneering days but there were no sports facilities closer for skiing than Banff, a full day's journey by road.

150

We had found ourselves for the very first time in a completely classless society. There was the radio; virtually no television because of the appalling reception and few if any attempted to use this form of entertainment before the arrival of cable transmission. We played bridge with the school inspector and shopkeepers, since some of the farmers with whom we had 'lunch' or coffee didn't participate. Our neighbours were, all hospitable and friendly, but many were older farm people with whom we shared less in common. We felt most at home with some of our medical colleagues, particularly those who were recent immigrants like ourselves. We became firm friends with the Green's in Shaunavon, while in Climax we were befriended by the reverend George Cunningham, the Anglican minister and his wife Agnes a delightful couple with a large brood of well-mannered children.

Somehow we didn't make many friends in Climax, and I believe our own attitude was largely to blame. Perhaps the townspeople sensed we weren't particularly content to live in this antediluvian community. The absence of a source of water for a piped water supply meant there could be no modern sanitation. We clearly expressed our views and reluctance to compromise with the difficulties experienced in obtaining drinking water and adequate supplies of water for bathing and toilets that we take so much for granted.

The Hospital ladies guild asked June to bake a couple of apple pies for the cake sale, which was something of a problem, since she had never previously made a pie. Her problem was not in the filling but in making the pastry and she had recourse to cookery books for the information, rather than admit her lack of culinary experience. A month after our arrival we were invited to the home of another of our new neighbours for 'lunch' at 7.45pm. Imagining that this was the local term for a supper or dinner invitation, we arrived in anticipation of our evening meal.

As the night wore on we became increasingly famished. There had been no talk of a menu or culinary delights as we chatted and talked. The clock passed 9 pm when our hostess stood up and disappeared into her kitchen leading us to believe that our meal was soon to appear as we desperately attempted to suppress the embarrassing sound of rumbling tummies. She soon returned announcing the time had arrived for lunch. She set coffee cups and cake on the table and as she did so enquired did we take our coffee with milk or cream as she invited us to be seated round the dining table. It was then that we learned 'lunch' alluded to nothing more substantial than coffee and cake. An invitation to 'Tea' would have meant a more substantial evening meal at about 6 pm, that we would have called dinner.

In my office, June assisted me utilising her secretarial and administrative skills. She made the appointments, typed letters and reports and collected the deterrent fees that I often failed to collect because through reluctance or embarrassment. She filled in the invoices that we had to submit to the various insurance groups, chief amongst which were those for Health region No. 1; which were submitted at the end of each month. Failure to do so would mean that we had no income, since I was no longer a salaried employee with a reliable fixed income. The harder I worked the greater my income, providing my accounts were correctly submitted on time.

In addition to my duties as a doctor I was at times inveigled into dental and even veterinary work. I was periodically required to extract a severely diseased tooth under a local anaesthetic, since the closest dentist was more than 110 miles distant. That was not as bad as having to treat a dog that was brought to me by its owner. Both were in great distress. The dog had approached one of the huge porcupines that were occasionally to be found on the prairie.

The porcupine belongs to the same family as our hedgehog, but is a giant in comparison. A rodent, it is generally harmless and when fully grown is about 2 feet tall and looks even larger and fiercer when its quills bristle upwards. When attacked, it rolls into a ball, but does not shoot off quills, so much as releasing them into the mouth and throat of an unsuspecting adversary. Each quill up to three inches long imbeds itself up to an inch deep, scores of microscopic hooks at its tip cause the embedded quill to work its way even deeper. These barbs also make extracting the quill extremely difficult and painful. An unwary animal that acquires a mouth or throat full of quills will ultimately die from a resulting wound infection, or starvation.

The owner asked me to help remove a large number of quills that had been released into the face and throat of his unfortunate dog, which was in great pain. Tugging them out of its face with a pair of pliers was a difficult enough task. To remove them from the back of its throat would be an impossible assignment without an anaesthetic. I used chloroform, but suddenly the animal had a cardiac arrest and there was nothing more that I could do.

One of the perennial problems we experienced living in a prairie town was where to go when we wanted to have a night out, or more importantly to celebrate a birthday, or anniversary. In addition there was the difficulty that I was always on call, unless we were away from the town. The main dilemma we confronted when leaving home and travelling was that the nearest city in which the facility of an acceptably good quality hotel and restaurant could be found involved a journey of some 500 miles or more round trip which meant some ten hours of car travel. To the west was Cypress Hills Park and Calgary, to the east Regina and further still, Moose Jaw.

We selected Great Falls as the destination of our choice, a Town of 60,000 persons, not including the military personnel on a large US Air Force base and a large surrounding population, 250 miles to the south in Montana. There were two department stores, several acceptable hotels and restaurants and somewhere where we knew we could shop, dine and relax. A further advantage was that food and household goods were one third less than in Canada, with a far greater choice of merchandise. The only trouble was that the journey, weather permitting, was a little over five hours each way.

Our first foray away from home was Labour Day weekend at the end of October. We left Climax Friday after lunch, having arranged with Norman Green to provide emergency medical cover in my absence and travelled south. At the US customs we were warned not to proceed further as there had been a fall of snow just south of Turner. Undaunted in our ignorance of prairie winter conditions we chose not to turn back. I was an experienced driver and there was a spade in the car. I didn't intend to allow a trifling fall of snow spoil our weekend.

A few miles further on, we came across a fifty-yard stretch of road in a small hollow covered in snow. It didn't appear to be much of an obstruction. I stopped the car and walked over the section, hoping to avoid having to shovel a path through it. At its deepest the drift seemed no more than knee deep, but perhaps too deep for the car to drive through. I checked there were no hidden obstacles. Apart from two feet of soft snow there was no other barrier. Full of ingenuity I rationalised that in order to save time and effort I could drive through at speed. June warned that it was a foolhardy idea and that we should turn back, but I was convinced so minor an obstruction was no real obstacle. The momentum of a vehicle weighing in the order of 2 tons travelling at say 50 miles an hour in a straight line must carry us through 150 feet of snow, in two seconds (M16), which meant we'd be through in no time. I backed the car a short distance, engaged the forward gear and telling June;

"Hold tight!" we sped forward ploughing into the snow at almost sixty miles an hour. Later I admitted that while it might have been time saving, it was not one of my better ideas. Each second can be subdivided arbitrarily into ten parts and it's a remarkable revelation to discover precisely what can happen in say eight tenths of a second, which is a single heart beat.

The car ploughed into the snowdrift at speed, throwing snow in every direction. Instead of maintaining the anticipated straight trajectory, it slewed, rocked and bucked dangerously out of control, close to overturning, before the wheels regained traction on the other side of the drift and I could bring the vehicle to a halt. The whole ill conceived process was over in little more than four heartbeats. It was unlikely that we might have been killed had we overturned in the snow but we might have been stuck there for several days. It had been a dangerous hair-brained scheme.

The journey to Great Falls took a little over 5 hours, where we spent the first of a number of pleasant weekends over the period of our Canadian stay. We shopped during the day. June purchased her first maternity dress and I found a down padded parka with a fur collar, which I still use during the more severe winter weather, and a hat with fur lined ear flaps to match. We purchased sundry household items for our home. In the evening we went dinner dancing, relaxed and thoroughly enjoyed ourselves, without disturbance from patients.

The next morning following a late breakfast we started on our return trip, the trunk of our car laden with all our purchases, knowing that we would not be back for several months until late spring. Our journey was uneventful until we came to the same snowdrift that had previously barred our way and which had not been cleared. Unwilling to attempt my earlier tactic, I drove gingerly off the dirt road and bumped slowly over the prairie for several hundred feet, skirting the blocked road before returning to the highway. As I proceeded I noticed tyre marks and reassured, realised that others had earlier used this more sensible, alternative route. I was learning.

Back in Climax there was Halloween and our first experience of the local youngsters dressed as witches and all manner of fancy dress knocking on our door calling out.

"Trick or treat?" Our response was to dole out treats of candy, cookies and fruit to each child. We settled in to prepare for the long rigorous winter everybody had warned us to expect. We had equipped ourselves with our warm parka outer garments and hats, and fur lined outer boots fastened with buckles which would be easier to release, rather than zips which would freeze. We worked and went about in conventional clothing, and only when venturing outside did we bundle up with outer garments and over-boots that could easily be shed when home or work place was entered.

The car radiator was drained and the coolant replaced with pure antifreeze. A block heater was installed in the sump and we were constantly reminded that this had to be plugged in to an electrical outlet at night or whenever we made a stop of more than an hours duration, or alternatively the car engine would need to be started and run for several minutes. An additive was regularly introduced to the fuel line to prevent the petrol from sludging, or freezing and tyres were replaced with those with new deeper treads. Snow tyres were never needed on the unpaved grit roads. Gearbox oil would sludge and freeze when really cold, making it impossible to start any vehicle left in gear, even though a block heater was used. Similarly brakes were never left on. If any moisture were present in the brake lining it would freeze, locking the wheels. Headlamps were protected with Perspex covers while a spade, flashlight and blanket together with a sealed box of biscuits and a spare can of fuel were always kept in the car trunk. Cracked windscreens were a recurring hazard, which while unsightly, could be ignored.

Canadian driving tests had to be taken, in spite of the fact that we held valid British and US licenses, and we each successfully obtained a Saskatchewan drivers licence on our first attempt. Saskatchewan licence plates, termed tags were issued annually, the cost of which included a compulsory car insurance provided by the provincial government, but which did not cover glass insurance, which required separate cover. Doctors were allocated clearly identified tags with a number 33 as a prefix, but most declined this privilege, in view of the risks of having a vehicle broken into by drug takers in towns.

We were constantly warned that in the event of a breakdown in winter we should always remain in the car, check the exhaust pipe was clear of snow and wait for assistance, no matter how close the lights of a farm or village might appear. We were more likely to be found in the vehicle than wandering down a road or across the prairie and developing frostbite, or more probably dying from hypothermia. Distances were deceptive and unwary travellers had paid with their lives when ignoring this advice. Clear air and flat terrain made visibility particularly good. Lights could be seen at night twinkling in the distance that might appear just a few hundred yards away, when in reality they could be up to twenty miles distant. We were also instructed to advise somebody by telephone where we were going and our anticipated time of arrival. Failure to observe these simple precautions hazarded health and life. During my stay in Canada, I never saw a chilblain, although I did have one or two patients who in years past had lost tips of ears, fingers or toes from frost bite, most often from falling asleep briefly in the open after a drinking session.

Prior to our second wedding anniversary in December 1959 the problem arose of where were we to go to celebrate and what gifts to give each other. On one of our frequent evening visits to Norman and Barbara Green we had admired an oil painting they had recently purchased. Norman confirmed they had acquired it from an art dealer in Regina who periodically visited them in Shaunavon to show them his new portfolio of canvases. Should we be interested in seeing this dealer's selection of artwork he would ask him to contact us when he was next in this area.

Some weeks later we received a 'phone call from Edmund Ujvare, who with a marked Eastern European accent announced he had just visited one of his clients, Dr Green, and understood from him that we might wish to see some of the paintings he had for sale. Since he was in the area he would be able to call on us with his collection that same day. An appointment was made for him to visit us later that afternoon after I'd finished seeing my patients.

Ujvare was a lean middle-aged man of medium height who spoke with a broad Hungarian accent. He related that in 1956 he and his wife had seized the opportunity of fleeing from Hungary, when for a period of ten days the borders were unguarded following an uprising against the communist regime. Amongst many hundreds of like minded citizens they trudged their way on foot to one of the many unguarded custom posts, where they simply walked across with whatever they could carry by hand, before the borders were sealed by a newly installed communist puppet government.

Previously an art dealer in Hungary, he and his wife struggled to carry as many rolled up canvases as they could manage, in order that he could establish himself in the western free world. Once across the border they had immigrated to Canada and opened his art dealership business in Regina. Through word of mouth he had acquired a growing number of clients amongst doctors and other professionals in the region. He showed us a number of framed oil paintings, two of which we particularly liked. Although by different Hungarian artists the matching frames were of closely similar size and with a related subject matter they could have been a pair. My wife and I agreed each of these paintings would be our second wedding anniversary gift to each other. Thus in spite of debts, which still dismayed us, we settled on the purchase of our first serious art objects. A purchase price was agreed, the dealer reassuring us that, if for any reason we tired of them, he would buy them back at the same purchase price.

Impatiently we hung them on the wall in our living room, with child like exuberance, assisted by Ujvare, who magically supplied picture hooks and wire for the task. Our new acquisitions replaced a pair of Tretchikov **(2)** prints, which had earlier adorned our apartment in Baltimore. One was of a Chinese woman and the other, of a fresh orchid lying discarded on a flight of steps, which we then relegated to decorate walls in our bedroom.

Five days before Christmas 1959, an unconscious inebriated farmer was brought into the Climax Bracken Hospital. In spite of his severe injuries, his good fortune was that shortly after rolling his horse drawn trailer over into a ditch and smashing several ribs as it crushed him, somebody had come across the accident scene shortly afterwards so that neither he nor his horse had frozen to death. Luckily he had sustained no discernable damage to his lungs or other viscera. In the hospital he was treated medically and over a number of days regained consciousness and slowly improved.

On Christmas Eve it was a local custom that the church choir, most of whom were young children, visited the hospital to sing to the patients. The children were dressed as angels, with a pair of white wings and a gold halo headdress complemented by a deep red cape. Each chorister carried a torch lantern as they progressed slowly, from bedroom to bedroom, the children adorably angelic, sweetly singing one, or more verses, of a Christmas carol. Although they had been specifically requested not to visit our unconscious farmer, somehow the message was not understood and the choir entered and sang in his bedroom. A week later when he had fully regained consciousness and was well on the road to recovery he confided that he'd first become aware of his surroundings on Christmas Eve as the choir awakened him. He went on to divulge that seeing the children dressed as singing angels, he thought he was dead and had arrived in heaven. We had a good chuckle as he recounted this experience. I reassured him the event might have been reality, had it not been his good fortune to have been found and rescued, so soon after his accident.

In December, with the approach of June's expected confinement some four weeks ahead, one of our neighbours who was particularly friendly and lived opposite arranged a 'shower' for June, which we found particularly generous and kind. At about this time, we considered our precarious finances had improved sufficiently to employ a live in mother's help. We had enormous debts, but these were being repaid on time and our financial situation was improving, as my practice grew and we discovered how little was available on which to spend our income with the complete absence of any local dining, or shopping facility.

Following our enquiries, somebody recommended Theresa, a 16 years old girl, the eldest daughter of a large family living in Claydon, a near by village, who'd just finished convent school. Arrangements were made to hire her, without interview, or reference since we considered a convent education would have produced a well-mannered, reserved young lady, ideal to assist my wife in our home and in the care of our new infant. She appeared late one afternoon in mid December, a sole passenger on the local bus, where I met her at the bus station and brought her to our home.

As we were concluding our first evening meal together, in our kitchen there was a knock at the side door. Theresa's acned 17 years old boyfriend Freddie, a farmhand on his father's farm, had called. Theresa stood up, left the table and moments later reappeared with her coat. Without any by your leave, thank you for dinner, or offer to help with dinner plates and dishes, she sped to the door and as she disappeared with her waiting beaux, she turned to utter those stereotyped teenage words.

"See you later."

Astonished, we decided as first time employers that a few ground rules, which had obviously not been covered in her convent education, were needed. At this juncture, June had industriously been assembling quantities of foods day by day that she labelled with contents and date that she set by in the freezer for use in the days that would follow her confinement. Freddie's arrival was always preceded with a brief tap on the door following which this gangling youth would march in, without the formality of an invitation. He had evolved the habit of calling regularly at our home each evening to remove our mother's help. On the second weekend following Theresa's arrival and just a few days before Christmas Freddie declared his parents kept turkeys on the farm and confided they were fresh, and of excellent quality. This being so, he enquired whether I would like to buy one, assuring me of a competitive purchase price, possibly half that which I would pay for a similar bird in the store. Never one to ignore a bargain, I agreed readily to procure a fresh 12 pound bird, to be delivered three days before Christmas and arranged for payment to be made on delivery. Three days before Christmas, Freddie, a now familiar, transient figure in our home, called to deliver our turkey as arranged. A creature of habit, he arrived when we were in the middle of our evening meal. As was his standard unembarrassed custom he tapped on the side door and promptly entered without waiting for the door to be opened or to be invited in. Striding in, accompanied by the usual blast of freezing arctic air he unconcernedly announced.

"Evenin'. I've brought that turkey you ordered Doc, it's in this bag." Indicating a large woven straw carrier bag he was holding in his arm, while with the other hand he clutched the handle.

"Where 'd you like me to put it?"

"That's very good of you Freddie. Just leave it on the floor over there." I replied, indicating a suitable place near the kitchen sink, "And I'll pay you for it right now."

Freddie did as I instructed, striding across the kitchen to leave the bag where I'd indicated, as I sought to retrieve my wallet to pay for what was destined to be our Christmas dinner. He placed the bag on the floor. No sooner had he released his grip and started to walk towards me for payment, when to our astonishment there issued forth an almighty squawk, as a turkey head raised itself over the battlements of the straw bag in which it had been confined.

Now unrestrained and released from its fetters, it proceeded to scramble out of the container with a further loud screech. Sighting his recent captor, it attempted to escape. My wife and I were momentarily startled and transfixed as we sat at the dining table. A twelve-pound turkey particularly in a confined space appears to be a frighteningly large beast. It seemed even more immense with fully extended wings violently flapping as it raced round uttering coarse gobbling cries as it attempted to find somewhere to hide, or preferably an opening through which it could escape. Startled, June and I both leapt to our feet.

Never one to commune contentedly with any form of unfettered nature, June screamed as she desperately attempted to seek some security behind me, while the bird flapped and squawked ghoulishly round our kitchen..

"Get that damned bird out of here." I yelled at Freddie,

"I thought you wanted a turkey?" Announced Freddie, unperturbed at the sight of the town's doctor, huddled together with a screaming wife, who days away from her confinement, repetitively shrilled.

"Get it away! Keep it away from me!!"

We clung together for mutual comfort and security, as Freddie, unmoved, apparently waited, for payment.

"Catch that Turkey and get it out of here immediately." I shouted, in duet to June's repeated piercing clarion call of. "Keep it away from me! Take it away!"

"Freddie, when you offered me a turkey I'd every right to imagine that you'd supply one ready for the oven. I don't want your live turkey so grab hold of it, and remove it right now." I bellowed.

The hunt ensued in full cry as he chased the screeching gobbling bird round the kitchen. Hurriedly I bundled my distraught wife into our living room for safety, carefully closing the door to deny this scrabbling feathered monster, with Freddie in hot pursuit, access to any further portion of our home that he and his avian friend seemed bent on disrupting.

"You said you wanted a fresh turkey." Freddie announced in his aggrieved whining teenage voice as he lunged first this way and then abruptly in another direction as the bird accelerated each time with a further loud shriek and loss of tail feathers avoiding capture each time. Puffing from this unexpected exertion, Freddie chased in pursuit of his gigantic fowl, which was evidently in better physical shape as it evasively darted round table legs, under chairs, and over toppled furniture, which was sent flying in all directions hindering the pursuer more than the pursued.

"You should've told me you wanted a dead bird, not a fresh one, an' then I wouldn't have to go to all this trouble." Panted Freddie over his exertions as with a further flap of wings the bird was able to leap over what was rapidly becoming a huge internal obstacle course, hurdling and creating mayhem in its ungainly wake.

Finally Theresa valiantly threw herself in a rugby tackle at the animal's legs. Making contact, she rolled in a heroically dishevelled heap on the floor and finally managed to subdue the struggling bird long enough for Freddie to secure it. With the kitchen in complete disarray Freddie rapidly carried the turkey upside down, still gobbling excitedly and with wings flapping, outside to the farm truck. Within moments of Freddie vanishing with his squawking adversary, I breathlessly surveyed our kitchen. It was a shambles, and more closely resembled something akin to a 'wild west' saloon following a barroom brawl. To my astonishment, an apparition clad in her hat and coat suddenly appeared. It was Theresa, striding towards the side door, obviously intent on following Freddie. Hastily I stepped between her and the door.

"Not so fast young lady. We're not running a hotel for your benefit, or a circus for Freddie and his delinquent farm birds. You've eaten, now clear the table and clean up the mess in this kitchen before you go out."

She pouted and looked as though she was about to make some riposte, but I continued before she could respond.

"Those are our house rules. If you don't like them you don't have to stay."

Theresa sulkily removed her hat and coat, cleared the kitchen debris and toed the line. The next day I purchased an oven ready turkey from the local food store, and for the next four weeks everything went well.

Farmers often gave the doctor various food items as gifts and occasionally attempted to pay their fees in kind with eggs, vegetables, or other farm and garden produce. Most often these fresh foods were welcome, while at other times they created problems and somehow the nuisance ones are those I tend to have remembered. In December of our second year one grateful farmer gave me a plucked goose, which was trussed and frozen.

"It's oven ready for Christmas." He declared. Remembering the live Turkey scenario of the previous year, I expressed my thanks and gratefully accepted it. Gleefully taking it home I presented it to June, who placed it in the freezer for use three weeks later.

Two days before Christmas June removed my patient's festive offering to defrost it prior to cooking. As the thawing process proceeded June discovered the entrails were still within the bird. A less than enthusiastic wife admonished me never again to accept a bird in this state. How was I to know the farmer's definition of oven ready was not the same as mine? As penance, it fell to my lot to remove the unwanted half frozen innards. The problem didn't stop there however. We'd been warned to expect a considerable quantity of fat when cooking a goose, but no one explained that the oven would be deluged with an unbelievable quantity of goose fat. Suffice to record, that after hours spent cleaning the oven interior, June never attempted to cook another goose. On another occasion a grateful patient delivered a brace of pheasants. Fortunately we found somebody in town willing to pluck and prepare them for us.

The best quality beef that one could buy was when a farmer could be persuaded to sell half an animal he was slaughtering for his own use. The carcass would be delivered to the meat locker plant where it would be butchered and cut into small portions, which were then packaged, labelled, frozen and stored for use over ensuing months. Every community had a locker plant and in this manner one was assured of excellent quality, inexpensive meat. Occasionally a farmer might ask if I'd like to buy fresh dairy produce, or vegetables that he or his wife had grown. I soon discovered after some trial and error which farmer could be trusted to sell produce of marketable quality and when to politely decline such offers.

As each bleak cold January day succeeded the next, June passed her expected date of confinement. On Sunday afternoon the 17th January, more than two weeks late, labour contractions started in mid afternoon. By late evening her labour was progressing well and shortly after 11 pm. I had the privilege of delivering our first child. Within moments of delivering him as I suspended him upside down by his ankles, grasped firmly in my right hand, he yelled and cried unappreciatively. Perhaps it was the sight of the masked, gowned adversary who'd assisted in evicting him from his earlier warm lodging, as he proceeded to show his disdain in the only way possible. My immediate response was one of sheer relief, blended with happiness that everything had gone without a hitch.

Once I'd completed my obstetric duties and checked our new born 7 lbs. 8ozs son, receiving congratulations from the duty staff I changed and left the hospital. It was well after midnight and in the crisp cold night air I gazed up at the countless stars plainly visible in the deep purple above, overwhelmed with an inexpressible sense of happiness. We'd been blessed with a healthy child and June was well. A completely new chapter had opened in our lives.

In the morning we telephoned the good news to both sets of grandparents, being unable to convey the news any sooner, since the telephone service worked only between 9am and 6pm. It was a terrible service. The line was poor and we were always aware that the local 'phone operator was listening in to our conversation as we heard laboured breathing on the telephone line. If that weren't enough, the calls cost £1 a minute, with a minimum of three minutes, a fortune at the time. June's mother was aghast to learn that her daughter would be returning home four days after her confinement, and gave me a long distance tongue lashing as she expressed her disapproval querying my medical and mental competence in permitting any maternity patient and her daughter in particular to return home so soon. Worst of all, she was berating me with the operator eavesdropping, while I'd paid for the call.

There were no florists within 110 miles of Climax. Flowers and plants were delivered by bus and were wrapped carefully in newspaper to protect them from the ambient air temperature, when being taken from the bus into a waiting car and then from a warm car into a building, since even a moment's unprotected exposure to the subzero atmosphere resulted in leaves rapidly turning limp and black. When ordering flowers the florist enquired.

"Would you like modern or antique?"

Perplexed, I asked for an explanation of the difference.

"Antique flowers are conventional flowers and plants while modern are artificial, made of silk or plastic." Came the response.

It was shortly after June went into labour that Theresa kicked over the traces. I was unaware initially of anything untoward, apart from having to hurry home each evening to see that she had something to eat. Her idea of the culinary art was somewhat basic. Rummaging in the larder to find a tin of food, she would then prise the lid open with a can opener following which she would heat and devour the contents straight from the container. She hadn't the faintest idea relating to anything more sophisticated than heating a kettle of water and pouring the contents onto a tea bag in a mug.

Two days after June's confinement I received an unexpected visitor at the hospital, in the form of the burly uniformed RCMP officer, jovial Bob Parnell.

"Doctor Powell, I wonder if I can see you for a few minutes about something private." He announced in a quiet, conspiratorial voice.

"Certainly Bob. Come into my office. I've just seen my last patient." I replied a little mystified.

"Doctor Powell, I'd like to offer you and Mrs Powell my congratulations."

"Well thank you Bob, that's very kind of you, but surely that's hardly a private matter. Is there something wrong?"

"I hope not. But I think I should tell you that the young woman in your employ is spreading rumours that you've been interfering with her." Bob replied, as his voice dropped to a whisper.

"You must be kidding. What absolute nonsense." I replied indignantly.

"Well that's precisely what I thought. I think however that you'd be very unwise to have her stay in your home alone with you, while Mrs Powell's in hospital."

"I agree with you entirely. The problem is that we've employed this young woman to help my wife with the baby when she returns home in a couple of day's time."

"That's wholly up to you but I think you shouldn't have her living in your home."

"Bob, I share your opinion and I'll just have to give her notice. In fact I think I'd better do it this afternoon, but I wonder if you'd accompany me back to the house. Before I tell her to pack and leave I want her to retract those allegations with you as my witness. She might even claim that I assaulted, or even raped her if I spoke to her alone, so I'd be greatly obliged if you'd accompany me both as my chaperone and witness."

Bob agreed to accompany me. We immediately drove the short distance to my house in our separate vehicles and on our arrival, found two trucks barring our way in the drive and a third parked in the road. Mystified I entered the house through the side door accompanied by the rather daunting uniformed figure of Bob, with holstered revolver at his side. In the front room we were confronted by a dozen or more teen-agers in the midst of a party, smoking, dancing and eating. The place was a shambles and much of the food that June had packaged and prepared had been opened and was strewn on the furniture and floor. Aghast, we promptly sent them packing. Theresa was the last to leave, while Freddie waited for her in his truck. I challenged her concerning the allegations she'd made in front of Bob. She categorically denied ever saying anything of the kind, or of making any accusations to anybody concerning my behaviour.

Theresa was a thoughtless immature girl and we should never have employed anybody that young, and certainly not without a reference from a previous employer. As she drove off with Freddie I thanked Bob for his help and concluded the matter was now at an end. I thought that would be the last I would see of Theresa, but there was an unforeseen sequel. One of the hospital cleaners kindly helped clean and tidy the house, so that June might at least return to an unsoiled home even though the food stocks had been seriously depleted. June returned home on the fourth day, in spite of the absence of the mother's help that we'd planned and the food she had earlier prepared so meticulously.

On the eighth day following our son's birth we returned to the hospital where with June holding a prayer book open, at the appropriate page, and one of the nurses holding our infant, the traditional biblical instruction was put into practice. Unencumbered by the influence of grandparents I felt that June, who'd been at greatest risk in the process of parenthood, should be given the opportunity of choosing a name for our son. In this manner we chose Robin, while my contribution, with June's agreement was his middle name.

With Robin's arrival I consulted a Sun Life of Canada insurance broker intending to increase the insurance cover on my life and at the same time to take out an endowment insurance on my newborn son's life. I learnt that State Law prohibited the latter form of insurance. The agent explained that during the years of the 'depression', so many fatal accidents had taken the lives of insured young children under suspicious circumstances that legislation was introduced to ban all such insurance practice.

Some days later I was summoned to the hospital to see four people suffering from burns. The first person I saw was Freddie's father. Theresa had been staying with Freddie and his parents since she had left our employ. After two weeks Freddie's parents had expressed their dissatisfaction at Theresa's disinclination to help with the household chores. There had been a disagreement at the dinner table. During this altercation, a fight had ensued

163

between Freddie and his father when the oil lamp, positioned in the centre of the table to provide light, had been knocked over. There was a fire, and in the ensuing melee several persons received burns, before the flames were extinguished. In the process Freddie's father's hands were badly affected with second and third degree burns. Realising that skin grafting would be essential I provided analgesics, treated and dressed his burns, and arranged for the air ambulance to convey him to Regina next morning for skin grafting.

Freddie's burns were less severe and were treated as an outpatient as were his two younger siblings. Just over a week later I received news that Freddie's father had successfully undergone skin grafts to both hands, but had suddenly died following a pulmonary embolus. Two irresponsibly foolish adolescents had indirectly claimed this farmer's life.

Our stay in Climax was born out of necessity. We had arrived in a state of penury and needed to borrow considerable sums of money. The people in Climax were warm and friendly, but my constant need to obtain fresh drinking water and the absence of an adequate water system made us very dissatisfied when we compared living conditions with those with a mains water supply in Shaunavon and Swift Current. As our economic situation improved my thoughts turned increasingly to finding a community, which could provide better living amenities where I could practice. With my wife imminently due to give birth to our first child during January we were in no position to move. I decided that as soon as the weather improved, I would search for a practice in a town providing better facilities.

In the first week of the new-year I heard from one of the drug company representatives that Dr. Morrison, a bachelor living in Eastend, a town 20 miles to the North West, situated on Frenchman's Creek, was planning to leave his practice and that no medical replacement had been found. I telephoned him and learned of his intention to vacate his single-handed practice at the end of February, the average duration of stay for any doctor in these outlying areas seldom exceeded 3 years. I expressed my interest and arranged to visit him the following weekend, to learn more of his practice and the community.

The journey to Eastend took thirty-five minutes travelling time, since by road it was almost 40 miles. The discernable difference between Eastend and Climax was fresh water. Frenchman's Creek, a small river to the west of the valley in which Eastend nestled had been damned. This provided a modest freshwater lake, which had then been engineered to provide an abundant supply of potable piped water creating an environment with modern waste and irrigation systems in which a community, sheltered in a pleasant valley, could thrive. In comparison with Climax, the town's population of 1,000 persons was more than twice as great, with a larger busier hospital and medical practice. In addition there was also a branch surgery in Consul a village some 50 miles to the southwest. The only drawback was the absence of living accommodation for the doctor, while Dr Morrison's rented office space was small and cramped compared with my current rent free house and office in Climax.

June and I agreed that this town would afford a far better environment in which to live providing my application to use the hospital facilities was accepted, and we could find a suitable home. I immediately wrote to the hospital board requesting hospital privileges and enclosing my CV.

Within the week the hospital board asked me to attend for interview. A meeting followed, at which the board agreed to grant me the hospital access that I requested and confirmed this would be sent to me in writing. Unfortunately I was unable to find any rental accommodation. I was advised to see the town's attorney, Mr Ray Snyder who also acted as a real estate broker. I called on him in his office, where his wife who was his efficient legal secretary. They advised me that there was a timber frame house with two bedrooms and a spacious basement at the west end of town sitting on a plot of an acre and a half owned by Luke Lajeunesse, which was for sale and would be suitable for my purpose.

Luke owned one of the garages in town and currently lived in the house, which was now too small for his growing family of three adopted children. He had recently built a larger home and would soon be moving. We inspected the house, which we felt would be adequate for our purpose, and since Luke was unwilling to rent it to us, we were compelled to make the best deal we could. He accepted our offer of $6,000 (£2,000) and completion was arranged for March 7th the first Monday in that month.

I decided that I would give my notice to the Climax hospital board at the end of January and until that time kept my intended move secret.

(1) Munchausen's Syndrome. An 18th century German aristocrat and soldier Baron Munchausen was a skilled storyteller. His accounts were extremely far fetched and however fantastic were told with such conviction they often fooled the gullible. In 1785 Rudolph Raspe compiled a collection of these tales one of which two centuries later was made into a film. Munchausen's syndrome is a psychiatric illness in which an individual pretends to have symptoms, or deliberately harms themselves in order to gain repeated admission to hospital. There is also Munchausen's syndrome by Proxy where a parent induces illness symptoms in a child to gain the child's hospitalisation. These illnesses may go undetected for years and waste medical time and resources. See 'The Million Dollar Man'. Robin Powell Maudsley Hospital, published 1993 in the British Journal of Psychiatry.

(2)Vladimir Tretchikov, (13 Dec 1913- 26 Aug 2006) An artist born in Siberia, who survived the Russian revolution and later imprisonment in a Japanese prison camp in Java. In the post war years he achieved fame and wealth comparable to Picasso. Seldom did one enter a home in North America without spotting one of his identifiably popular prints adorning a wall. Serious art aficionados disparagingly described his art as 'kitsch'.

"Art can reach the heart, but kitsch can make you rich." Alleged one cynic.

His studies were exquisitely executed and brought pleasure to vast numbers. The most popular and recognisable of his prodigious output were a series of portraits of Oriental young women, and another of flowers.

(M16) Speed in miles per hour when increased by a half gives speed in feet per second: 40mph = 60feet/sec. Halved, it gives your speed in metres per second: 40mph = 20 metres/second, 'a heartbeat'.

Chapter 10

EASTEND SASKATCHEWAN

1960

Dr Morrison left Eastend at the end of January, at which time I tendered my resignation to the Climax Hospital board providing 4 weeks notice. Prior to taking possession of our new cottage, in March, we continued to live in Climax, and for our last three weeks I commuted daily between both towns, in the hope of maintaining my new Eastend practice. On my first visit to Consul in late February, there had been no doctor for three weeks. I arrived mid afternoon, accompanied by June who was determined to view the village. Robin, then three weeks old, was left at home, bottle-fed and cared for by Nellie, our latest mother's help.

The weather was dry, with brilliantly clear visibility when we arrived but had grown bitterly cold. In the waiting room I left my car keys on a table in the centre of the room so that one or other of the patients would periodically take them to start my car and leave the engine running for a few minutes every half hour, to avoid the engine freezing up. There was never any thought of vehicle theft or loss of contents.

Within the consulting room, one could hear the occasional abrupt staccato crack of the roof joists as the timbers contracted with the sharp fall in temperature outside. Working non-stop, apart for an occasional cup of coffee, brought in by Mrs Beach, the wife of RCMP sergeant Beach whose home and office was next door, I saw my last patient shortly after midnight.

The temperature outside was minus 42 degrees Fahrenheit (74 degrees of frost), the lowest we'd ever experienced. As we left the office the air struck our exposed skin like a harsh whiplash. The car started easily although the interior was barely warm and on our journey back to Climax the car jolted over every bump in the road and behaved as though there was no suspension, as the brutal effect of the cold made the springs and rubber tyres lose all suppleness. The heater blowing hot air at its maximum seemed not to function, as I peered through a tiny crescent of clear glass at the bottom edge of the windscreen, which was otherwise coated in frost and ice both inside and out. June constantly scraped the interior deposit of ice away to provide a minimal area of clear visibility, without which I would have been unable to drive, as I crouched down to look through the tiniest aperture of clear glass.

We arrived home at half past two, the journey taking almost twice as long because of the severe icing on the windscreen impeding my vision. After connecting the engine block heater to the electric power supply we fell into bed, warm, but exhausted.

There was no garage shelter for the car. While I could start the engine easily when the block heater was hooked up, it required a period of time with the engine running, for the gearbox oil to unfreeze to enable the gears to function and have the car heater blow sufficient warm air to make the interior comfortable and clear the windows of ice. Some mornings following a severe cold spell I might need to leave the engine running for up to fifteen minutes before the vehicle could be used. Occasionally first thing in the morning when there was a hospital emergency and the doctor was needed urgently, somebody would call to fetch me in their own vehicle, since there would be too much time lost in the delay to activate my own car.

There was no sudden transformation in our attitude towards life on the prairie. Initially we heartily disliked and resented the dry, unyielding environment in which we found ourselves compelled to live through dire economic necessity. I'd made a dreadful mistake in naively responding to an advertisement without obtaining advice to assess the conditions under which we would be required to live. When considering the state of our finances, the availability of a rent free house and office provided by the hospital, together with the certainty of an income exceeding our wildest expectations were major contributory factors in my decision to undertake a five-day car journey into Canada. To her credit my wife stoically accepted the changed situation in which we found ourselves and loyally supported me, without reservation, once I'd dealt with the problems of water and sanitation.

Without being aware of it, we had slowly been adapting to our Spartan new environment as our feelings gradually changed with the passing weeks. As we acclimatised to the semi arid conditions of the prairie with its insensitive and unforgiving milieu our experiences moderated our outlook. We started to enjoy our surroundings and the farming community in which we lived and imperceptibly began to accept that we were in the midst of a marvellous adventure of a lifetime.

It was impossible not to be impressed by the awesome grandeur of immeasurably vast open spaces that bore comparison to an enormous ocean. There were innumerable areas where one could stand in one spot, slowly rotating through 360 degrees where sight would be unimpeded by a tree, fence, or any man made object, viewing an area exceeding a thousand square miles at a glance. One could gaze out in every direction, on a dust free day, allowing one to see more than 20 miles to the horizon of this dry grassland.

Other than a sign indicating the name of a town or village there were no signposts or billboards and none of the detritus and refuse which is the plague of modern living. In large measure this was virgin land as it had been created.

Previously this had been one unimaginably vast tract of virgin countryside, frequented by herds of roaming buffalo and tiny groups of antelope, deer and gophers. In the mid 19th century the buffalo, of which there were an estimated thirty million in North America, were hunted to the edge of extinction by predatory white hunters, until just a handful survived in captivity. Within a few decades of this debacle, ranchers had introduced herds of cattle to the prairie, while nomadic native tribes of Indians were corralled into reservations. In the first decade of the 20th century farmers displaced ranchers as gigantic farms with hundreds of thousands of acres under cultivation, were encouraged, growing wheat, with more than 50 % of Canada's vast wheat crop produced in Saskatchewan. Occasionally a small oil pump might be visible with its brown rotary arm slowly, rising and falling, rhythmically pumping oil from some deep subterranean reservoir, reminding the viewer that in addition to the farming wealth above ground, a vast mineral resource existed beneath, the ownership vested in the state, since mineral rights were specifically excluded when plots of land were sold under the Homestead Act.

The pace of life was relaxed and the people friendly. Doors were rarely locked, and the crime of theft from ones neighbour seldom occurred. Unfortunately farm mishaps of every kind seemed to abound, from the trivial to the most serious, with a relatively high morbidity amongst the young from accidents. Farms were huge and only successful with a minimum size of one to two sections (640 to 1,280 acres). The wheat yield at about 24 to 27 bushels per acre was meagre, the wheat short stalked due to the poor rainfall, but nature's compensation has been to provide grain with a much sought after high protein content.

The heavens, particularly in the late summer and fall, presented magnificent daily abstract art displays we had never seen previously, or imagined possible. With the approach of sundown as the huge solar orb changed from brilliant gold to burnished orange, we were treated, to some of the most vivid and remarkable sunsets imaginable, with phenomenal radiating subtleties of colours as the sun's blisteringly luminous disc slowly plunged into the horizon. There were infinite variations of colour from vivid orange, pink, and yellow giving place to deepening shades of fiery chameleon reds. Spectacular shades and hues were cast as the setting sunlight reflected atmospheric particles caught in its rays to reveal a prismatic spectrum of marvellous colour subtleties amidst the fading light, where no artist's palette had ever hinted that such a range could exist.

At this time should one reluctantly drag ones gaze to glance, in the opposite direction eastwards, there was the brief opportunity to view a remarkable contrasting exhibition of a dark blue band above the horizon, topped by a deep pink cover, which swelled like some gigantic upturned shallow saucer, as the sun descended. This dark colour arose as a product of the curved shadow of the earth, projected out into space, blocking the sun's rays while the pinks, were those same atmospheric particles reflected in the rays not obstructed by this planet's silhouette. The magic of each of these daily colourful sunsets deserve to be listed as one of the seven natural wonders of the world, the silent equal of any tumultuous waterfall, or inspiring snow capped mountain peak.

As nightfall rapidly ensued, the kaleidoscopic display of sunset was soon replaced by the Aurora Borealis, which was most pronounced in mid winter. This bewitching exhibition of another of nature's heavenly illuminations commenced with broad drapes of faintly coloured light, appearing like some ephemeral curtain covering the horizon and then emerging as swathes of parallel bands of light tinged with colour, akin to larger versions of wartime searchlights sweeping the night sky. Originating from just above the northern horizon they performed a majestically slow ghostlike choreographed dance across the firmament, orchestrated by an unseen dissonant hand, weaving first in one direction and then another, leisurely gyrating to no discernable pattern, or design. Occasionally in the silence of the night one could detect the barely audible staccato crackle, of static electricity, bursting out like the sound of far off faint accompanying applause from an otherwise distant silent audience of shimmering stars clearly visible in the Milky Way, with the moon suspended, in a cloudless deep purple sky.

On the prairie there were none of the dense fogs we had experienced in London, nor the torrential blinding rains following in the wake of late summer tropical storms verging on hurricane force, that we experienced in Baltimore. In her frustration nature gave the prairies westerly and northern winds. Not the fierce gales of the tornado, but wind unobstructed by anything to interrupt its path. Throughout the sometimes searing hot summer months this created dust blizzards for one or two days at a time. Inundating dust that obstructed and stung vision, turning day into a pale twilight, leaving thick layers of a dark grey powdery grit everywhere, while gorse bushes bowled jauntily along, bouncing and rolling without obstruction for mile upon mile over open prairie, until caught by some wire fence when there was the appearance of dozens of these huge dry balls, like prisoners held against an almost invisible perimeter fence, caught while attempting to make some mass escape.

In winter the wind could at times produce devastatingly cold wind chill factors, with periodic snowstorms that at once were impenetrable and terrifying, should one be caught out doors. These storms were the result of wind blowing the powdery snow that had lightly fallen some days earlier in a thin coating over the prairie, into a fierce coldly spinning translucent miasma. Repeatedly we heard tales of one or more children leaving a school house to go to the toilet and being found days later frozen to death, lost in one of these dense swirling clouds of snow. Lost and unable to find the door, hidden by a snow haze denser than any London fog, that could provide security and warmth when but four or five paces away. Ropes had often been tied round the waist of a child leaving a schoolroom to use the toilet to avoid such a calamity.

June found herself driving towards Shaunavon in the middle of winter when suddenly overtaken by such a snowstorm. There had been a light fall of snow some days earlier, too scant to be of real account, coating everything in its powdery covering. Under a clear cold blue sky she had set off for Shaunavon when a wind unexpectedly blew up. Not particularly fierce to begin with, but sufficient to cause the snow to become airborne, where it could be driven in every eddying current of air. What had started earlier as little more than a breeze freshened into something stronger. More snow was picked up driven by an ever-increasing fiercely cold arctic wind creating an opaque pall to become as impenetrable as any smog and far more deadly for anyone caught out doors.

She found it a harrowing experience, but was fortunately able to follow a truck's lights for several miles at a snail's pace before arriving in Shaunavon where, with considerable difficulty, she was able to find her way to the home of our friends the Green's. There she sheltered and phoned me in my office with her intention of remaining the night in Shaunavon. I showed little understanding and insisted she drive back home. "Who's going to baby sit if I'm called out in the middle of the night?"

"You'll just have to bundle him up and take him with you." Was her unsympathetic rejoinder.

Never having witnessed one of these alarming 'white-outs' it was only after I'd left my office and ventured into the street that I started to understand June's difficulties and her mistake in venturing out without listening to the weather forecast. My half-mile drive home took more than half an hour.

Little snow remained on the prairie grassland as the slightest wind swiftly turned the light powdery covering into a small whirlwind of opaque ice particles which were blown and then trapped in small drifts in any lower lying area where they remained before the next gust of wind carried them onwards, or until a Chinook wind (c) turned them into temporary pools of icy water. By mid December, arctic conditions unrelentingly prevailed as dry cold temperatures plummeted to hover between zero and minus 10 degrees Fahrenheit. At these temperatures one felt far more comfortable and life was altogether snugger on the prairie with double-glazed windows and central heating than at 35 degrees Fahrenheit in London.

Periodically there were the warm Chinook winds, which blew from the west from a few hours, to two or three days. A rapid elevation in temperature by anything up to 30 degrees Fahrenheit within a matter of minutes could take place, which caused snow and ice to thaw and melt as though some gigantic hot air drier had been turned on. The winds were an advantage to the wild grazing animals, since it gave them access to vegetation that might have been covered by ice or snow. At this stage although the surface ice and snow melted it was unable to soak into the frozen ground, resulting in mud and puddles everywhere before the wind ceased and temperatures plummeted with amazing rapidity and surface water froze again. Once solidified, conditions under foot became perilously slippery and in town there were the additional hazards of enormous pointed icicles hanging every where, from telephone and power cables, roof gables and tree branches, ready to plunge earthwards with any upward fluctuation of temperature, or when dislodged by any moderately severe wind.

*   *   *

When June returned home with Robin after her confinement I initially donned sterile gloves and facemask to prepare his day's formula, but soon realised these precautions were unnecessary. The horrific news at the time of eight newborn babies dying in a major Saskatchewan hospital as a consequence of a nurse mistakenly adding salt instead of sugar to a batch of feed made us increasingly vigilant when preparing each bottle. Without domestic help we urgently hunted for a more mature and reliable replacement to Theresa. Nellie, a young woman in her mid twenties from a large Catholic farming family in Val Marie answered our advertisement and the person given as her reference recommended that we could confidently employ her.

Nellie arrived with her suitcase, brought to our home by Teddy Lucartz, her boyfriend, whom she hoped one day to marry. As she settled in, she immediately revealed that she'd had an illegitimate child fathered by Teddy that had been adopted soon after its birth displaying a treasured framed photograph of the infant. She also showed June the wedding dress she had purchased some years previously and the white plastic bridal bouquet, all in readiness whenever Teddy might say the word.

Our new mother's help was as strong as a horse and a cheerful extrovert. She skilfully took responsibility for Robin as she had undoubtedly cared for younger siblings in her own family. The manner, in which she fed Robin and induced him to burp after his feed, left us in no doubt that she was experienced in such matters. No sooner had she settled and begun work, we were told by one of my patients that Nellie's family were a shiftless bunch and she, as with the rest of them were habitués of the demon drink. There was little that we could do other than to keep a strict weather eye open for any sign of trouble.

Nellie was a reliably industrious woman who cared for Robin in exemplary fashion during his first weeks. All went well until we decided to take a weekend vacation. It was a late Easter weekend break and we hadn't had any recreational time away from my practice and work in almost six months since the Labour weekend. I found that being constantly on call every day for weeks at a time became very stressful causing me to become increasingly irritable and at times short tempered. Unwilling to leave Robin, we took him with us together with Nellie to care for him during our three days break.

We motored the five-hour journey to Great Falls without incident and checked into the hotel where we booked two adjacent en-suite bedrooms for two nights. Our intention was that we would sleep in one while Nellie with Robin would sleep in the other. We sent Nellie to the hotel's dining room for her evening meal and baby-sat as we unpacked and dressed in preparation for our evening out, dinner dancing. When Nellie returned we gave her the phone number of the restaurant where we had our reservation, with instructions to call if there were any problem and left her to watch her bedroom TV telling her to lock her bedroom door for security.

Three hours later we returned to our hotel and as we passed Nellie's bedroom door en-route to our room June gently knocked to check that all was well. There was no response. The door remained firmly locked but we detected an ominous and prolonged scuffling noise from within. Further scuffling ensued and the door remained closed. June turned to me and quietly said.

"Arnold; I'm sure she's got a man in there. Make her open the door."

I knocked on the door more loudly and in an authoritative voice called out. "Nellie, is everything alright? Could you please open the door?" The scuffling continued, with no other response.

"Arnold. She's got my baby in there with some strange man. Do something." The sound of shuffling from within was all that I could detect as I placed my ear against the door. A note of hysteria crept into June's urgent whisper.

"Make her open the door."

"What do you want me to do, break the damned door down?" I huskily replied as I knocked more insistently. "Nellie; would you kindly open the door and let us in." I demanded in a more commanding voice. There followed the muffled sound of a key slowly grating as it was turned in the lock and an even more unhurried removal of a security chain from the slot on the adjacent architrave. As the door started to open June whispered urgently.

"You go first and I'll come in right behind and collect the baby."

I sensed that June intended this was now to become an unarmed military style SAS operation without training, or stun grenades. As the door sluggishly opened fully, there stood Nellie in her cotton pyjamas, the spacious bedroom empty apart from the bed in the centre and a huge wardrobe and chest of drawers on which stood the bulky television set, showing a late night movie. Once the door was fully open we had a full view of the interior. To our alarm there was no sign of our portable cot, which had been placed beside the bed and even more disconcerting; our three-month-old child had disappeared. June tore past me in a maternal frenzy.

"Where's Robin? What have you done with my baby?" She veritably screamed, as her eyes frantically scoured the empty room.

"He's in there June." said Nellie defensively, as she pointed innocently to the bathroom. June immediately opened the bathroom door and rushed in, ignoring the possibility of finding a man as in a Hitchcock movie, ominously skulking behind the door, or in the shower cubicle. There, reposing peacefully asleep in the mobile cot, which had been placed in the empty bathtub, was Robin.

"In heaven's name what is he doing in there?" remonstrated June "and in the bathtub for goodness sake." as she hastily swept our sleeping infant into her arms.

"Why on earth did you lock him in the bathroom? How dare you do such a thing like that to my baby?" An angered and worried mother is an awesome figure, not to be challenged lightly with any sort of response.

As Nellie started to mumble something about not wanting to disturb the sleeping infant with the sound from the television June turned to me in her fury and coldly enunciated, as though this were all my doing.

"Bring the cot into our bedroom N-O-W and get Nellie to help you."

No sooner had Robin been installed safely in his travel bed, unperturbedly still slumbering, June instructed Nellie to return to her room. Within moments of our door closing June announced quietly, as though fearing she might be overheard, that she was leaving our bedroom to watch the access to Nellie's room from around the corner in the corridor. The next moment she'd whisked out through the bedroom door, which she left slightly ajar, to hide and observe Nellie's room. Within a couple of minutes she returned from her covert extension of the earlier commando operation.

"I was right; as I suspected. A moment ago a strange man skulked out of her bedroom and has just gone down the stairs. I wonder where she had him hidden?" She breathlessly announced in a nervous conspiratorial tone.

"I suppose that huge wardrobe. That was the only place we didn't look." I replied in a whisper.

"I bet she just picked him up when she was downstairs having her evening meal."

The following day, feeling upset and betrayed that we could no longer trust Nellie; we cancelled our reservation for the second night and returned home.

There were no accusations or recriminations, but Nellie precipitously ended her employment four weeks later at the end of May. We didn't dismiss her, nor give her notice; she simply left of her own accord. We'd invited Norman Green and Alan Fletcher with their wives to dine with us. Nellie, who normally ate with us at meal times, felt put out that she was not to join our company at dinner. She didn't voice her angst, but we could see it in her demeanour. She took her meal alone before the expected arrival of our visitors. With the entrance of our guests she appeared sullen and morose. Our friends and I conversed as June prepared the finishing touches to our meal. June noticed that Nellie, who should have been assisting, barely helped. Instead she disappeared from view. As we commenced our meal Nellie resurfaced to sit on the back door steps, sampling can after can of lager. Our meal continued as we became aware from the soft and discordant bawdy songs she lamented into the night air that Nelly had become inebriated. To all within earshot it became apparent with her unrestrained and increasing amplitude that she had become more than slightly intoxicated. This incrementally mounting noise, which initially had caused us some amusement, now reached an embarrassingly disturbing level.

Excusing myself from our friends, I left the dinner table and strode outside. There I found Nellie seated on the topmost back doorstep moodily singing, interspersing each few bars of her thirst making solo lament, with a drink from one of several beer cans resting at her side. Politely I explained to Nellie that her singing was not greatly appreciated and could she please either stop, or sing somewhere farther away from the back door steps to avoid disturbing our dinner guests.

Without demure, Nellie complied with my request and stopped singing. I returned to June and our guests, seated at the dinner table. Thinking the matter resolved I resumed my meal and rejoined the conversation. Within a few minutes, dissonantly, but at first softly, Nellie was at it once more. This time to add to her evening's recreation, she appeared to have lined up a few of the empty beer cans on the fence and was trying to knock them down with poorly directed stone missiles banging against the fence. The clatter and sound increased as though I'd not spoken to her previously, while her raucous singing threatened to engulf our dining room, obliterating all conversation.

June looked at me, sitting at the opposite end of the dining table, too far to be prodded with a genteel tap to the shin, her encouraging signal that as the male part of our team I was expected to stand up and 'do something'. I excused myself from our guests, who were smiling as this embarrassing dramatic domestic comedy unfolded and walked outside, announcing to our guests.

"Sorry for the disturbance, I'll be back in a moment."

Once outside, in the cool dark evening air, I followed the clattering sound of stones being jettisoned against the fence accompanied by Nellie's raucous vocal renderings. There I found Nellie, seated with her back to the side wall of the house singing mournfully to the stars, while occasionally lobbing yet another poorly aimed missile at the cans strewn close to the fence.

I explained that she was causing a disturbance to our dinner party. I clarified this was my second time of asking if she could possibly be a little quieter or move right away from the house and if she felt she couldn't co-operate I would need to call the RCMP. Not a threat, just a statement of fact of my intention, if she failed to desist immediately, or move much further away. We both knew the closest RCMP was almost 30 miles away in Shaunavon and it was highly unlikely there would be any response to deal with so common a problem as a young person, having had a little too much to drink, and sitting in a backyard serenading the moon and stars.

Some-how she took umbrage. I didn't comment adversely about the bawdiness of song, or the quality of her voice. I made no remarks about the cans she had set up on the garden fence and was trying to knock down with poorly directed projectiles, or the resulting clatter that periodically rent the night air. Without raising my voice, I made a simple and very polite request that she should desist.

"Nellie; would you please make less noise." I'd requested earlier. I didn't cajole, shout, or otherwise intimidate. She knew the suggestion that I might call the RCMP was not to be taken seriously, and yet she took offence. No sooner had I turned my back and walked inside the house, when she strolled off quietly into the night and disappeared. She simply vanished without.

"Goodbye." Or even. "See you later." Not even an exasperated "I've had enough, I'll be back to pick up my things in the morning." No. She was simply nowhere to be found.

We didn't know where she'd gone. There was certainly no wheeled transport available, and in her inebriated state she could never have mounted a rocking horse let alone a conventional live animal, should one have been at hand. Unsteadily, she just slowly swayed with an uneven gait away into the evening air and vanished, leaving her wedding gown, her case and what few possessions had earlier accompanied her, behind in her bedroom. Nellie never made any attempt to regain these belongings, which included her unused plastic wedding bouquet and cherished baby picture.

Almost miraculously we briefly glimpsed her two weeks later. Returning home late one night, as we drove along a very narrow country lane, having taken a short cut, we caught up with a small truck weaving from side to side ahead of us. Suddenly it stopped and a figure, caught in our headlamps jumped out and ran in a coarse reeling stumbling fashion, obviously the worse for drink, into one of the fields. We recognised it was Nellie. We stopped, called after her, but she remained hidden in the dark and made no response. The driver of the truck was none other than Teddy, who was also intoxicated. Briefly we spoke to him and he arranged to collect Nellie's case and effects the next day. It seemed that Nellie felt too embarrassed to face us to return for her belongings.

Our next live in mother's help, Mrs. Lacree, was an older lady in her fifties. She had answered our advertisement, had been interviewed on the telephone and we had spoken to the people she had given for references. Her complexion was rather swarthy and she spoke with a strange accent. She stayed with us for about two months during which time she somehow managed to break most of our small china and glass bric-a-brac, invariably concealing the damage, but when caught out, always blamed Robin, who now able to crawl was unable to stand or refute these spurious allegations. In the end we dismissed her. Shortly after her departure a letter arrived for her from the Department of Indian Affairs and we realised she was from one of the reservations and was a Cree Indian.

With three unsuccessful live in mother's helpers in a little over six months, we decided upon a different strategy, which later proved to be our finest choice. Martha Kuysterman, a friend and neighbour, recommended a friend of hers, Kay Vanderzaan, a thin gangling lady from the Netherlands, who had immigrated to Canada soon after the Second World War, when the Dutch government paid the transatlantic fares of those willing to migrate. An extremely kind conscientious person, she had a growing family of three girls, the youngest Yokkeey, a sweet adorable child of 7 years of age. Living less than half a mile away, Kay would walk over to join us in the morning at 9 am and would stay until 5 pm from Monday to Friday. A tall sensitive intelligent mother, she had experienced periods of great hardship both in Holland during the Nazi occupation, followed by hunger in the first two post war years and financial difficulties as she and her husband endeavoured to eke out a living on the prairies. Coupled with this there had also been a horrifying tragedy in more recent times.

Somehow one of her children aged three had been left unattended in the kitchen during one of those brief pauses when Kay, an industrious housewife, was elsewhere in the house. Kay had not been unduly perturbed since there was no cooking at the time. There were no hot pots of food, steaming kettles, or hanging electric flexes, this was simply a busy Monday morning in summer when the first load of family washing had been pegged out to dry in the yard and other household linens were being collected for the next wash. A normal adventurous child, she climbed onto the top of the top-loading washing machine next to the kitchen sink. Whether the lid was closed and she lifted it up, or whether the cover had been left open, is an academic matter, since the mechanism only locked the lid automatically during a wash cycle. It was half full of water in readiness for the next load of washing when the little one attempted to peer inside. Fascinated as she stared further into the gloomy interior she had lost her balance and fallen headfirst into the machine. Accidents of every kind appeared to be rampant in these seemingly tranquil rural communities. Reliable and trustworthy, Kay remained in our employ for2½ years, an exemplary mother's help..

My replacement in Climax, arrived four months after our departure. He was a Canadian doctor who'd been in partnership practice with his wife in Gull Lake, 70 miles north of Climax. After many years of marriage an acrimonious separation followed. She remained in Gull Lake and he moved to Climax to live in the hospital cottage. Rumours abounded concerning his behaviour. He'd a habit of taking swigs of Coca Cola from a bottle he carried in his pocket when consulting and conducting ward rounds. Adding credence to the rumourmongers, that the Cola was fortified with brandy, was his increasingly unsteady gait and slurred speech, that all could witness as the day progressed.

We were told that he frequently went hunting and had a pair of hunting dogs, one of which tended to be more boisterous and disobedient running ahead when told to "Heel boy; Heel!" When it had ignored his command once too often he decided to teach it a lesson with some buck-shot from a barrel of his twin barrelled shot gun fired into its posterior. Of course he never intended to do anything but teach it an unforgettable lesson, but alcohol and lead shot, when the luckless animal was too close, proved an unintentionally lethal combination.

On another occasion he took exception to a neighbour across the street whose radio music was blaring too loudly and discharged a round of shot into the house, "In justifiable protest." as he put it when the RCMP arrested him. Fortunately nobody was injured in the incident. The judge bound him over to keep the peace and the neighbours were far more watchful in regulating the volume of their radio from then onwards.

(c) The Chinook were a tribe of Indians who lived in coastal northwest America. A translation of the name was 'snow eater', from the rapidity with which warm westerly winds melted the snow. Moist winds blow in from the Pacific Ocean. As they pass over the Rocky Mountains the moisture condenses in the colder altitude producing clouds and rain on the summit and western slopes. Passing over the mountains the wind having lost its moisture warms up as it descends the eastern slopes. The warm dry wind then races eastwards, blowing rapidly and pleasantly, while at other times gusting with tornado ferocity and dramatically raising temperatures, anywhere along a front from Colorado in the south to Montana and Saskatchewan in the north. The temperature rises are dramatically rapid from well below zero to warm spring within an hour or two. The wind might last up to two or three days after which temperatures plummet precipitously within minutes with an even more unbelievable rapidity back to bitter arctic winter.

Chapter 11

EASTEND SASKATCHEWAN

Spring 1960

We moved into our timber-built cottage in Eastend the first week of March. It rested solidly on an extensive breezeblock foundation. The basement, eight feet high, with narrow high-level windows ran under the entire house, empty except for an oil fired furnace standing in one corner, which delivered prodigious quantities of ducted hot air no matter the depths of cold outside. Our immediate task was to construct a bedroom, playroom and laundry-room in this space. Within days, Mr. Lacey, a handyman carpenter created our additional rooms at minimal cost.

This very first home that we owned, with the help of a bank overdraft, stood on a lot of just under two acres and we decided to manage the huge rear garden on a 'crop share' basis. There was no spring as we understand it in Europe. The weather changed from bitter cold to summer in a matter of days and lasted little more than four months. The moment the warm weather arrived there was an intense hive of industry in the farming community as seed was sown.

We arranged with a local farmer to plough our garden in April and provided the seed, which Kay Vanderzaan, helped by her daughters planted in early May, after which they were responsible for weeding and irrigation. Finally we harvested the crop in late August, before September's frost, which was then shared, each of us taking half.

In our first year we planted rows of beetroot, green beans, potatoes, turnips, cucumbers, carrots, melons tomatoes, and corn on the cob. The virgin land produced the most prolific crop during those four summer months, which kept Kay's family and us in fresh and frozen vegetables until the following year. Beetroot made splendid jam in addition to wonderful beetroot borsht and we discovered with delight that freshly picked corn on the cob could be eaten raw when it was succulent and sweet. However left for no more than a few hours after picking, it then needed to be boiled and cooked in the conventional manner.

Living in a small town, irrespective of office hours and an appointment system, patients were constantly knocking at the door with some medical problem, which they perceived to be urgent. The single living room ran the length of the house and this often proved an awkward problem, particularly when we were dining or entertaining. Lacerations and fractures could be dealt with easily enough by sending the patient to the hospital where I could telephone the staff to arrange for an X-ray or a suture set to be made ready and then appear a little later to deal with the problem. Other difficulties could not be dealt with so readily and frequently disrupted our home life. Once we made the decision to extend our stay for a further year, I drew plans to build a room on to the front of the house and arranged with Mr Lacey, to construct it. From the town's frontier days of 50 years earlier, each homestead farmer had been compelled to build his own home, barns and outhouses, which meant that there had been no demand for specialist trades people connected with the construction industry, apart from a plumber.

The room was completed in the summer of 1960 and provided a front door through which patients could enter an anteroom of about 120 square feet. Furnished simply with four chairs and a table this avoided their having access to the living room within, which gave my wife and I a measure of privacy. A minor design mishap occurred when the framed double-glazed window was delivered. It had been ordered 6 feet wide and four feet high, but on delivery we found the measurements had been reversed. Since time didn't permit us to wait for the window to be changed, it was installed, with the window ledge running vertically, which looked a little odd, but was perfectly functional. We decorated the room and June painted the exterior of the front door a vivid lilac colour. I was in my office at the time June attended to the front door. One of my patients passed the house and noting the colour dashed breathlessly into my surgery with the news.

"Doctor Powell you must go home. It's your wife. She's plum gone out of her mind. You'd best go home straight away an' stop her from painting that door of yours that awful colour." He was quite serious.

Patients who called out of hours were never turned away. Martha K. who lived in the next street came to consult me with her 18 months old son. A devout Catholic in her mid thirties she had emigrated with her husband from Holland shortly after the war. When she appeared at my home, she had a grossly distended abdomen and was expecting twins. She arrived as we were eating lunch, beside herself with worry. Peter, her little boy, was driving her to distraction. She explained that she feared he was going to die of starvation, since he steadfastly refused to eat any of the wholesome foods she placed before him and ignored all her pleas and entreaties to eat just a little. I did my best to reassure her, explaining that it was unknown for children of this age to wilfully starve themselves to death.

She broke down, wept and could not be reassured. In sheer desperation I invited her to sit at our table, drew up a high chair for Peter and asked June to give the child a dish of ice cream, which she set before him. We continued talking and I asked Martha to ignore her son. A few minutes later, to her immense relief, she observed an empty bowl. I explained that the little boy simply wanted to exert his own authority over what he chose to eat and not accept his mother's choices of the 'good nutritious food' she wished him to have.

June became very friendly with Martha often visiting her on the days I consulted at Consul, and helped her with the washing and ironing for her large brood of children. Following her confinement I was greatly honoured when she named one of her twin sons after me.

A few years later when living in London Martha sent us a distressing news cutting relating to her twins and Peter, the child who wouldn't eat. That winter of 1968 the twins then aged 7 years had gone cavorting and skating on the lake with their older brother Peter aged 9 years. The ice, which had appeared solid enough, had been subjected to a 'Chinook' over the previous days. Suddenly it cracked and gave way jettisoning the two younger boys into the freezing water. There was no adult in the vicinity and no time to summon help., Lying on the ice Peter inched forward and miraculously managed to extract each of the boys from their watery trap. In his haste to join his wet shivering brothers now waiting on firmer ice, he stood up too soon. The ice gave way, plunging him into the water. He attempted to extricate himself but the margins of the ice kept breaking and within no more than a couple of minutes this brave little fellow tragically succumbed to the cold, and drowned. Martha, a practicing Catholic wrote a brief accompanying note telling us how proud she felt that heaven's angels, particularly lonely at that time, had taken her Peter for company.

Accidents seemed all too prevalent on the prairies, particularly where the young were concerned and drowning was not an uncommon phenomenon in this arid region. I recall two further episodes from this period, one of which providentially had a happy outcome. The first relates to another child. In the spring of 1960 I had delivered a young Hutterite couple of their first child whom they also named Arnold. June likewise had a little girl named after her, by one of my patient's from the same colony the following year.

The Hutterite commune had constructed an extremely large sluit (pronounced slew), the size of a small lake, some 50 yards in diameter on their farm, although these water storage channels usually tended to be long and narrow. Round the periphery were chickens and other domesticated small farm animals and swimming in the middle were a group of ducks and geese, creating a delightful rural idyll.

In view of the proximity of this lake to the living accommodation with the presence of young children I suggested to John Walters, the senior member of the community, where each member bore that same surname, the water should in some way be fenced off to safeguard the smaller children who could be at risk. He rebutted this advice by saying that adults were always working in the area and in the 50 years the community had lived in Eastend, while some had fallen in, there had never been a fatality.

My namesake in the summer of 1961, a toddler of 18 months, had chased after the colony's small flock of ducks. He followed them into the sluit where he fell over. This episode was witnessed by one of the community wives, who immediately rescued him, wet but unharmed. This was undoubtedly a vindication for John Walter's argument against installing a fence. The little fellow was chastised and told not to follow the ducks or to go into the water a second time. The very next day little Arnold Walters once more toddled after the ducks. As on the previous day he entered the pond, and within seconds had slipped over in water, no more than a few inches in depth. This time his guardian angel had deserted her post for no more than five minutes. His mother anxiously searching for him a little later, found her infant lying face down in the water where he had fallen some minutes earlier. An unguarded few minutes had resulted in a preventable tragedy. Some weeks later I had reason to visit the farm and noted the perimeter of the small lake remained unguarded and there was no power that could enforce the erection of a fence.

It was a Sunday afternoon, when I was involved indirectly in another young person's drowning, or more correctly, resuscitation. It was in the summer of 1961 and the circumstances were very different as was the outcome from the previous accident. It was a typically hot dry day, when the prairie was covered by a shimmering haze as the sun unrelentingly blazed, through an azure cloudless sky. Even the insects had been lulled into a noontime quiet, with no breath of cooling breeze. One would need to drive hundreds of miles and still not find a lake as pleasantly cool and inviting in which to swim as the four youths who had driven over from Shaunavon had found.

The teenage friends, one of whom was Chinese Canadian, had motored over in their farm truck, not for the first time, two sitting in the enclosed cab and two in the open flat top rear and parked it close to the water's edge. All fit athletic young men they changed into swimming shorts and eagerly plunged into the somewhat murky, but refreshingly chill water. There was a diving board close by and a certain amount of horseplay and shouting was in progress, as one would expect amongst a group of exuberant young men when someone noticed that one of their companions had disappeared.

Suspecting the worst, each friend immediately dived under the water searching for his companion. They directly located their friend lying motionless under the water, where his swimming shorts had somehow become entangled in some underwater snare. They were able to drag his unconscious body out of the water and at once instigated artificial respiration they had been taught at school. They lifted his seemingly lifeless body into the back of the truck and continued their attempts at resuscitation as they sped to the hospital, in their frenzied attempt to save his life.

I was summoned urgently to the hospital where I found this young man on his back on a trolley in the accident room. Unconscious and barely alive, but sporadically breathing, I had him turned on his side and instigated suction of his respiratory tract, attempting to aspirate as much of the debris and muck that was laying in his mouth, throat, and upper air-passages. As the nurse continued with the suction and as his unconscious respirations improved I placed the youth in an oxygen tent and put up an intravenous drip of normal saline, hoping to overcome the effect of the vast quantity of water that he had swallowed producing an electrolyte hyponatraemic (salt) imbalance. I next added a hefty dose of a broad-spectrum antibiotic, and then rushed to the phone to call the air ambulance. As luck would have it, no air service could be available for 48 hours due to engine problems. In some desperation I attempted to locate a consultant anaesthetist who could give me any form of guidance in the management of this case. I succeeded in locating an anaesthetist in Regina who chatted reassuringly, but stated that it was too far for him to travel for a domiciliary.

The next morning found the patient feverish, barely conscious, but alive, with a mottled chest x-ray indicating he had a severe bronchopneumonia. In his favour was his youth and fitness. He made immense progress in an oxygen tent with a high dosage of intravenous antibiotic therapy and accompanying respiratory physiotherapy as his consciousness improved. Within a few days his status had improved significantly and we knew we were gaining in our struggle. The following weekend after his narrow escape I discharged him from hospital, to continue his recuperation at home under the care of his own family doctor.

The heroes of the day were the young man's companions. Directly they found their friend missing, they urgently and methodically dived and searched, feeling for him and relying only on touch in the murky water. Once found and on land, they had instigated immediate cardio pulmonary resuscitation, which they had continued until medical help was at hand. The patient's parents ran a Chinese bakery in Shaunavon and my wife and I were the happy recipients of a regular supply of pastries and cakes from a grateful family for months thereafter.

During my first weeks in Eastend a teacher at the local school, a woman in her mid thirties, consulted me complaining of severe lower back pain.

Following two further consultations when there had been no improvement in spite of following advice to avoid lifting combined with analgesic and muscle relaxant therapy, I advised that her persistent back pain would benefit from hospitalisation where she could be treated with a few days conventional treatment of complete bed rest with traction. She steadfastly refused my recommendation stating her pupils and teaching were a far greater priority and she couldn't spare the time. I compromised, providing her with more analgesics and muscle relaxants, even though they provided no more than temporary relief.

This state of affairs continued for several weeks, as she steadfastly refused hospital treatment and her intractable back pain persisted. Then she consulted a doctor in Shaunavon who finally cured her problem when he hospitalised her and provided two weeks strict bed rest with traction.

During that time Dr. Henderson, the town dentist, visited me in my office accompanied by his wife, a woman in her fifties, whom I'd never met before. She too was complaining of severe lower back pain. Radiological investigation of her spine proved unremarkable and I recommended a period of bed rest with traction in hospital. She refused this advice, preferring to remain in bed at home with analgesics.

She visited me a week later accompanied again by her attentive husband. She complained her discomfort was far worse, describing it as agonising and explained that in two weeks time she had to be well enough to make a long car journey to attend a family wedding in Alberta. Once more I recommended traction in hospital and explained I could see little likelihood that she would make her car journey unless she followed my advice. She adamantly persisted in her refusal to be hospitalised. Her husband asked if I could give her some stronger analgesia and I explained the only stronger medication would be Pethedine, or Morphine, which I would be unwilling to prescribe other than in hospital.

"Look I'm a qualified professional like yourself. If you would prescribe something like Demerol (Pethedine), say for one week, I will make myself personally responsible for the correct administration."

At this juncture I should have told them that unless they were prepared to follow my advice they should find another doctor, but I had been practicing no more than 3 months in this town and needed to build my practice. There could be no better way than through the recommendation of another professional person and so I reluctantly agreed to his proposal.

"Alright. On that basis I'll give Mrs Henderson a prescription for twenty Pethedine tablets of 50mg. to be used no more frequently than one every eight hours. I'll do this on the understanding that you keep them in your possession, and keep a record of the date and time when it's used. If there's no improvement within a week then I'll insist that she must be hospitalised."

Dr Henderson agreed and I wrote out a prescription, arranging to reassess the patient in one week.

Saturday night, five days after that consultation, I was awakened by the telephone. Eastend, unlike Climax, had a 24 hour automated telephone service. The ringing roused me from a deep sleep shortly before midnight. Through habit I looked at the illuminated bedside clock to confirm the time. It was 11. 50 pm. On the other end of the line a hoarse, barely audible voice said.

"Doctor Powell, Dr. Henderson here. Please come quickly. It's my wife. I think she's stopped breathing."

"Did you say stopped breathing? What do you mean?"

"Please come straight away? I think she's dying."

"Good heavens. Can you feel a pulse?" I enquired, now fully awake.

"No, I can't feel a pulse anywhere." He responded in distress a few moments later.

"Alright, I'll be over straight away. Leave a light on in the front porch so I can find your house." Leaping out of bed and telling my wife where I was heading, I grabbed a pair of trousers and slipped on a dressing gown and slippers. I rushed out to my car and sped to the dentist's bungalow on the edge of town. I arrived in record time finding my destination very easily, as there was both a light blazing in the front porch and a distraught husband nervously waiting at the open front gate, dressed like myself in dressing gown, pyjamas and slippers. As I pulled up I grabbed my medical bag and rushed out of the car, following Dr Henderson into his house.

He rapidly ushered me into the bedroom where I saw Mrs Henderson slumped face downwards on the floor. An examination indicated that she was dead, but from the coolness of the body and stiffness of her limbs I believed she'd been dead for at least four or five hours.

"What on earth's happened? Why's your wife on the floor? " I asked incredulously.

"We'd both gone to bed early. My wife and I were reading magazines as we usually did, when I must have nodded off to sleep. A sudden noise roused me. It was my wife who'd fallen out of bed. The light was still on and I called to her to see what was wrong. When she didn't answer me, I got out of my side of the bed to assist her. I called her name and when she didn't respond I tried to help her up. It was then that I noticed she didn't seem to be breathing and called you straight away."

"Did you give Mrs Henderson any Demerol today?"

"Yes she had one tablet this evening at 6 o'clock. I've a list here of the dates and times she had her medication and I've still got 12 tablets that weren't used."

"There's absolutely nothing I can do for your poor wife and I certainly can't give you a death certificate. As you know, where there's been an unexpected death the matter must be reported to the coroner, which is what I'll need to attend to first thing in the morning. There'll have to be an autopsy to determine the cause of her death and depending on the pathologist's findings the coroner may consider an enquiry is needed."

Taking my leave I hurried home, and first thing the following morning phoned the coroner. I gave him a brief summary of all that had happened in the past week explaining that when I examined the deceased, the body had cooled and rigor mortis was setting in which suggested that the lady had been dead for some considerable time, at a guess possibly four or five hours at the very least. That being the case it seemed a little unusual that a corpse could leap out of bed. Having leapt or fallen out of bed, it seemed bizarre that the husband, who claimed to have been wakened by this event should have waited several hours before phoning and telling me that he thought his wife was dying. It all seemed highly suspicious. I wondered whether there might be some foul play.

Later that morning I dictated a full report to June, who was my secretary, which she typed out for the coroner with a carbon copy for the pathologist. Following an autopsy, the truth relating to Mrs Henderson's unexplained death was revealed.

Mrs Henderson, childless and with very few friends, had lived in Eastend for many years, seldom socialising with her neighbours and keeping very much to herself. I was aware that she took the occasional Seconal barbiturate sleeping capsule, in the evening before retiring to bed, and had warned her and her husband not to combine this with her Demerol. That evening at 6 pm, she had taken her single Seconal capsule in addition to which she had taken her 50mg of Demerol to relieve her pain. This in itself might not have been sufficient to depress her respiration, but unknown to me, and concealed by Dr Henderson was the knowledge that his wife was an alcoholic. For many years she had been habituated to drinking large quantities of alcohol and as was later revealed, so too was he. While he worked during the day in his dental practice, she languished at home. To while away the hours of boredom and loneliness she regularly imbibed up to two bottles of wine each day. In the evenings when Dr Henderson returned home he shared a further couple of bottles of wine with his wife.

The cause of her death was from inhalation of vomit followed by respiratory arrest, due to the combination of alcohol, barbiturates and demerol. The week following the autopsy and internment Dr Henderson placed a simple sign on the door of his dental practice stating 'closed' and left town, never to reappear. His house was sold and thereby revealed the family secret. Empty wine bottles were discovered everywhere. There were bottles of every colour, shape and size in every bedroom where these secret alcoholic pillars of society, had discarded them over the years.

The autopsy finding left two questions unanswered. Why did Dr Henderson claim that his wife had just fallen out of bed when he telephoned me, knowing this was patently untrue? Secondly why as a qualified professional person did he claim that she was dying, when in fact he must have known that she had been dead for several hours?

I discussed the case with the coroner and the RCMP. We were of the opinion that when Mrs. Henderson died her husband might have been too intoxicated to know what had happened until some hours later. An alternative theory was that he spent several hours clearing the empty wine bottles out of their bedroom, since at the time of my visit there was no trace of a bottle to be seen anywhere and I had been unaware of any smell of alcohol. Possibly it was a combination of both these circumstances.

This incident taught me a number of vital lessons. There was the confirmation that alcohol could be a lethal cocktail when combined with relatively small quantities of medication. Added to this was the realisation that an alcoholic like any drug addict is a deceiver, who invariably finds methods to conceal the quantity of alcohol used. I resolved from that time onwards that when in my professional judgement I considered hospitalisation to be advisable, should the patient ignore this advice, then I also had the right to explain in unequivocal terms that I would be unable to provide further medical counsel, or care.

Following Dr Henderson's swift departure from town, the closest dental practice to be found was in Swift Current, a round trip of 210 miles. The community made strenuous efforts over several months to attract another dentist to establish a practice in the area, all without success. The dentist's spacious premises were across the main street from my rather small office next to the Credit Union. As it remained empty with a 'to rent' sign I decided to move my surgery from its cramped location to his former office. My wife and I set about renovating the suite of rooms. We obtained assistance from a handyman to make bench seating and for the carpentry and painting works, while we undertook the task of papering the interior walls. With ceilings in the waiting room 14 feet high it proved a daunting challenge, but we felt proud to have achieved this minor success, in our first attempt at paperhanging.

Shortly after our move to Eastend, driving over rough terrain, miles from anywhere, the underside of our reliable Olds struck some rocky outcrop. There was a sickening jolt accompanied by a grinding sound. We were travelling to Shaunavon and proceeded onwards, thinking that nothing was amiss when suddenly I became aware of the oil pressure light showing up on the dashboard. The initial reaction was to tap the little red light in the hope that it had developed a fault. It hadn't. The significance was that I had damaged the oil sump and had lost oil, which meant no oil pressure. I could undoubtedly drive slowly for a few miles before the engine seized up but whatever I did would not be good for the mechanism unless the punctured oil sump was repaired and the oil replaced. We drove to the only car show room in Shaunavon and since we had 100,000 miles on the clock I left June with instructions to exchange our vehicle for a new car, as I walked to the nearby hospital to visit a patient. Her car choice was a patriotic English Vauxhall Envoy coloured green. I returned to the showroom some thirty minutes later to discover that June had been experiencing immense difficulty with the salesman, a true prairie male chauvinist, who had ignored her request to inspect the car. She then said that she wanted to purchase the car and asked him to prepare the documentation for her to drive it away that afternoon.

Unrelentingly he continued to ignore her as though she were invisible until I arrived. Only then did this sexist bigot sit up and take any notice. The cost was $1,800 minus $325 for our Oldsmobile. We showed a profit of $25 on a car we'd driven over 35,000 miles. I later discovered that patriotism or not, an English saloon car was not a robust enough piece of mechanical engineering for this remote corner of the world, when 26,000 miles later following a year of prairie road travel I had to replace the engine.

At the time of our motor vehicle change we'd been in Saskatchewan nine months and planned to return to London to let our parents see their new grandson and to celebrate my younger brother's marriage. Our original objective had been to remain in North America for two years. With the end of our second year approaching we made our decision to stay for a further year. We lived in a pleasant small town where there was both water and sewage. I felt that with my medical practice flourishing and growing, it would be foolhardy to give it up at this juncture when everything appeared to be going so well. We had cleared a considerable portion of our debts, in spite of having to replace our car and fortunately June was amenable that we should remain for a further year.

With this decision we flew home. June went ahead with Robin, flying first to see our friends in Baltimore and then on to London, where I joined her three weeks later. We remained in London two weeks more, before flying back to Canada to embark upon one further year in practice.

Chapter 12

EASTEND SASKATCHEWAN

1960

The town of Eastend derived its name as the most eastern area patrolled by the North West Mounted Police stationed at Fort Worth, in the Cypress Hills. It was incorporated as a village in 1914, when connected by a branch railway line of the CPR (Canadian Pacific Railroad) and later as a town of some 1,000 people in 1920. Situated in the Frenchman river valley through which flows the Frenchman River, a small tributary coalescing with other rivulets, which ultimately flow southwards to form the majestic Mississippi River, the town had many advantages over other local prairie communities. Its chief asset was a copious source of potable water, which could be used for drinking, irrigation, washing and sewage. The Eastend Union Hospital, while designed along similar lines, was larger with its 16 beds than the hospital at Climax. The community had three churches, a large school into which children were bussed from surrounding areas, two banks and more shop and store facilities. In addition there were more professionals; Dr Vic Millions, a Canadian doctor, Mr Ray Snyder a lawyer, Dr Henderson a dentist, Bob Hickerty, a pharmacist and Ross Smith the town policeman, who with his brother Glen, a very competent pilot, were proprietors of the town's hardware store. There was a landing strip and the latter two gentlemen, amongst others, owned planes.

Once we had moved to that pretty township, where the fossilised skeletal remains of a 65 million year old Tyrannosaurus Rex was found in 1994, we first met a group of Hutterite homesteaders who lived in a large communal farming community some miles from Eastend and who became my patients. Their family name was Walters, named after Jakob Walters who had led his family from South Dakota in 1918 into this area of Canada.

The Hutterites, named after Jakob Hutter who was burned at the stake in 1536 as a heretic were a group of Anabaptist Protestant farmers who lived in Moravia in the 16th century. Due to religious persecution they moved to the new world and established farming communes. The family group jointly owned the farm. Each family lived in their own room with communal dining and working facilities. They lived in a peaceful, non-violent, but illogical time warp, of their own making. They dressed in the same style of attire their forebears had worn 400 years earlier, like so many religious sects, such as the Amish and Mennonites in Pennsylvania and Ohio and some of the Chassidic Orthodox Jewish groups and many other like-minded peaceful communities. All the adults and children dressed in dark hand made clothing, the women wearing black and dark navy full length skirts, frequently with floral aprons and always a small bonnet, with coiled braided hair, while the men wore trousers and jackets made from coarse heavy fabrics, with buttons for fastening and invariably wore dark hats while the married men were bearded.

This extended family group accepted modern technology to the extent of a single electric light bulb in the communal area, with a radio for listening to weather forecasts and no other use. They used candles and oil lamps for lighting in living rooms, but unlike the Amish, utilised trucks and tractors for farm work. Schooling was compulsory by law, and so a small government schoolhouse, in which lived a non-Hutterite schoolteacher was provided. Before attending school, immunisation was mandatory and so all the children were immunised against diphtheria, tetanus, whooping cough, polio and smallpox. As children grew to adulthood, marriages were arranged. The girls of marriageable age left the community with their large, beautifully crafted, hand made, wooden dowry chests full of linen and clothing that had been diligently sewn, embroidered, knitted and painstakingly accumulated over the years. In similar manner, a young woman from another communal farm, would arrive to marry a suitable bachelor and would join the communal farm where he lived, bringing with her, her own heavily laden dowry chest of carefully prepared clothes and linens.

In contrast to the Chassidim, there was no place for any schooling beyond the legal minimum required by the state and no encouragement of a college education, making them dependent on others for every professional service. Marriage, other than to another Hutterite seemed unknown, although I did learn of one young man who married a non-Hutterite young lady and was thereafter rejected by his family and community. I was never aware of any divorce amongst members, although I never specifically enquire about such matters.

When a community prospered and became too numerous, a satellite community was financed and started some distance away. Prosperous through their own industry and hard work together with the application of religion in every day life, I found some of their commercial practices didn't always match their religious zeal, but this might apply in any community. We had arranged with the colony to buy half an animal to be delivered to the locker plant for our beef supply, where it would be cut up and packaged for our use throughout the ensuing months. Some members delivered the top half of the animal, instead of the normal vertical half, where many of the better cuts of meat were to be found. The locker plant alerted me to this anomaly and the order was cancelled.

Ruth Sigurdsen, was the Eastend hospital matron who supervised all nursing care. Slim, tall and dignified, she was a middle aged Canadian nurse who was ably assisted by a number of auxiliaries and nurses, many of whom were British. There were Margaret and Nelda, who married the Verpey brothers and Marion who married Robert Benz amongst a group who had earlier arrived from England. With larger North American salaries and unaccustomed disposable incomes they had all succumbed to the temptations of buying fur coats, large luxurious cars and other extravagances, which left them in debt for many months. They had likewise not been immune to the charms of some of the young men who abounded in this rural community and many had married, only later to discover that a handsome cowboy did not always make a suitable husband. Successive post war British governments, with their failure to amend deplorable conditions of employment in the National Health Service had much to answer for in the loss to North America of so many young nurses and doctors. Particularly was this so amongst numerous highly qualified fellowship and membership doctors who like Alan Fletcher were compelled to emigrate in droves due to the absence of consultant posts within the NHS.

Mr L, the dour chairman of the board was an efficient but unsmiling farmer of French origin. Having once met his wife one could understand and forgive his seemingly cheerless disposition. Dr Vic Millions was the other doctor in Eastend. A tall rotund gentleman in his sixties, who was at the best of times well inebriated, had a small practice of loyal like-minded supporters. I seldom had the inclination to speak more than a few words with him when we met, as I endeavoured to shun his grossly intoxicated bonhomie.

In addition to my main medical practice in Eastend there was a branch surgery at Consul, a tiny village some 50 miles to the southwest. The citizens there had built a small centrally heated office suite adjoining the RCMP office. It had a comfortable waiting room and a spacious consulting room with an examination room and a bathroom. The sole upholder of the law in this remote corner of what became my practice was RCMP Corporal Beach, a cheerful childless fellow in his mid-fifties, whose wife made herself responsible for maintaining the doctor's office next door.

I visited Consul twice a week, Friday morning and Monday afternoon. The office hours on Monday commenced as close to 3pm as I could time my arrival and continued until I had finished seeing any patient who needed to consult the doctor. At times the surgery continued until midnight. I never stopped for refreshments while consulting, although if the surgery carried on well into the evening Mrs. Beach would always appear, unbidden, with a cup of welcoming hot coffee.

During the winter months, patients would take it in turns to pick up my car keys, which I left on the waiting room table and start my car every thirty minutes or so, since there was no electrical outlet into which my car's block heater could be connected. I found it astounding to find that patients would arrive from farms 50 or 60 miles distant, from both sides of the border to consult a doctor. The sparsely populated area covered by my practice was immense, well in excess of 1,200 square miles. On my journey to Consul I would often stop enroute to see one or two incapacitated older patients.

At these domiciliary calls I was invariably plied with cups of coffee but after a time I called a halt to this hospitality since the coffee's diuretic effect often made life extremely uncomfortable when driving. Seldom were house calls made. Distances were very great and the possibility of becoming stuck on some off the route track, was very daunting. Patients were always encouraged to visit the doctor, where all the investigative facilities were immediately at hand, unlike the GP's practices in the UK.

One morning in late April 1960, shortly after sunrise, we were rudely awakened by a tremendous bang with resulting shock waves that shook and rattled every window and door in the house. Startled from our slumber and instantly awake, I glanced at the bedside alarm clock to check the time. It was 6 am.

"Good heavens! What on earth was that asked June?"

"I've no idea. It sounded like a bomb, but it's more than probably Nellie, falling out of bed." I replied in jocular fashion.

"Don't be so silly. You'd better check to see if there's anything wrong."

Jumping out of bed, I hurriedly put on my dressing gown and slippers, checked Robin's room and confirmed he was still sleeping as Nellie emerged yawning in her sleeping attire, from her basement room.

"Mornin' Dr Powell, did you just hear somethin'?" she enquired.

"Heard the same thing as you and I thought you might know what it might have been." I replied. "I'm just going to check the basement to see if anything's wrong with the central heating furnace. You'd best get dressed and make Robin's milk and breakfast ready." I instructed.

Having checked the house and found everything in order I proceeded to wash and dress when June, who was making breakfast, looked out of the kitchen window and announced there was something strange happening outside.

I joined her at the window where we saw several small groups of people in two's and three's rapidly walking and jogging along the road out of town and the occasional vehicle speeding by. Wondering where they might be hurrying, we looked along the road, ahead of them. As we stared into the distance, each of us suddenly noticed that the motel we could normally see some quarter mile down the road at the west end of town appeared to have diminished in size. The twelve room motel of timber and plaster board construction had lost most of its roof and had timber joists sticking into the air at bizarre angles as though it had been struck by a tornado. A small number of people who had reached what seemed to be the shrunken remains of the motel were busily tearing at the protruding wooden beams. From the distance of our home, the people resembled clusters of giant ants while the wooden structures appeared like a large pile of disorderly telegraph poles.

"Looks as though there's been some sort of accident at the motel" June exclaimed.

"I think I'd better hurry down to the hospital to organize some emergency preparations for anybody who might have been injured." I replied.

We hadn't long to wait. Two men were brought in as casualties and fortunately they were the only people to have been injured. Both were coated in a thick film of grey dust, with singed hair and eyebrows. Apart from neither being able to hear and with a few minor lacerations they appeared to have been otherwise uninjured. The motel, which had been closed during the winter months, had been preparing to reopen with these two workmen attending to the general renovation and redecoration of the bedrooms.

The story unfolded that they had been visiting friends on a nearby farm. Claiming they had drunk no more than a couple of beers, as they played cards, they had left just before sun up to return to the motel to snatch a couple of hours sleep, before continuing their work. Upon alighting from their truck, these worthies entered the motel, where they immediately noticed a pervading odour of gas.

Two years later in 1962, a mains natural gas supply was introduced to communities in this region of Saskatchewan, a logistically fantastic operation since gas pipes had to be buried at least 8 feet below ground to avoid the 'frost line'. Prior to that time gas would have been provided from one or more propane gas cylinders located outside the building.

Having smelt gas, the sensible approach would have been to open windows and doors to clear the atmosphere, before checking the gas cylinder and its connections. One might conjecture they may have been a little the worse for imbibing a few more than the two or three cans of beer they admitted drinking, since that might explain their subsequent behaviour.

They decided they must go immediately in search of the source of the leaking gas, probably a tap that had been left on the previous evening, and turn it off. It was dark and some form of illumination was essential. Having left the only flashlight in the truck, they decided there should be no going back. Unable to find the light switch they recalled seeing a candle stub standing in a candleholder placed forlornly in the centre of a bedside table, with a convenient matchbox alongside. One of them struck a match to light the wick, when there was a violent explosion.

Fortunately the timber construction collapsed in such a manner that serious crush injuries had somehow been avoided. Had the building been built more solidly of brick there might have been a rather different outcome. There were no broken bones and any resulting injuries appeared to be the result of the blast and sudden short-lived burst of flame.

I decided that both men should be admitted and kept under observation. One of the men, apart from a perforated eardrum, appeared to suffer no other untoward signs of his accident and was discharged after two days. His companion developed an ileus (absence of bowel sounds), which caused me considerable worry. Having no experience in traumatic blast injuries I telephoned the air ambulance at Regina and arranged for the patient's transfer. Some days later I received a report stating he'd made a full recovery without surgical intervention.

Twelve months earlier I'd been on A&E duty in Baltimore, when a gentleman in his 70's had been brought in one evening by ambulance. The bumper of a passing taxi had struck him while he was crossing a road. He had been thrown backwards out of the path of the vehicle, which knocked him down. Fortunately the taxi had been travelling slowly and hadn't run over him. He sustained a fracture to the tibia of his left lower leg, and some minor bruising. Under an anaesthetic, his fracture was reduced, and a plaster of Paris cast applied, following which he was admitted to the ward with a dextrose saline drip in situ, and his vital signs monitored.

During the night it was noted that his pulse rate was rising and his blood pressure was maintained by increasing the rate of flow of his intravenous fluid. Some four hours after admission he had a cardiac arrest and expired. Although there had been no reported abdominal injury, nor any trauma marks on the abdomen or pelvis, autopsy revealed that he had a ruptured spleen, which had resulted in the patient bleeding to death without this condition being identified.

This preventable death had been presented the following week at one of the case conferences, which were a regular feature of the hospital's postgraduate education programme. As a consequence, although unfamiliar with blast injuries I was mindful of the possible complications that might have followed the explosion and therefore chose to transfer the victim to a major hospital.

Days later, an agitated farmer arrived at the hospital with his wife who had taken a drug overdose, asking the nurse to summon the doctor. The nurse called me on the phone and prior to my arrival, Mrs Anderson, conscious and tearful, admitted to the duty nurse that an hour earlier she'd swallowed half a bottle of aspirin tablets, washed down with a bottle of beer. When her husband returned from work she confessed her action. He'd immediately bundled her into his car and had driven straight to the hospital. She was given a glass of milk to drink as I prepared to pass a naso-gastric tube into her stomach to perform a stomach wash out.

Once this procedure was over she was given further milk to drink with the addition of bicarbonate of soda, to neutralize the acid. She expressed the desire to return home and in order to keep her under observation I set up an intravenous infusion in her forearm. Some 48 hours after admission when appearing to have made a perfect recovery she suddenly collapsed complaining of severe abdominal pain. Sweating and with a rapid pulse, examination of her abdomen revealed a tenderness that had not previously been present and I diagnosed an acute peptic ulcer perforation. A naso-gastric tube was passed for a second time and a strict regimen of nil by mouth and continuous suctioning of her stomach contents was started, while maintaining her fluid intake by intravenous infusion. This technique of conservative 'Suck and Drip' management could often result in a perforation healing without the need for surgical intervention, providing there was no major bleeding and the regimen was commenced within the shortest possible time to avoid the peritonitis that would inevitably follow if the perforation was left unattended.

The patient was monitored closely and after seven days we were able to relax knowing that the emergency had passed and the perforated ulcer was healing without the need of surgery. During Mrs Anderson's prolonged hospital stay she confided that she'd taken her overdose just before her husband was due home to gain his attention and not because she wished to kill herself. An industrious woman, she felt her husband had been neglecting her, causing her to feel particularly lonely and isolated on their farm. Her action had been more a cry for help for she was not clinically depressed. She rarely saw neighbours and seldom came into town. She begged that under no circumstances should I reveal her secret to her husband and I agreed providing she undertook never to jeopardize her life by behaving in such an irresponsible manner. I did however take the opportunity to explain to Mr Anderson that living on the farm, miles from neighbours and friends, his wife felt isolated which had made her feel depressed. I recommended that to remedy this difficulty he must permit her to meet friends and allow her to shop in the local stores at least a couple of times every week, to which he readily agreed.

One amusing incident from this period occurred one Saturday evening some months after moving to Eastend. While dining in Jack's Café after visiting the evening cinema show, I was summoned urgently to the Eastend Hotel across the street to see a gentleman from out of town. Leaving my wife and assuring her that I'd return as soon as possible I hurried off, wondering what the emergency might be. The hotel receptionist rapidly directed me to the room of my unknown patient. Hastening up the stairs I knocked on the first floor bedroom door opened it and walked in. There I found a middle-aged man smoking a cigar, whom I'd never seen before, sitting at a desk on which rested a glass and a half full bottle of whiskey.

"Good evening, I'm Doctor Powell. The hotel called me to say you needed a doctor urgently."

"Sure, that's right. I asked them to call you. Come on in and have a drink." As he spoke and moved he appeared mildly inebriated.

Placing my medical bag on the bed, I opened it, and as I removed my stethoscope replied.

"Not at the moment thanks. Maybe another time when I'm not on duty. Now what seems to be the trouble?"

"No trouble Doc."

Mystified, I enquired. "What do you mean no trouble? There must have been a problem. Why else did you ask the hotel to summon a doctor urgently?"

"Naw, they musta got the message all wrong. I jest said to call the doctor. I didn't say nothin' about no emergency, or urgently. I just thought that it bein' Saturday night an' all, you'd have nothin' to do, so I thought you could give me a check up."

The chutzpah! I was speechless. My choice was either to storm out and returns to my wife and my unfinished meal, or to make the best of a ridiculous situation. I took out a notebook, recorded his name and details and requested him to remove his top clothes. Very briefly I checked his heart and blood pressure, before advising that he needed to refrain from smoking, should drink less alcohol and advised him to attend his own doctor for a blood test at the earliest opportunity. I then packed my bag and told him my fee was $50 for an out of hours weekend call. This was an outrageously high fee, but which he paid without demur, more than adequately defraying the cost of our meal and cinema tickets.

On another occasion I was called to the same hotel late in the evening. Earlier that day a visiting member of parliament from out of town consulted me with a painful shoulder. A rotund middle-aged gentleman, he had considerable limitation of movement and felt that the pain had become too unbearable. I recommended an injection would alleviate much of his pain and at the same time give him greater mobility. I gave him an injection of a corticosteroid, 'Depot Medrone', together with a local anaesthetic. Within minutes he was able to move his shoulder freely without pain. He volubly expressed his thanks and went about his political business.

I received an urgent call to visit him in his hotel room. When I arrived and walked into the bedroom I saw the patient sitting up in bed in great distress, with his arm raised vertically above his head, unable to lower it. He explained that being pain free he'd extended his arm up above his head to turn off the bedside light and suddenly discovered that he was unable to lower it. The earlier success had been short lived since he had dislocated, (subluxated) his shoulder joint. With some difficulty I was able to reverse the dislocation and then supplied him with a sling and advice on how to manage his shoulder over the ensuing weeks. The following day he returned to Ottawa and I heard nothing more.

Joseph, an 18 year old college student from a city on the Eastern seaboard had arrived in Eastend to spend some time on a farm, prior to undertaking his further education. Perhaps he'd imagined seeing himself in the romantic role of a cowboy driving herds of cattle, but the reality was that he had been working as a farm hand for one of the local farmers. The work may have been a little dull, but with quantities of good food and copious fresh air and exercise he rapidly developed a healthy tan and had been thriving.

During the previous month's spring planting he acquired that minimal skill, controlling a huge red Massey-Ferguson tractor. Slowly and monotonously he would drive up and down some of the largest tracts of prairie farmland, planting the spring wheat crop, which made him over confident and perhaps a little careless handling this machine. There had been an unusually heavy three days rainfall in the first week of June, during which time most farm work temporarily ceased. The day following this downpour, young Joseph had been driving his lumbering red leviathan, when he came to a cattle gate through which he needed to pass. Leading up to the gate was a small incline which would have seemed barely noticeable to the casual observer. It was here that he chose to park his vehicle. Setting the brake, he left the engine running, opened the gate, walked the few paces back to the tractor and drove through, up the almost imperceptible incline, where he stopped. In his effort to gain those extra few seconds of time he left the engine running as previously, but only partially applied the brake. Confidently he sprang lithely from the cab and walked briskly back to shut the gate. As he swung the gate closed, with his back to his stationary vehicle he was unaware that the tractor was rolling silently towards him down the incline, slowly gaining momentum.

Momentarily he became conscious of an irresistible force pushing against his back, shoving him downwards onto the gate, which partially swung open as the tractor forced him into the ground its several ton weight of water filled

198

tyres and steel machinery passing over his body, compressing his pelvis and skull before demolishing the gate and stopping in the field at the bottom of the incline. Some minutes later his crushed body was found, partly compressed into the ground. The tractor with its inadequately applied hand brake and engine still idling waited innocently in the meadow, but fifty paces away. It was Joseph's good fortune that somebody had walked over to investigate where the driver of this tractor might be and why he'd left both the engine running and the gate open.

Joe was brought into the hospital, where I was urgently summoned to see him. He was conscious and in great pain whenever he attempted the least movement. X-rays were taken and amazingly the only bone injury he had sustained was a fractured pelvis. Apart from a small laceration on the side of his forehead, there had been no injury to limbs, urethra, bladder, kidneys, or any other viscera. After suturing his laceration and apart from treating him with analgesics and bed rest he was commencing to make an excellent recovery when three days later his extremely anxious mother flew in from the east coast. She immediately requested that I transfer her son to a major medical centre and an air ambulance was organised that same day. Had this accident happened the day before the rain, or days later when the soil would have been unyieldingly hard, the outcome would have been gravely different.

About one year later, almost to the day, I was called to the hospital to see the eldest child of Bent and Karen S. Bent was the manager of the Co-op store. Charming intelligent people, both he and his wife, had been born in Denmark and spoke perfect English with a marked Scandinavian accent. They had two children a daughter aged 6 years and a son of 3 years. Over the previous months we had visited each other's homes, dined with each other and were on very cordial terms.

That Sunday morning Bent had gone out to the nearby golf course to play nine holes of golf. He had taken his son with him as an observer and had strictly instructed the child to stand well away when the golf club was being swung. At the second hole he had teed off and missed with his first swing. After a few seconds pause he swung his club a second time, just as his little boy stepped forward, unnoticed. As Bent swung his club back it struck the youngster on his forehead, knocking him out. Bent was in a state of shock when he bent over his son and saw blood spurting from a huge gash across the line of the child's eyebrows. Terrified, he picked his unconscious son up, placed him in his car and rushed him to the hospital.

When I saw the youngster, he'd regained consciousness. I examined the wound in preparation for suturing when I discovered loose fragments of bone from the anterior portion of the frontal sinus in the wound. I hurriedly applied a temporary dressing, gave him a covering antibiotic and anti-tetanus shot, and immediately had him transferred to a trauma centre by air ambulance.

After three days, Bent returned with his son. The injuries had not penetrated the posterior portion of the frontal bone, and thank heavens there had been no damage to the brain or its coverings. When accidents occur luck always plays a key role in the degree of damage sustained and the outcome. In both these cases, good fortune was definitely on the patient's side. Sadly as my next experience relates, luck was not on the side of the young and innocent.

Mr. and Mrs. A lived with their three children, a boy aged 8 and two younger girls aged 4 and 2 in a modest 3 bed family home on the outskirts of Shaunavon. The previous day, a Sunday, there had been a birthday party for the 4 year old and a number of neighbours children had joined the happy celebration in which there had been the usual party games, balloons and food followed by a large iced cake with 4 birthday candles. The two younger children were dressed in their best frilly party clothes and as the birthday child blew out her candles everybody sang happy birthday. At the end of the party, the younger children were put to bed and the remains of the birthday cake, with its partially burned candles were left on a coffee table before a settee in the front room.

The following day the little boy attended school and Mrs A busied herself with her daily chores, but for some reason did not remove the cake from where it had been left the previous afternoon. After their noontime meal she put the two children to bed for a nap. The day was oppressively hot and quiet and Mrs A decided that she would take the opportunity to have a little shuteye in her bedroom while her young charges slept in the next room.

A little later she was awakened by what she initially imagined was a dream in which she heard the muffled scream of one of the children. It was then that she also first detected a burning smell. She arose and left her room to investigate, when she noticed smoke drifting upwards. Calling her daughters names she rushed into the children's bedroom, to find both beds empty. With the smell of burning more noticeable and now frenzied with worry, she dashed round the house, into each of the rooms, shouting her daughter's names. The door to the front room was closed. As she opened it, she was met with a wall of flame and intense heat that prevented her entry. Not knowing if the children were in the room, or where they might be, she frantically rushed outside screaming and shouting to summon help from her neighbours.

Following the autopsies on these children, I chaired the Coroner's inquest that was held some days later in Shaunavon, into their loss of life. Prior to the inquest, the RCMP escorted me, at my request, to the scene of the tragedy. There I saw the devastation caused by the fire. The badly burned room, with the persisting all pervading odour of burnt wood and fabric and the incinerated remains of the settee, pushed away from the wall, behind which these innocents vainly sheltered to escape the flames. Although the bodies were partly burned, the pathologist confirmed death had been from smoke asphyxiation. The mother, the chief of Shaunavon's fire department, the RCMP and neighbours all provided evidence.

The circumstances strongly indicated that as the mother slept, the elder child had woken from her nap, and led her younger sister out of their bedroom, without awakening mother. She had then taken matches from the kitchen table, where they were kept next to the cooker and both children had walked into the front room, where the door had been left ajar. Having opened the door, which was hinged on rising butts, it closed firmly behind them once they were inside. The height of the door handle was such that they would have been unable to reach it unaided.

Within the room they doubtlessly tried to re-enact the events of the previous afternoon. Several matches had been struck, in an attempt to light the candles still present on the birthday cake sitting on the coffee table. Remains of the matches somehow survived the fire and were identified on the floor. In some way one of them must have ignited the dry fabric covering the couch. Unable to open the closed door the children had fled to seek refuge in the space behind the couch where their bodies were later found.

At the conclusion of the proceedings I recorded the two deaths to be by misadventure; the saddest family and communal tragedy that I had been summoned to witness.

Whenever I see very young children enjoying a birthday celebration with a cake and accompanying candles, I'm reminded, with foreboding, of those horrific scenes that are forever seared into my memory and with them the need to keep matches well away from young children. The same message must equally apply, to keep all tablets and medication in a secured position well out of the reach of the very young.

Chapter 13

SASKATCHEWAN

Spring 1961

Located prominently on Main Street was Jack's Café, owned and managed by the Shourounis brothers, of Greek origin, who also owned a substantial farm and ranch just beyond town. A centre of friendly convivial social activity it was the only restaurant in Eastend. The menu was basic but the generous beefsteaks could only be described as enormous, matching the abundant helping of fries and vegetables. There were four brothers, Spiro, Nick, Jack and Pete the youngest, who told me how he'd made his way to Canada from Greece as a youth of 14 prior to the war. Next door and to the west was the dentist's office, while to the east was an empty plot and then the most substantial building in town, the brick built Bank of Montreal.

The security system at the bank was unimaginatively simple. During office hours there was an alarm bell that connected the bank to Jack's Café, where it would ring, once activated by a bank employee. On hearing the alarm, the proprietor would 'phone the RCMP at Shaunavon 25 miles to the north east and Consul 50 miles to the south west to summon help since these posts covered each of the main roads connected to Eastend. It was seldom ever activated to check the system's efficiency.

A couple of years before our arrival two aspiring young scoundrels, unknown in the area, held up the Bank. Armed, they had driven up in a saloon, which they parked outside the brick building just after opening time. They strode into the bank, waited their turn at the tellers counter and then pulled out pistols demanding money. Terrified staff and customers were forced to lie on the floor, while the manager was compelled to open the timed combination lock on the safe, at gunpoint. As he waited for the timed lock to respond his fears for the Bank's money were assuaged, since unknown to the interlopers, he had activated the alarm connected to the café next door and knew one of the Shourounis proprietors would alert the RCMP.

Two of the brothers were present in the restaurant when they heard the alarm bell. Pete turned to his brother Nick and commented.

"Isn't that the alarm? Wonder what they're fooling around with at the Bank? I guess I'd better drop by and tell them the alarm's gone off so they can shut it down." At a leisurely pace he proceeded next door, opened the bank door and announced.

"Hey guys, do you know your alarm's been ringin'..." and then his voice trailed away as the gunmen indicated he should lie down with the other occupants on the floor.

At the conclusion of the raid the armed villains rushed out of the bank into their getaway vehicle. Pete immediately strode into action. He telephoned the Smith brothers at the nearby hardware store, alerting them of the robbery. Ross Smith, one of the two brothers who were the proprietors of the local hardware store, was the part time town policeman, since Eastend had no RCMP, while his younger brother Glen, an experienced pilot who provided an invaluable crop spraying service also gave flying lessons.

Glen drove to the bank, picked up Pete Shourounis and together they drove to the nearby airstrip where Glen's Piper Club was always fuelled in readiness for flight. During the war Glen had been an RAF pilot instructor in Alberta, and reminiscent of his days with Hurricanes and Spitfires, soon had his plane taxiing down the runway. They were airborne within minutes and as they gained height headed east. They were shortly able to spot the bandit's car as it raced eastwards towards Shaunavon leaving an enormous cloud of dust. Using his two-way radio Glen communicated the information ahead to the RCMP who had been alerted by the bank manager. Within thirty minutes of leaving the scene of the crime the suspected bank robbers were stopped, searched and the stolen money recovered. Some time later the bank provided a token financial reward for the apprehension of the villains and introduced a more reliable direct alarm system with the RCMP.

In the late spring of our first year the last patient to consult me at the end of the day was Mr S, a farmer in his early sixties who worked part time at Jack's Cafe. He complained of nothing more onerous than a painful left elbow. It had come on quite recently and appeared to be increasing in severity. There had been no injury, he had a full range of movement and there was no local tenderness. There seemed to be no reason for this trouble and the only other symptom was what he described as an occasional 'emptiness' in the right side of his chest, when his elbow was most troublesome. Mystified, I arranged for him to return to the hospital for an ECG (electrocardiogram) the following morning, to exclude the possibility of angina. The next morning he failed to appear at the restaurant and neither did he keep his hospital appointment. Somebody called at his home where he was discovered in bed, where he'd died during the night. An autopsy confirmed death had followed blockage of a coronary artery. I had suspected but failed to identify his angina. Had a diagnosis been made, apart from advice and glyceryl trinitrin tablets, there was no other treatment then available.

A fortnight after we moved to Eastend we received a 'phone call from Mary Hyman, the wife of Dave Hyman a storekeeper in Gull Lake, some 70 miles north of Eastend. She'd heard a rumour that a Jewish doctor had moved into the area and with Passover approaching said she would be delighted if we could join her and her twin teenage daughters for the Passover dinner. We readily accepted her invitation and thus commenced a delightful friendship, during our stay in Eastend. As a consequence of this contact I was requested to help make a 'minyan' (a quorum of 10 adult males) for services that were held in Swift Current at the time of the Jewish New Year and Day of Atonement, for which I had to make a journey of 220 miles round trip. The previous year one of Mary's daughters had successfully undergone thoracic surgery to remedy a 'Fallot's tetralogy' and when they left school, both became nurses.

In Shaunavon, I developed a very close working relationship with Norman Green, a Leeds graduate who was keenly interested in ophthalmology and competently performed many minor ophthalmic surgical procedures under local anaesthesia. Alan Fletcher FRCS a London University College Hospital surgeon joined him in the middle of 1960 and our patients were able to benefit from the increased range of surgical procedures that then became available, rather than needing to travel to Swift Current or Regina.

Many of my maternity patients had reason to be grateful to Alan Fletcher. One evening shortly after his arrival we'd invited him and his wife with a number of the Eastend hospital nursing staff to dinner at our home. Following dinner Alan gave us a spontaneous demonstration of hypnosis. Amusingly his volunteer remained unaffected but one of the observers proved to be a very susceptible subject. I discussed the applications for hypnotherapy and decided to use the technique. One of the more troublesome problems in practice was nausea and vomiting of pregnancy. Professor Scott Russell who occupied the chair in Obstetrics and Gynaecology in Sheffield had advocated a small morning dose of honey, which occasionally worked well, but not always.

This demonstration coincided with the introduction of a new drug in 1960 called 'Thalidomide' which drug house representatives were encouraging doctors to use for insomnia and hyperemesis (nausea associated with pregnancy). Thanks to Alan Fletcher's instruction, I started to use hypnotherapy for these very conditions and found it to be remarkably effective. As a consequence I never prescribed medication for this problem and thank heavens never endangered the health of my patient's with what proved to be a catastrophically dangerous drug to the unborn foetus.

Pharmaceutical companies constantly bombarded doctors, to use their products. Their representatives provided us with information, literature, and copious quantities of samples, encouraging the use of the latest pharmaceutical advances. This was useful on a number of fronts. It provided samples, particularly antibiotics and vitamin supplements that I could use for the children of some of my poorer patients. In addition the reps were a useful source of information relating to ones colleagues in other parts of the province. The other side of the coin was that patients would consult me, asking for the latest wonder drug they had read about in the most recent issue of The Reader's Digest, or some similar publication. There seemed little realisation that something new was not necessarily better than something older and proven.

One of my patients, a very pretty young woman of 16 years, came to see me. With the sacrifice of a frog, the test confirmed her pregnancy. Her boy friend, three years older, was delighted with the news. A church wedding was arranged four weeks later as they hastily put up their marriage banns. Unfortunately just seven days before the wedding she miscarried. A beautiful young bride dressed in virginal white, she was married the next weekend,. Three months later she again consulted me and once more I was able to confirm she was pregnant. This time there was no miscarriage, but as the pregnancy proceeded she went into premature labour and in the 36th week of gestation I delivered a healthy male infant weighing just over 5 pounds, nine months after her marriage. Both mother and child did well following the confinement, but gossips amongst the town elders agreed the reason this young mother had married nine months earlier was because she was pregnant. They were completely wrong, but patient confidentiality forbade enlightening them.

Mrs. Kieghley consulted me. She was in her thirties and had seven children. Known to be a strictly practicing Roman Catholic she had unsuccessfully used every means of birth control at her disposal and now in desperation wished to be sterilised. I suggested that to preserve anonymity she should have this relatively simple procedure performed elsewhere. She refused. I arranged for her to be admitted and organised an anaesthetist and surgical assistance with Dr Green. There were no laparoscopic procedures. Since she knew the nursing staff, many of who were Catholic, a strategy was devised to deceive them. Her admitting diagnosis was of persisting abdominal pain that necessitated an 'Exploratory Laparotomy'. She was admitted for surgery during which both her Fallopian tubes were tied and cut, following which her healthy appendix was removed. None of the nursing staff were able to observe our covert action and the patient made a perfect postoperative recovery.

In June 1960 the news media bombarded the public with the fantastic story that Israeli Mossad (1) secret service agents had captured Adolf Eichmann in Argentina and it was at this time that Mr. H, brought his wife in to my office for a consultation.

A kind and genteel middle-aged childless couple, formerly from England lived in a picturesque but remote farm some 20 miles north west of town. Mrs H suffered from multiple sclerosis, and now confined to a wheel chair, travelling had become increasingly fraught. As a consequence I visited them on their farm when requested. Before setting out I would always telephone ahead to let them know of my departure in order that should I not arrive when expected, somebody could drive out to discover where I might be stuck. Mrs. H's elderly mother, a woman of ninety two lived with them. In her childhood she had been raised in Windsor and had often seen Queen Victoria's children at play in the great park. Her father had been the first bank manager of a branch, which was opened in Finchley Road, opposite John Barnes, just north of Swiss Cottage before the turn of the century. This lady consulted me concerning a lump on her chest. I diagnosed that it was a cancer of the breast and recommended that in view of her age surgical treatment was not to be considered. I explained that these tumours tended to be far less aggressive in the elderly. Two years later this genteel lady died of old age, the tumour having caused her no trouble other than the realisation of knowing that it was present.

*   *   *

Napoleon Bonaparte is alleged to have enquired of his advisors prior to appointing a general to his senior military staff.

"Is the man lucky?"

The converse could be said to have applied to the Mc Kinnon family that I first met in the spring of 1961.

Shaun McKinnon lived with his wife and two adult sons on a single section farm in the hilly region to the northwest of Eastend. He'd been one of the earlier settlers in the region having emigrated from Ireland some years prior to the First World War. He was the fourth of a large Irish Catholic family and his anticipated share of the small family farm his wife explained, would;

"Barely have supported a couple of chickens, let alone a man with a wife and family."

He responded to a glowing coloured poster that he'd seen in a railway station in 1909, showing sheaths of wheat standing shoulder high with their abundant golden heads of grain, in vast picturesque fields, with a clear deep blue sky overhead. The advertisement's wording indicated that in the province of Saskatchewan, in the Dominion of Canada, he could purchase a quarter section plot of land of 160 acres for just $10 Canadian Dollars. He could hardly believe his eyes. One hundred and sixty acres, larger than any farm he'd ever seen for the equivalent of two weeks work in Dublin. It was like manna from heaven.

He hastened to enquire further and was told that to acquire title to his 160 acres dream farm he would need, under the Canadian Homestead Act of 1885, to make a single payment of $10 and fulfil a number of simple requirements. These included living on his chosen quarter section of land for 5 years during which time he would be required to build a home and have cultivated at least 40 acres of land for the growth of cereals. At the completion of 5 years he would acquire full title in perpetuity, excluding all mineral rights, which would rest with the crown. In addition at the end of five years, should he wish, he could exercise the right, as a bonus, to acquire an adjacent 160 acres quarter section for a further payment of $10.

This was too good to be true. Shaun scrimped and saved for months to scrape his fare together. In addition he saved an additional sum for the land purchase and sufficient to buy a few basic tools and implements, before setting off. He bade farewell to his family, crossed the Atlantic and entered Canada through the St Lawrence Water seaway and then proceeded westwards by train. He found his homestead, laid claim, and then commenced the backbreaking task of clearing the land of rocks and stones, an acre at a time, in preparation for ploughing and planting. His first major problem was drinking water, which he had to haul in an ox drawn cart from Frenchman creek, a full two days return journey. The prairie area was predominantly flat grass land as far as the eye could see, with gentle undulating hills, devoid of any trees to break the winds that periodically swept across the land, blowing the course sage grass, snagged in brambles into large spherical bundles some two and three times as large as any medicine ball rolling playfully for scores of miles across the open land, watched only by gophers, lithe acrobatic land squirrels that lived in small colonies that maintained look out positions standing perpendicularly to attention on their rear legs, and the occasional deer and antelope.

The lack of trees created problems other than the absence of a windbreak or natural shade. There was no kindling wood with which to make a fire and no timber for the construction of a rudimentary home. While the water he laboriously hauled in for himself and his pair of oxen was free at the point of acquisition, every piece of timber had to be purchased, when one had the money, from the nearest township a journey of at least two day's round trip. The home he was required to build he made of oblong pieces of prairie sod laid one upon the other, like a flat wide brick, to form a giant truncated igloo, roofed over by thinner slabs supported by sparingly placed timber joists and abutting this a small barn to shelter his livestock.

The climate was harsh. Summer temperatures could reach into the high nineties Fahrenheit, without the benefit of any shade, with plagues of summer mosquitoes and occasionally locusts. Winter would produce plummeting sub zero temperatures for days on end from December until April, apart from those episodic two or three days when an easterly blowing Chinook wind miraculously turned the harshest mid winter into a series of mild, spring like, mud squelching days before hard ice dramatically reappeared as the Chinook mysteriously vanished and temperatures precipitously tumbled down to former arctic levels. There was no real spring season. In late April from harshest mid winter, summer suddenly appeared, and with it the need to feverishly plant crops, that could germinate grow and be harvested before the inevitable frost in the first days of September. After that vestigial autumnal September chill, annihilating the myriad insect pests there was an 'Indian Summer', when temperatures stayed in the mid sixties and seventies Fahrenheit before collapsing in late November. The fall weather was arguably the most delightful that could be found anywhere on the North American continent.

However in the region of southwest Saskatchewan termed 'Palliser's triangle' this was not the entire picture. There were the endless days of pale sapphire blue skies, with no sight of a rain cloud, the parched prairie grass and failing crops, desperate for the merest bead of moisture or morning dewdrop. There were the times when the wind blew incessantly, for days on end, uninterrupted by any natural shelter, sweeping over the prairie, with layer upon layer of dust creeping into every man made nook and cranny.

In winter there were the snow blizzards. The days when instead of dust, fresh powdered snow, lying on the ground were blown by fierce gusts of wind, into an impenetrable fog, disorientating the inexperienced, and where the unwary could become and were lost within three or four paces of cabin or outhouse door and froze to death.

This was the area where Shaun McKinnon and countless land hungry immigrants accepted the offer of free land and unwittingly paid for it many times over. Paid daily in unimagined hardship. Paid in unbelievable squalor and loneliness, miles from the help and comfort of neighbours and anything that civilised society might offer. Some could not endure the solitude, others could not create sufficient funds to sustain themselves and occasionally, some surrendered their lives, particularly the few young children who had accompanied parents. Many of the disillusioned gave up and moved away, broken, lonely and impoverished. Only the banks and a few legal advisers who taking advantage of this slow exodus were able to acquire huge tracts of land for a pittance, benefited.

Having acquired his quarter section and purchased a further 160 acres with his saved $10, as his economic status began to improve his thoughts turned to finding a companion, a mate. Due to shortages occasioned through the ravages of the First World War and the first years thereafter, wheat and grain prices of every kind peaked. The Canadian prairie farmers were entering one of the first of the very few periods of financial prosperity.

There were fewer women than men who endured the rigors of the early immigrant life and finding a female partner from amongst these settlers was virtually impossible. With the tremendous loss of young men in Europe following the Great War and the following influenza pandemic of 1919, there were many unattached young widows and spinsters. He wrote to his family in Ireland requesting they assist him in finding a suitable bride. They could mail him a picture of the young woman and if he approved, arrangements could be made for him to send the steamship and rail tickets for her journey. He mentioned his 320 acres farm and in Eire they considered him to have become exceedingly wealthy.

Once these formalities had been completed, Shaun met his chosen bride to be, some months later, in 1929, for the very first time, when she alighted wearily from her marathon journey in Eastend. He had arranged with the local priest that he and his fiancée would be wed the day of her arrival and following the wedding he immediately took her to his home in his horse drawn cart. However poor her family circumstances in Eire one can barely imagine her shock and disillusion to discover the domestic conditions in which she found herself thrust, in total isolation, with a constant shortage of water and every amenity, in complete contrast to her expectations of marrying a wealthy farmer. Unknown to them in their remote prairie homestead, within a few weeks of her arrival, the world's economies staggered from the October 1929 Wall Street stock market crash. What the McKinnon's and their farming neighbours soon learned was that the bottom had simply dropped out of the Canadian wheat market. It was costing more to take their produce to market than they were receiving. The consequences were disastrous. John Steinbeck in his book "The Grapes of Wrath" admirably portrayed the prairie years of the depression and the dust bowl resulting from poor farming practice aggravated by scant rainfall.

In time the McKinnon's had several children only two of whom survived the rigors of pre-antibiotic life in the harsh isolated prairie environment into which they were thrust. At the time I first met them the older son Ted was aged 27 years and his younger brother Ian, who idolised him was 21 years old. Neither brother claimed any love or respect for their father whom they considered a tyrant to them and their poor overworked mother. Ian described him as a mean skinflint and a hardhearted disciplinarian.

Ted consulted me in late March 1961 for what he imagined might be VD (a venereal infection). He believed this because he and his brother had taken a couple of days off to drive across the border for a fun weekend in one of the Montana border towns. Having sown a few wild oats with some of the town's readily available young women they had returned home and all had been well for a number of days until Ted had experienced some irritation and itching in the more private areas concealed by his underpants. Closer inspection had revealed some small crawling creatures, which I identified for him as Tinea Cruris, pubic body lice.

I took a blood sample and other tests to exclude the possibility of a venereal infection and gave him a prescription for a lotion to rid himself of his unwanted parasitic guests, arranging to see him the following week. The next week he appeared as arranged. The lice causing his irritation had disappeared and I reassured him that his tests to exclude a venereal infection were clear. In great consternation, he said he found it difficult to accept that he had not somehow picked up VD and asked if he could see me once more to have the tests repeated to make absolutely certain. I assured him this was not necessary but agreed to see him in a month's time to repeat the tests should he wish.

I thought no more about the matter until the end of April when the RCMP called to interview me concerning an apparent accident on the porch of the McKinnon farmhouse earlier that day. There had been one of a series of ongoing arguments between Mr. McKinnon and his elder son. Fathers and sons working together seldom seem to see eye to eye. Following this last of many altercations, Ted had later sat brooding for a while in a rocking chair on the porch. He then went to his room and returned with his shotgun and a short length of timber. He fashioned a small notch in the end of the wood with his knife, leaving the wood chips on the porch, where they were later found, and then sat back in the rocking chair. Placing the end of the loaded shotgun barrel into his mouth, he rested the butt on the floor and using the short length of notched timber activated the trigger.

Ted's younger brother claimed that Ted had been very withdrawn and seemed worried and depressed since his consultations with me. He blamed the death of his brother on their father with his father's incessant criticism and the frequent resulting arguments. He swore retribution in front of all and sundry.

"I'll get the old man for doing this to Ted."

Apart from the gunshot wound, the post mortem revealed one other abnormality that related to some unexpected primary changes in the spinal cord, from an undiagnosed early pernicious anaemia. Anaemia of this kind producing neurological changes might well have been responsible for depression and its consequences. After the autopsy there was a brief inquest following which Ted was buried in a family plot the McKinnon's had purchased in the Eastend cemetery after the shooting. Ted's brother Ian, had selected the burial casket and bizarrely had asked the undertaker if Ted could be buried in a double width casket so that when he in turn died, the bier could be opened, when he could then be buried next to his brother.

It was at this time that Mrs McKinnon, dressed completely in black, consulted me. Pummelled by the severity of her existence, she had aged prematurely. Her wrinkled, sun battered skin and general stooped appearance made her appear wizened and shrunken far beyond her years and depression had now been added to her burdens.

Planting time had commenced in the first week of May. In mid May my old friend Bob Parnell of the RCMP visited me once more. He greeted me by announcing.

"Morning Doctor, there's been trouble again at the McKinnon homestead."

"What kind of trouble?" I enquired.

"Old man McKinnon vanished two days ago and I wondered if you might be able to throw any light on the disappearance?"

"Sorry Bob, I can't help you. He wasn't a patient of mine and apart from seeing him at the time of his son's inquest, I'd never seen him before and I haven't seen him since. Can you tell me anything about his disappearance?"

"It appears that he and his son completed some hours of seeding and then leaving his son to continue, he returned to the farm house, where he had a coffee in the kitchen, left the mug on the table and then walked out. It was kind of hot and he left his coat and pocket book in the kitchen. He just strode outside and disappeared without trace. He couldn't have run off because he didn't take his wallet, or use any transport. We've had groups of people searching the property for two days and we've found no sign of him anywhere."

"Well everybody heard Ian threaten to 'get the old man'. What if he did just that? He could have buried him in a shallow grave and seeded over the ground. You'd never find him."

"Doctor Powell, I think you've been reading too many Agatha Christie detective novels. In his distress Ian may have said many things about his father but that doesn't mean he did anything that he shouldn't."

It was a week later when a farm hand found the body of Mr. McKinnon some half a mile from the farmhouse amongst a small copse of trees where, it was conjectured, he must have crawled for shelter. While the daytime temperature was warm and pleasant, at night it fell to a little above freezing. Autopsy revealed that he'd died following a perforated stomach ulcer. Judging by his growth of facial stubble it seemed that Mr McKinnon must have laid in great pain for some time, out of earshot, before he died. It was thought that he had been out walking when he collapsed from a burst stomach ulcer. Too weak to return home, he'd crawled to the nearest shelter from the elements that he could find and there, after laying for perhaps two to three days he died from peritonitis.

His funeral took place following his autopsy and he was interred in the family plot in Eastend, at which time something untoward was discovered. Ted, due to the undertaker's error had been interred in the wrong plot. Some days later Ted's remains within the huge grey bronze-handled sarcophagus were exhumed and then re-interred in the correct plot.

One busy Saturday afternoon in June, I was in my office when Ian McKinnon came to see me without an appointment. He complained of feeling unwell and had amongst his symptoms experienced intermittent diplopia (double vision) since the previous day. Increasing in severity over the past hours he claimed he had twice almost driven off the road on his journey to Eastend to consult me. His general malaise was of very recent onset and was rapidly becoming worse. It needed no great diagnostic acumen to notice that his eyes looked yellow, even in the artificial light of my office. I checked the mucosal surfaces of his tongue and mouth, which confirmed that he was severely jaundiced. I arranged his admission to hospital for some blood tests. The next day he was febrile and extremely ill, his jaundice having deepened. With the rapidity of onset of his symptoms I felt that he had a fulminating hepatitis. I telephoned for the air ambulance and had him transferred to Regina. Later that week, I was informed that my patient had lapsed into a hepatic coma shortly after his arrival. His condition continued to deteriorate rapidly and he died two days later. His body was returned to Eastend where he was buried alongside his recently interred brother and father.

Mrs McKinnon dressed from head to toe in mourning black moved into Eastend, a pathetically depressed, prematurely aged, walking spectre. There was no way in which she could manage her homestead farm, which was put up for public auction with its contents, livestock, and all its vehicles. A new owner purchased Ian's Ford Edsel automobile. He decided to save money by not taxing or insuring the vehicle for the remaining taxation period of eight weeks but would wait until October 1st. when he would then licence and insure the vehicle for the ensuing twelve-month period. The car was moved to his farm and stored for safekeeping in the barn, closest to his house. At the end of September there was a fierce thunderstorm, which became the talk of the town. The barn in which Ian's Ford had been housed was struck by lightning. The building burned down with the loss of its contents. Ian McKinnon's car, while uninsured, was burnt out and totally destroyed.

That late summer, a family who owned the block of land behind our cottage decided to build their home. Soil was rapidly excavated for the basement and construction was started using cement breezeblocks, manufactured locally, in a small factory to the west of Eastend. Unfortunately the night frosts, as one might have predicted, had an adverse effect on the cement, causing it to crumble. Antifreeze was added to the water and as the winter progressed pure antifreeze was ultimately used at a considerable additional cost. A central heating boiler was installed, with a chimney, which protruded through the centre of the plywood floor, the latter providing a temporary roof for the basement when covered with thick plastic sheeting and weighted down. To our amazement the whole family then took up residence in the middle of winter.

Characterizing many prairie homes was the varied appearance of their unfinished state. As funds became available year-by-year more of the home would be completed. It was a standing joke to observe that putting the finishing touches to a home invariably indicated that a family house would shortly be offered for sale.

I found it a strange anomaly to see so many of the farmer's wives shopping for eggs and milk in the grocery store. Apart from the Hutterite colony, very few farms maintained a cow to provide milk or kept chickens to lay eggs. What had once been normal good housekeeping practice had gradually died out, as farms became larger and their owners endeavoured to enjoy the good life. This meant intensive work on the land for the short season between seed sowing and crop reaping, using huge farm machinery in the process, following which the farm house would be closed up enabling the farmer and his family to enjoy an easier life in town with the option to access warmer climes during the severest cold.

Wheat could only be sold at the grain elevators. The government controlled the price paid for wheat, which was considerably less than in the US and permitted farmers to sell their production at the grain elevators on a strict quota basis, which had the effect of reducing the value of farm land on the open market.

A further strange practice was the manner in which farmers in this area lavishly purchased 'top of the range' motor vehicles and other equipment when harvest yields were good and wheat prices were high. This harvest bounty was completely unpredictable and might happen no more frequently than every three, four, or more years. Since this was the normal state of affairs there seemed to be little provision made for the years of poor harvest, when farmers claimed they were 'broke', were unable to pay for essential goods and services and occasionally had to relinquish their homes and farms. Perhaps the severe economic depression in the decade leading up to the Second World War had conditioned this community, inhibiting forward economic planning.

This strange psychological absence of scheduling reminded me of a visit I made to Paris in Easter 1947, when I visited and stayed with Serge, one of my French cousins who had lived in Vichy France throughout the terrible war years. He appeared to spend money lavishly on food in extravagantly expensive restaurants while living in a very meagre deplorable apartment. Young and uninhibited I had the temerity to enquire why he didn't conserve his resources by spending less on food, thereby providing the finances to secure more suitable accommodation. He explained.

"During the war we lost everything and were fortunate to have survived. Some of my family didn't. Food in the belly was a better investment for survival when we were in hiding than property and goods, which were confiscated and stolen. I'm still uncertain about the future and I find it hard to change my habits."

*   *   *

The majority of our winter days were passed with temperatures hovering in the region of zero Fahrenheit. The air was crisp and dry, which made these low arctic conditions more acceptable, since one always left and returned to an environment that was pleasantly warm. Taking walks with our son, instead of a pram or pushchair we had a small sleigh which with Robin suitably bundled up, glided effortlessly as we pulled it over ice and snow under the prevailing cloudless blue skies.

In the winter of 1961 at the time of Robin's first birthday I seized my opportunity to visit a patient by horse drawn sleigh. The occasion was a visit to the Hutterite colony. The minor roads close to the colony had become impassable to all but horse and tractor. One of my Hutterite patient's had returned by air ambulance from Regina following major surgery. I had arranged to escort her back to the colony and at the same time examine a couple of sick children who'd been unable to make the journey into town to see me. We drove out by car from the landing strip to within about three miles of the colony where we were met by two sleighs each drawn by a pair of horses. Leaving my car we sat in the sleigh and were each wrapped in, highly odorous rugs which were none too clean,. The driver cracked his whip and our journey continued accompanied by the steady muffled sound of horse's hooves through the snow and the gentle hiss of the sleigh's runners over ice. The journey was completed in fifteen minutes and after safely delivering my charge and examining my two young patients I was escorted back to my car, by sleigh.

It was a captivating experience and one that I could fully recommend to any doctor making house calls in winter. There were no hazards from roaming

214

wolf packs and the whole exhilarating experience must have been the closest that I would ever approach to the lives of my grandparents more than seven decades earlier when they had lived in rural Poland.

(1) The Mossad is the Israeli secret service. In June 1960, following information from Simon Wiesenthal (1908-2005), an architectural engineer who dedicated his life to tracking down and bringing to justice Nazi war criminals, a group of Mossad agents discovered Adolf Eichmann the most senior Nazi SS officer responsible for the arrest, deportation and murder of millions of Jews during the war. Having identified him, hiding with a false alias in Argentina, they were then able to kidnap him. Drugged and concealed in a carpet he was transferred to Israel where he was put on trial for war crimes. In 1961, in spite of claiming that he did none of these things and even so, he was acting under orders from his superiors, he was found guilty. The death penalty was passed and implemented for the only time in that state's history.

Chapter 14

EASTEND SASKATCHEWAN

1961

We journeyed to Great Falls in April 1961 for our first, long overdue, weekend break in more than six months. The following day was Passover. Arriving at our hotel June purchased a local newspaper where she found an advertisement for a 'Communal Seder' Passover supper to be held at the Rainbow Hotel. She telephoned and reserved two seats at $15 a place. The next evening we found ourselves seated next to Colonel Sid Wasserman, his wife and 3 children. Most of the participants were from the US Air force base near by as was the officiating rabbi.

Befriended by the Wasserman's we had a most enjoyable evening. They invited us to their home the next day, and we were given an escorted tour of the base. From then on, we made a point of visiting them whenever we journeyed to Great Falls. Sid was the senior officer in charge of aircraft maintenance on the base. The last time we saw him was in the aftermath of the Cuban missile crisis in October 1962, although his eldest son Jay visited us twice in England, before his premature death from leukaemia.

With June's help as secretary and receptionist I had rapidly built up a flourishing medical practice and in 1961 with little recreational activity on which to spend money, the signs of a surplus in our bank account appeared for the first time in our marriage. It was at this stage we arranged our vacation in the middle of the year to visited London for the wedding of June's brother Brian to Annette Liss. By that time we'd been away from home for three years and decided to make our final preparations to return sometime during the latter part of 1962, failing which we felt we might have reached a point of no return and would be tempted to settle in North America, which had never been our intention. We might have returned to the UK in 1961 but had long ago promised ourselves an extended touring holiday of the western USA, and decided that this couldn't be accomplished until 1962.

We travelled to England for the June wedding, flying from Great Falls. Garaging our car, I purchased a new white Chevrolet Impala (m12) sedan, with pale blue trim and arranged to take delivery from Currie Motors in New York the first week of July, intending to drive the new car from New York to

Great Falls on our return and then garage it ready to use the following year for our touring vacation and then ship it back with us to the UK.

Our return flight from London to New York's Idyllwild airport (later renamed JFK after the November 1963 assassination of President Kennedy), coincided with the arrival of 'Hurricane Donna' which had been reduced to a tropical storm as it journeyed north from Florida. The downpour reached alarming proportions, with a prodigious 2 inches of rainfall in two hours. Umbrellas were useless in the gusting wind, while car window wipers made no impression on the water deluging onto windscreens. It was as though we were beneath a huge waterfall. Continuation of our journey was impossible as wind and rain was of such intensity that all flights and transportation services were cancelled. We were provided with a taxi to convey us to a nearby airport hotel for the night, sharing it with a middle-aged couple, who'd been on the same flight.

Once in the hotel we proceeded to our room to freshen up and then entered the dining room for a meal. There the couple that had shared our taxi invited us to join them at their table. They were Mr and Mrs Ginsberg, from Baltimore, Maryland. We revealed we'd lived there recently and spoke of friends and acquaintances that the others might know. June mentioned Esther Segal, her former department head of the Baltimore Housing Authority. At this, Mrs. Ginsberg said she knew Esther extremely well and frequently met her in her work at the Johns Hopkins Hospital, as the senior social worker, where she had to liase with the Baltimore Housing Authority when accommodation was needed for many of the hospitals poorer patients. June then exclaimed,

"Good heavens then you must be the Sadie Ginsberg I used to call and speak to at Esther's request almost daily."

They were meeting for the first time. Thereafter we exchanged Christmas card greetings for many years.

The following morning the storm had passed. We took a taxi into New York, to collect our new car and set off on a three days journey via Chicago to Great Falls, where we garaged it and reclaimed our Vauxhall, before continuing the last portion of our journey to Eastend. The first of our many preparations had been made for our return to the UK the following year.

Shortly after our return to Eastend we realised that our plan for June to conceive had been successful and we estimated that a baby would be due sometime in mid March 1962.

Our last Christmas in Eastend was disturbed at 1.15 am on December 26 1961, after we'd retired for the night. There was an insistent knocking at our front door, which aroused me from my sleep. Slipping on a dressing gown and slippers, I hastened to turn on the lights and open the front door in the hope that the knocking wouldn't awaken Robin, now almost two years of age. A stranger stood on the doorstep, bundled up against the cold.

"Are you the doctor?" he enquired.

"Yes" I replied. "What's the trouble?"

"I've a sick child in my truck out there. Would you mind takin' a look at him?"

"Of course not, bring him in."

The man scuttled back to his vehicle and returned with his wife, clutching a young child wrapped up in her arms against the cold and a slightly older child, holding tightly to her mother's coat. By this time my wife had joined us and seeing this group had proceeded to the kitchen to prepare hot drinks for the adults and hot milk for the children. As they entered and closed the front door I sat them round the table and with pen and paper started taking notes. The family came from a farm some 20 miles to the west, and the patient, whom the mother was holding was almost 18 months old. The older child, a girl of five years, clinging shyly to her mother was well, but too young to have been left alone, asleep, in the farmhouse.

"What's been the trouble?" I enquired.

The mother explained that her son Billy had been running a fever and had been crying but had seemingly settled down although his fever persisted. He was a chubby well-nourished little fellow who appeared very flushed. I checked his temperature and found it raised. The only other positive findings were a sticky, purulent yellow, discharge from one ear and some prominent lymph glands, in his neck. The child had so far received no medication for his fever or his pain.

"When did you first notice anything wrong?" I enquired.

"It started two days ago with a fever and he begun trowin' up an cryin'."

"And what about this discharge from Billy's ear?"

"That was a bit later, the night afore last I reckons."

"Christmas eve?"

"No the night afore that."

"Do you mean to tell me he's had this problem for over two days?" I asked incredulously. My wife at that moment had returned with the warm drinks and I seized the opportunity to reconstitute a supply of oral penicillin powder that I kept in our refrigerator for emergencies and had the mother give the child his first double dose, having confirmed there were no known allergies. I gave the mother the remainder of the medication and printed instructions to give the medicine strictly every six hours until the course was finished. I asked

218

them to bring the child back to see me in five days, or sooner, if he appeared no better and gave them some medication to bring the child's temperature down. I emphasised the need to keep the child's head out of water until I could confirm the ear had healed. The drinks finished and as Billy was being dressed I asked.

"You told me this started the night before Christmas Eve. Why didn't you bring him in to see me sooner?"

"In case you was gonna keep him in hospital, we didn't wanna spoil his Christmas." The mother responded. My wife and I looked at each other in amazement, hardly crediting the reply.

Later that morning, after my ward round I recounted the night's event to the matron , as we sat drinking coffee and eating the last of the mince pies in her office. When I announced the names of the parents there was a startled gasp of surprise.

"Yes I know it's too incredible to believe that they should imagine a sick 18 month child would need to stay home so as not to miss Christmas." I said.

"Dr Powell you don't know the half. Three years ago they brought two sick children in here straight after Christmas. They were both hospitalised. The little girl of two recovered, the younger one, a boy, a little over a year old died of pneumonia."

I had to assume Billy recovered, since his feckless parents never returned for me to check his ear as I'd instructed.

One of the more amusing of these early morning calls came one cold night in the fall of 1961 when two plump women, almost beyond the recall of middle age, arrived at about 3 am awakening me with their insistent knocking. In dressing gown and slippers I let them into the front room and offered each a seat. They lived on neighbouring farms some 25 miles to the west of town and the elder of the two, who was in an almost frenzied state of worry, spoke first. She explained that there had been a domestic upset which resulted in her having a furious argument with her husband, who'd as usual, been drinking. She admitted that her husband's periodic binge drinking, which had been a regular feature of their marital life always descended into discord and argument, although the following day when sober he was always apologetic and considerate, promising he would never let it happen again. At the culmination of their most recent disagreement, he had leapt out of bed without a stitch of clothing on. Clutching his bottle, he'd rushed outside, completely naked, and had fled in his truck, driving erratically into the night.

When three hours had elapsed and he hadn't returned, she was beside herself with worry. She alerted her neighbour, whose husband went out searching for him, as did his two adult children who lived at home with their parents. The neighbour's wife, who was at her side, had driven her into town to solicit my help. I sympathised with her problem and asked how I might help.

"He's gotta bad heart an' with nothin' on, this cold aint gonna be doin' him no good at awl, will it Mary?" turning to her friend for confirmation. "Would you please come out an' help us find him."

"I don't quite see how I can find your husband, particularly in the dark, if you don't know where he is. Even if I found him I can't lasso a moving truck can I? I'd suggest your best bet is to call in the RCMP."

"I can't do thet. If the mounties finds him wit' an open bottle in the truck they'll be bound to trow the book at 'im. He's already on the Indian list an they'll be sure to put 'im inside an takeaway his driver's licence."

At this juncture Mary, the neighbour explained that her neighbour's husband had a long-standing drink problem with a number of convictions for driving while under the influence of alcohol. The nub of the problem was that if the RCMP were to find him in charge of a truck in his inebriated state, or regardless of his sobriety, with an open bottle of alcohol in a motor vehicle, he would in all likelihood receive a custodial sentence, since the judge had warned him at the time of his most recent conviction, less than a year ago, that he'd have him thrown into jail.

At this point the wife, the elder of the pair pleaded, almost in tears. "You gotta help me find him, afore the Mounties gets to him first."

This woman wasn't disturbed about her husband's heart or his exposure to the elements. She was more concerned that family and friends should find her alcoholic husband before the police found him in his intoxicated state, in charge of a motor vehicle. I persuaded them that there was no way in which I could help at this juncture but would be pleased to see her husband if he felt he would like assistance in dealing with either his drink or heart problem. Some twenty minutes later, they reluctantly left, allowing me to return to my bed and sleep.

* * *

Norman Green had taken flying lessons and was a qualified pilot. He recommended that this was one of the safest modes of transport mile for mile and that I should give it a try. He subsequently purchased a twin engine machine for long distance flights. The flat open prairie was certainly an ideal place for aviation and I arranged with Glen Smith to give me lessons. Glen who co-owned Eastend's hardware store with his brother Ross, had spent the war years training RAF pilots in Alberta and was a highly skilled pilot and instructor. In addition to giving flying lessons he also provided a sought after crop spraying service.

He gave me a number of weekly lessons, which I thoroughly enjoyed. After I had completed several hours of instruction and was preparing to fly solo, my wife put her foot down. That week there had been an aircraft accident in the nearby town of Lethbridge. Two doctors had taken to the air just before dusk to make a short journey. Neither had any instrument rating in their flying experience and had cut the timing for their journey a little too finely. On descending to land, they apparently failed to remember, or with the failing light to heed the power cables on the runway approach. In the twilight, the plane's wheels collided with the cables. It crashed and immediately burst into flames. There was no fire fighting equipment at the landing strip and there were no survivors. Both doctors were married and between them had seven children. News of this accident spread rapidly, particularly in the medical community, following which June, for the second and last time in our marriage, firmly gave me an ultimatum. She explained that she didn't want me to fly and if I were to persist she would return to England straight away. My flying lessons ceased that week.

A small number of people had planes that were kept at the small landing strip in Eastend. Bob Heggety the pharmacist was an owner. On one occasion he related how the previous day, to save time, he'd filled his fuel tank with gasoline with the intention of making an early start on his journey the following morning. The next morning he arrived at the airfield, made all his usual pre flight checks started the engine and taxied down to the end of the runway. There he turned the plane into the morning breeze, stopped and repeated his instrument checks, which included checking the fuel gauge which he'd omitted to do when he started the engine. It registered zero. He tapped the gauge which refused to budge. He wisely decided to taxi back to the parking area, where he cut the engine climbed out of the plane and made a visual inspection of his fuel level. The tank, which should have been full, was empty and had he taken off, he would have run out of fuel, with lethal consequences.

Theft of gasoline from farms or aeroplanes was one of the more troublesome problems to arise from time to time. Whether perpetrated by some of the youth for a prank, or simply financial gain there could be some unfortunate consequences. One such event occurred just after sunset. A farmer who had experienced previous problems with young 'joy riders' stealing fuel from the pump he kept in his yard to supply his tractors and vehicles, noticed a car at his pump. He turned on the electric lamps he had installed to illumine the area to enable him to identify the thieves. He then picked up his hunting rifle and ran outside, waving his arms to stop the miscreants. There were two young men who promptly leapt into their car, started the engine and ignoring the irate owner's demand to stop attempted to speed from the scene. Whether attempting to scare, or to stop them the farmer raised his gun and let fly with three or four shots at the rapidly accelerating car now partially obscured by a following cloud of dust.

I became aware of a crisis when I received an urgent call from the hospital to attend a young man who'd just arrived and had been shot. I rushed over to the hospital to examine him and there on a trolley lay a young man in his late teens in considerable distress. Pulling back the covering sheet he lay there with his trouser top open and partially pulled down. Raising his shirt I saw a collection of pale pink small bowel, with a number of perforations, staring at me like some exotic tropical insect eaten flower, protruding from an opening in the lower left side of his abdomen and in the centre, stamen like, was the shiny silver spent bullet. The bullet had struck the car entered through the patient's back at an angle just above the left sacro-iliac joint and travelling laterally had finally exited where I had discovered it, perforating the bowel.

Hastily I administered morphine for the young man's pain and put up an Iv drip, before placing a call to summon the air ambulance advising that I had a patient presenting as a surgical emergency with a perforated bowel from a gunshot wound. Within two hours the plane arrived and the patient was taken to the airstrip in the back of a pick up truck to be flown to Regina. Following his ordeal he returned home after some weeks with a residual limp. As the bullet passed through his back into his abdomen it had injured nerves of the lumbar-sacral plexus in the left side of his back. As a consequence of this nerve damage, considerable muscle weakness had developed, leaving him lame in his left leg.

Some three months later I was subpoenaed to appear in court to give medical evidence relating to the wounds sustained by my patient. Appearing in a court of law is a harrowing experience to be avoided whenever possible. Once sworn in I was asked by the prosecuting attorney to give my medical qualifications and occupation, together with a brief résumé of my clinical experience. He then asked me to describe briefly to the court the scene that I had found when I first examined the patient and to describe my course of action. When I had finished, it was the defence attorney's turn to cross-examine me.

"Doctor Powell, you say you were the first doctor to examine this gentleman."

"Yes sir."

"Further more you describe when you examined him that he had a bullet wound in the lower left abdomen."

"Yes, that's quite so."

"How doctor, did you know that it was a bullet wound?"

"Well for a number of reasons. Firstly an experienced duty nurse at the hospital summoned me to see a patient who she described had been shot. When I questioned the patient, he gave an account of seeing somebody with a gun running in his direction as they drove off in their truck. He recounted hearing a number of bangs followed by severe pain in his back and abdomen. When I examined him there was a wound in the abdominal wall with perforated bowel protruding through it and in the middle I could unmistakably see a bullet."

"Doctor you say that you could see a bullet. How did you know it was a bullet?"

"It was a shiny silver metallic object and I could see that it was a bullet. I've seen bullets before."

"Are you a ballistics missile expert?"

"No."

"Have you ever received training in ballistics?"

"No I haven't."

"Then how do you know for certain that it was a bullet?"

"Because it looked like a bullet."

"But you clearly stated you have no expertise with ballistics."

"That's correct, but in the same way I don't have to be a philatelist to recognise a postage stamp when I see one or a numismatist to recognise a coin, I don't need to be a ballistics expert to recognise a bullet when I see it." I replied becoming rather exasperated.

At this juncture the judge interrupted, addressing nobody in particular saying.

"I think you've made your point." Following which, the defence attorney announced.

"Thank you. I have no further questions for this witness."

Picking up my notes, I left the court, feeling as elated as any free man.

(M12) A new 4 door Chevrolet Impala automobile purchased June 1961 cost $2,200, with western springing, safety seat lap belts for front and rear passengers, a rarity at the time, and every conceivable extra was included, except air conditioning, which was unavailable.

Chapter 15

SASKATCHEWAN

1962

On March 23rd, almost two weeks late, June went into labour for her second confinement. There had been a normal pregnancy, apart from the time I'd returned home one afternoon two weeks earlier, in response to her urgent telephone call, begging me to return home at once. I entered to see my shivering pregnant wife seated on the couch with a tea towel draped round her shoulders, trying to dry herself and our two year old son at her feet.

June had been taking a bath and when she'd finished had stood up in the bathtub, picked up the bathrobe that she had left on a stool close by, and started to put it on. It was then that she noticed a short length of string protruding from the pocket. Placing her hand in the pouch to determine what the string might be attached to, she suddenly felt something warm and furry move. She emitted a shriek, dropped the robe in the bath and fled, not for the first time, when confronted with a 'wee timorous mouse'.

Unfortunately all the towels were kept in the bathroom cupboard, and fearful of facing her rodent adversary, the only cloth she could find with which to dry herself was a tea towel from the kitchen. When I retrieved the robe from the bathtub, having let out the water, I discovered the poor mouse; unable to escape from the towelling pocket had unfortunately drowned.

Once more I exchanged the role of husband for obstetrician and had the privilege of safely delivering June of the second of our children. My initial impression as this child slowly appeared was of an exceptionally tall bright-eyed baby. At 4.20am on March 24th when all was revealed, we discovered to our immense delight that we now had a daughter. Some days later we named her Melanie at which time, quite unexpectedly, I received a gift of a greatly treasured gold Parker fountain pen with a card from a nameless patient inscribed 'To my favourite obstetrician'.

*   *   *

In our paediatric training it had been drummed into our heads repeatedly that no sick child should ever be turned away without being seen, and no child should receive medication without first being examined. No story of my exploits in Canada would be complete without recording the saga of little Tommy S.

Tommy was the seven years old son of a farmer and his wife who lived 18 miles north east of Eastend. He was delightfully impish. A lively, wiry little fellow, full of fun with mischievous eyes, but who was unfortunately prone to eczema and severe episodic attacks of asthma, prior to the advent of inhalers and nebulisers.

One Saturday afternoon Mr. S, who suffered from marked ankylosing spondylitis attended my office. At the end of his consultation he asked me if I would prescribe some medicine for Tommy who was back at the farm and had recently developed a feverish cough, which was becoming more severe. I explained that I could not prescribe anything without first seeing the child.

"Aw c'mmon Doc, you've seen Tommy lottsa times before, and you know what he's like and how bad he can get, when he's one of his coughs."

"Sorry, I've a rule that I don't prescribe until I've seen the patient."

"But it'll take me a good hour or more to get to the farm to fetch him back here and his cough's bin gettin worse."

"Sorry Mr S, those are my rules."

"But the dust on the journey's bound to make him far worse. That's why I didn't bring him with me in the first place. Be reasonable, couldn't you wave your rules just this once?"

"I'll tell you what I'm prepared to do. I'm going to give you an antibiotic to give him prior to your setting out and an antihistamine cough medicine, just sufficient for one dose. You can only have this if you promise to bring him in straight away to see me. Do you agree?"

Mr. S reluctantly agreed. I gave him the starter doses of medication and Mr S promised that he'd administer the medicine and would return with his son within the hour. He then shuffled out of my office, extending his flexed head forward as best he could, his illness, forcing his gaze, to look constantly at the ground, as though subservient and diminished.

True to his word, Mr. S returned with his son just over an hour later. Tommy didn't appear at all well. He was in the midst of an asthmatic attack and had a slight fever. I arranged his admission to the hospital where I gave him a subcutaneous injection of adrenaline and organised that he be nursed in an oxygen tent with a humidifier. I increased his dose of antibiotic and left him under nursing supervision.

That evening we went to the cinema. The film show ended just after 9 pm and before returning home, as was my custom each evening before retiring, I visited the hospital to check my patients. I went into Tommy's room. The oxygen tent was filled with water vapour and it was difficult to see the patient in the darkened room through the mist. The nurse assured me the child was

225

sleeping comfortably but I insisted I needed to check him, and she assisted me in folding back the transparent plastic tent. There I found Tommy's condition, unobserved by the nursing staff, because of the dense mist, had deteriorated dramatically. He was showing all the signs of severe respiratory obstruction, his chest sounds were gurgling and he was unconscious.

The nurse and I immediately commenced aspirating the mucous blocking his airways, with a suction pump, but to little avail, while a further subcutaneous dose of adrenaline made little difference. Another member of the staff was sent to telephone the child's parents to summon them urgently, for I was of the opinion that he was about to succumb and there was no way in which he could be transferred by air ambulance to a specialist paediatric unit in time to save him.

Tommy, who had now received, without benefit, copious doses of antibiotics, antihistamines and subcutaneous adrenaline, was about to die. Inexorably his life was slipping from our grasp. Urgent measures were called for and I felt desperately inadequate. Terrified at the thought of attempting my first tracheotomy on so small an individual, I decided upon another strategy. I managed to find a vein in his slender young arm, into which I secured a line to administer intravenous fluids and medication. I immediately gave him a large intravenous dose of cortisone rationalising that as Tommy's life ebbed away we had nothing more to lose. Desperately we reinstated the oxygen tent hoping and praying, that its vaporiser pumping in clouds of cool moisture and oxygen might somehow help.

Within thirty minutes of summoning them, Tommy's distraught parents arrived. Prepared for the worst Mrs S. was in tears. The nurse drew back the oxygen tent cover that they might take one last look at their moribund son vainly battling for his life.

Tommy lay there breathing normally, peacefully asleep, soaked in the vaporiser's moisture. Miraculously there was no sign of the distress or bubbling respirations of but a few minutes earlier. His parents clutched each other and wept with relief and the staff and I could easily have joined them. Tommy remained in hospital for a total of 48 hours as his respiratory problem subsided, after which he returned home fully recovered. I dread to think what might have happened had I not undertaken to make rounds on my patient's that evening, or worse still had Tommy been put to bed at home with his medicine, unseen by a doctor.

One of the lessons I learned repeatedly was that a patient, taking a regimen of medication at home for an acute medical problem might fare badly, yet in hospital with the same dose often improved rapidly, suggesting a far better compliance when under strict nursing supervision.

Mrs Marsden, a patient who lived on a farm about 15 miles just beyond Consul was pregnant with her forth child. In view of the speed of her last two confinements and her great distance from the hospital, she decided to obtain board and lodging as a paying guest of a lady whose house backed onto the grounds of the hospital. She moved in approximately four weeks before her due date and intended that when her labour commenced she would simply walk the fifty yards from that house to the hospital's rear entrance, which was never locked. When at approximately 10 pm. her labour commenced she collected her packed bag and proceeded as fast as she could to the hospital. As she entered the back door she screamed out for help. Her baby was born on the doorstep just as the night nurse arrived to assist her.

One of the Hutterite ladies who attended me for her confinement was delivered of a healthy little boy. She elected to have him circumcised and we arranged that this would take place the following day. When visiting the hospital for my evening, ward round, close to midnight after my clinic in Consul, there was a message awaiting me, requesting that no matter how late it might be Mrs. Walters wanted me to call to see her, and to be awakened even should she be asleep, as she wanted to speak to me. Expecting that she wished to cancel the following morning's surgery I visited her. The room was in darkness, yet she remained awake. As I entered she immediately greeted me. Taking my hand in hers she entreated me with the words.

"Doctor, you will be careful not to cut off too much tomorrow."

I was able to reassure her that no more than was necessary would be removed, with which she kissed my hand, still clasped in hers and murmured.

"Thank you." Then releasing it turned over and went to sleep.

* * *

Politicians according to their own agendas invariably distort history and events. In the province of Saskatchewan there was no exception. Aided and abetted by the media creating and conjuring up news, a non-existent event was reported. The socialist New Democratic Party stated that in opposition to the intended provincial socialised medical reforms, a doctor's strike was planned in Saskatchewan in the summer of 1962.

Nothing could have been further from the truth. The medical profession, with many British graduates, had been simmering with justifiable concern over the proposed introduction of a socialised care programme in Saskatchewan, which would have closely resembled the 'Swift Current Health Service No. 1' insurance programme. The province voted for the conservative Mr Diefenbaker in Toronto but locally the New Democrats were now the prevailing majority party with Tommy Douglas their left wing leader as prime minister.

Representation to the provincial government, by the medical profession, fell on deaf ears. The medical leadership held a number of regional meetings

227

where it was decided to challenge the government to persuade the New Democrats to back down on the proposed introduction of their medical care programme. The doctors overwhelmingly decided that 75% of their members would take a month's summer vacations simultaneously, while the remaining 25% of the Colleges would be left to provide an emergency service, that there might be no hardship through loss of medical service. Further it was agreed that each of these doctors would work in a practice other than their own, giving none any material advantage, or gain.

The Provincial Government threatened that if this were to take place, they would recruit English doctors to replace what they irresponsibly labelled 'The Striking Doctors.' As events unfolded the provincial government claimed to have recruited 900 UK doctors to break the 'strike', which at one per 1,100 Canadian residents seemed excessive.

Flown from England straight to Regina, prior to the days of the Jumbo jet it seemed remarkable to have crammed so many into the solitary turbojet photographed with these many hundreds of medical saviours. Upon arrival, illegally dispatched to minister to the sick, since they were without medical registration, or prior hospital accreditation, they were provided with a car, the assurance of an inflated salary, and then sent out to deal with the ailing Saskatchewan public, simultaneously breaking the doctors strike. The sole beneficiaries were the news media who in the summer doldrums could send out reporters to create news stories, and the handful of British doctors, who funded by the provincial government availed themselves of a heaven sent opportunity to visit the province for work experience without need of immigration or other documentation.

It had taken me several weeks to have my credentials checked and authenticated by the Saskatchewan College of Physicians and Surgeons, to obtain my medical license and then to apply for hospital privileges. I never met any doctor, nurse or patient who ever saw any of these medical recruits, although I know of one who flew over and settled in Alberta. I'm convinced there were others, certainly no more than a token few and not hundreds as the provincial government alleged.

The media caught up with at least one 'strikebreaking doctor', who collected his car with his initial cash payment and proceeded to drive in a southwesterly direction. Apparently navigation wasn't one of his skills, since he missed all the signs enroute until he mistakenly found himself at San Francisco's Fisherman's wharf. There, an understanding police department re-routed him, to Regina assisting him with a generous, all expenses paid escort, in case of any further confusion in map reading.

I had taken two vacations, with a total duration of 5 weeks during my first two years in Canada, on each occasion returning to London for a family wedding. Fortunately these had coincided with the quietest time in the farming year before the August harvest period with its plethora of accidents and injuries. At holiday times I had arranged with a colleague to cover my practice in case of emergencies, while I reciprocated in like manner. The arrangements the college were proposing made no difference in my practice, accept that the colleague I delegated to render emergency care would similarly be on holiday and a completely unknown doctor would provide medical cover.

Our Canadian adventure had been extended incrementally, from one to three years. We believed that the educational needs of our children required that schooling should commence before 6 years of age and entry into the first grade. We needed to move back to London or relocate in a major city. The previous year we had made our decision to leave in 1962, but first was our planned tour of the west.

Poring over maps we plotted a 6,000 miles route that we would cover in 6 weeks, our southernmost destination, Tijuana, Mexico, just south of SanDiego. To help with the children, Kay Vanderzaan volunteered to leave her family and accompany us. We purchased a tent, camp beds and camping equipment, as this was to be a camping holiday, when weather permitted, since we intended stop-overs at a number of national parks en-route, which provided well equipped camp sites. In addition we contacted family and friends in various parts of California, whom we intended visiting.

Our vacation commenced by driving into Montana and changing to our more spacious new Chevrolet. From Great Falls our first destination was the picturesque Glacier National Park and then south into Yellowstone National Park. We then wended our way through Utah, and Nevada to Las Vegas, followed by Lake Tahoe and then on to Sacramento where we visited June's school friend Vera and her husband Lester Smith. Onwards we progressed to San Francisco and then south to Carmel, one of the most delightful west coast resort areas and then along the fearsomely tortuous coastal route to San Simeon and William Randolph 'Hirst's Castle', which had just opened to the public earlier that year. We proceeded south to Santa Barbara and Los Angeles where we visited cousins and enjoyed the wonders of Disneyland, which had opened in 1955, before proceeding to San Diego and then south into Mexico. In San Diego we were able to watch a historic, first ever coast-to-coast televised broadcast, made by President J.F.Kennedy from the White House via a satellite. We returned via Oregan to Seattle and the 'World Fair', witnessing the demonstration of a telephone that also transmitted a picture of the speaker. We then drove eastwards passing hundreds of miles of orchards, wheat and cornfields, until we returned home. I don't believe we would ever have been able to accomplish this extended vacation, had we not been living in North America at the time.

Arriving back in Eastend we were faced with a dilemma. We received news that my father who for years had suffered from high blood pressure had been admitted to Guy's hospital, where he lay incapacitated by a major CVA (stroke), affecting his speech and the use of his right arm and leg. While there was little I could do about this terrible situation, I felt that my presence in London might provide some moral support. My colleagues and friends Norman Green and Alan Fletcher were bent upon migrating to the US. The average time spent by most doctors in the harsh climactic conditions of the prairies was three years and we had now passed that watershed. The time had arrived to move on.

We decided to leave Eastend in mid November and return to London. The following few weeks were a sad winding down. We had originally considered returning via San-Francisco and across the Pacific but opted, due to my father's illness, for the shorter route, with the idea of visiting my father's sister who lived in Montreal and visiting friends in New York and Baltimore enroute. We booked our passage on the SS United States, the 'Blue Riband' trans Atlantic record holder, departing from New York at the end of November for Southampton. I continued my practice as we prepared to sell up and pack, crate and arrange the shipping of goods we were taking back with us.

The household goods that weren't accompanying us were sold in a garage sale in November. There were sad good byes to friends, colleagues and patients, the general consensus was that within a few weeks of life back in England we would realise we'd made a terrible mistake and would soon return.

Our penultimate visit to Great Falls and our American friends was in October. Sid Wasserman entreated us to postpone our departure. In September the US government had discovered photographic evidence of Soviet Russian rockets, capable of carrying nuclear warheads being assembled in Fidel Castro's communist Cuba. Worse still, further rockets were enroute to Castro on Soviet ships. The US had implemented a naval blockade on the sea-lanes to Cuba and midst mounting tension stated their intention of stopping further shipments. There was fear of this escalating into war. This might be the international flashpoint between the major nuclear powers, with the soviet leader Nikita Khrushchev challenging President Kennedy.

Sid pleaded with us that we place our departure on hold, until the crisis had resolved. He gravely informed me in confidence that his maintenance units were working flat out to sustain a flight of US bombers circling in Alaskan air space throughout 24 hours of every day. This was classified information, unavailable to the public. His concern was that every one of those bombers had a nuclear capability and was fully armed. If the cold war escalated with nuclear projectiles and bombs we would undoubtedly be safer in a remote prairie township than in London or some major centre of population. Many decades later, the Cuban missile crisis may seem to have been rather inconsequential, but at the time it was a major crisis heading the world towards a terrifying Armageddon and we seriously pondered the need to postpone our departure.

We hadn't been home for 16 months, our parents had never seen their granddaughter a beautiful child of 7 months and my father remained seriously ill following his CVA. Mentally we were attuned to return to the UK. I felt that if our stay was extended, the more difficult would be the period of readjustment in the UK and the greater possibility that we might be tempted to return to settle in the USA as our friends were doing.

Our last day in Canada was in mid November. The Soviet missile crisis had been resolved and we had said our final farewells. Packing cases had been shipped out. Our house remained unsold, but our attorney friend, Ray Snyder, assured us that given time he was bound to find a purchaser at the expected price. With suitcases packed with the clothes we would need on our journey we drove out of Eastend shortly after breakfast for what was to be the last time, with our two Canadian children on board, our first destination Great Falls, to retrieve our new car. As we reached the top of the small incline to the north east of town I stopped the car. We gazed back and suddenly a damn was breached, as tears uncontrollably flooded down.

Having initially hated this semi arid area when we arrived, to such an extent that had we had the finances to leave we would have fled to greener climes, I was unimaginably blubbering like a child deprived of some favourite toy. We had spent 40 months of our lives on the prairies and were now leaving never to return. I had enjoyed practicing medicine in this sparsely populated community and as I stared one last time at the prairie community that had been our home, little did I realise, that never would I find medical practice more varied and challenging. Life had been hard, and it seemed that seldom had there been a day without some fresh and often exciting predicament that had taught us great self-reliance.

Sadly we retraced our familiar route south to Great Falls, one last time, where I sold our Vauxhall and picked up our Chevrolet. We then proceeded eastwards to Baltimore to rejoin our friends the Kaplan's and to complete some last minute shopping, buying gifts for family members, most of which were stolen when our car was broken into in New York. We travelled to Montreal to visit my aunt Rebecca who had lived in that city since 1945 with her husband and son Russell following her wartime marriage to a Canadian serviceman.

We embarked upon the SS United States, in New York for Southampton on the last day of November, our car in the stowage hold and arrived in London five days later. Our household goods were delayed by a longshoreman's strike and arrived following a six months delay. On our return we stayed with June's parents in their home, greeted by the coldest winter since 1947. The British had learned nothing when compared to the provincial prairie Canadians when it came to coping with snow and ice. On the prairies with daily subzero temperatures we had never felt as cold as we found ourselves in London.

Our home in Eastend remained unsold for more than three years after our return to the UK. A former patient bought the house and Ray Snyder who dealt with the conveyance generously refused to charge for his services in gratitude for the medical assistance I'd provided during my brief tenure in the community.

Chapter 16

LONDON

1963

That first year on our return to London was the most depressing of my career, a period in which I was unable to secure a regular income, find a practice, or establish a home, and a year in which my grandmother and father passed away. One of the few happy events took place six months after our homecoming, when the last of our family arrived. Our new daughter, described by June as her 'English Flower', was named after my paternal grandmother Zosha, who died earlier that month. Delivered at the Royal Northern Hospital by UCH obstetrician Joe Holmes, the only difficulty was that experienced by the hospital staff who had to question each maternity patient in an attempt to identify the recipient for the huge bouquet of flowers sent for delivery to a Miss June Fraiman by Fred Fraiman, since there were no unmarried mothers and no one of that name in the hospital.

The winter was particularly cold, and while not comparable with Canada's arctic clime, with the absence of adequate heating and thermal insulation in home, work place and public transport, chilblains returned which made life uncomfortably miserable. We continued our stay as guests in my parents in law's home for fifteen months. Had it not been for their unstinting hospitality, I'm certain we would never have been able to persevere during the lengthy transition that proved necessary for me to establish myself in a practice and provide a home for my family.

Our preference was to live in proximity to family in North London. The acquisition of a home was beset by many problems two of which proved almost insurmountable. I was unable to purchase a home until I knew in which area I would practice, as I would need to live within close commuting distance when on call. No building society or bank would provide a mortgage facility in excess of three times the borrower's annual salary and since I had yet to establish a regular income, I found myself barred from access to funds needed to assist in the purchase of a house, while the requirements for renting a home proved equally daunting.

We searched for months to find a suitable home and in the autumn of 1963 found a spacious five-bedroom house constructed in 1928 that the original owner wished to sell. Located close to my parents in law's home in

Broadfields Avenue, it had been built for £2,400 (M13). A price was agreed, but before moving in, the thirty five-year-old dwelling needed complete renovation. Part of this process involved the installation of what many considered expensive novelties, such as thermal insulation, double-glazing and ducted hot air central heating. In the spring of 1964 we moved into our incompletely decorated partially furnished home and continued painting and decorating with the assistance of a part time handyman for several months more. That summer, in between locum work, running my new practice and seeing patients at any time of the day or night I was summoned, I spent my spare time wearing rubber gloves and painting the exterior of our home, instead of taking recreational time off, or a holiday.

I applied for every National Health Service post advertised in the Greater London region at that time. In a small number I was short listed for interview and attended along with a few other hopeful applicants, some considerably older than myself, only to later discover the post had been awarded to a more successful candidate. Once more I found myself in the unenviable environment of too many doctors chasing too few vacancies. In May 1963 shortly before my youngest daughter's birth, I had applied for a newly advertised practice vacancy and had then been eliminated at interview. Waiting, along with four other rejected short listed hopefuls, I was informed that my application had been unsuccessful. The other applicants dejectedly walked away and to the surprise of the committee, I had the temerity to knock and, re-enter the interview room unannounced.

I apologised politely for the intrusion and asked the chairman of the committee if he or the board could spare a few minutes to give me some indication why I'd failed and what I should do to improve my future chance of success. The chairman, taken aback, explained, as I stood there.

"This is all a little irregular but it was the group's opinion that having been abroad for such a long period you've insufficient experience of practice in this country to be a principal. We unanimously felt, that you'd stand a far greater possibility of success if you obtained work as an assistant or locum for another two or three years to gain more experience. There are of course vacancies in more sparsely populated regions where there is a great shortage of medical personnel and even at this stage; your chance of success would be infinitely greater."

He was implying that were I to work in the Orkneys or Outer Hebrides I could immediately find a practice opening. I felt as though I was back at Treelon attempting to gain entry into Canada. I couldn't find a post in a NHS general practice other than as a poorly remunerated locum since according to this committee, I lacked experience of practice in the UK, and yet I might be sufficiently experienced to work in the sparsely populated remote areas of the British Isles, with fewer amenities than on the prairies.

Thanking the chairman for his candour I strode out of the room feeling humiliated and angry. I was unaware of any significant difference in medical practice throughout the western world, apart from terminology and language and considered the advice illogical. I had trained and completed my house jobs here and I'd been employed in London as a locum over the past five months in several practices. I'd been qualified six years and laboured day and night in English and American hospitals followed by practice in some of the harshest conditions in one of the most remote corners of the world gaining clinical experience in a practice area far in excess of Greater London. I'd sutured wounds, set fractures, performed dozens of surgical procedures alone and while assisting others, and given anaesthetics. I'd delivered scores of babies without mishap. I'd immunised, cauterised, injected and investigated, counselled, rescued, resuscitated and even extracted teeth in the absence of a dentist. I'd cross-matched blood and given transfusions, set up intravenous infusions, taken blood samples for investigation, checked x-rays. I'd immersed myself in everything that I considered might prepare me to be a competent GP. The advice really didn't make sense and it was then that I resolved to start my own practice.

Since returning I discovered in my work as a locum that many single-handed practices were in 'lock up shops', or inadequate portions of a domestic dwelling and none were purpose built. Some were an unhygienic disgrace, lacking in almost every basic facility in comparison with those I knew in North America. Coupled with this was the absence of any facility to perform any minor surgery, or medical investigations, apart from a basic urine test or syringing wax from an ear. Invariably there was no secretarial or ancillary help, to maintain any order, or assist with correspondence. Patient records were housed in inappropriately small expandable antiquated wallets, designed in the days of Lloyd George, often crammed with misfiled indecipherable written cards, with patient notes unavailable, illegible and sometimes missing. Saddest of all was the revelation of the waiting to which patients were subjected for non-emergency procedures. Up to three months hanging around for a hospital appointment was commonplace, with all the attendant fretful stress for all concerned.

The time lapse between consultation and undergoing an investigative procedure followed by the protracted period that must intervene before any results could be obtained and relayed to the GP was a blot on the health service. A simple hernia repair might necessitate a wait of well over a year. The unnecessary increase in worry and anxiety to which patients and their families were subjected was totally unacceptable, yet in spite of these inadequacies, government constantly trumpeted that the UK had the finest health service in the world, which was complacent nonsense.

As a British G.P I missed the total lack of access to hospital beds. Student clinical instruction had been hospital based, as were two further postgraduate years of training. In Canada as a GP for more than three years, I had privileges to investigate and care for patients in hospital. In the United Kingdom GP's were totally excluded from both hospital beds and A&E departments. Something had to be seriously amiss either with student training, or the role allocated to the GP when reviewing the shortage of medical manpower within the hospitals, which created appalling bottlenecks and delay.

One of the worst of many paradoxes I encountered on my return was the 'Pap Smear Test'. This Papanicolaou test **(1) (M14)** provided a reliable means for the timely detection of cells, which untreated, could soon become malignant, resulting in cancer of the uterine cervix (neck of the womb). This test had been widely available in the USA and Canada at minor cost since the late 1940's. In the UK in 1963 and for twenty years thereafter this was only available within the NHS to a woman over the age of 40 and only once in five years. Younger women were inexplicably excluded. Privately it was readily available at minimal expense for a woman of any age. More than 12,000 women from their mid twenties onwards were dying each year from a disease that with timely diagnosis was preventable.

Had three coach loads of women passengers plunged off a road killing all 120 in the prime of life there would have been a public outcry. Had an identical number perished in an outbreak of cholera in a local hospital, somebody might have noticed and raised a question in parliament. Maybe some campaigning news reporter on the Mail, Telegraph, or Times might have earned their spurs by agitating for safer driving or cleaner hospitals and water; There was never even a mention on the popular David Frost TV show 'That Was The Week That Was', yet 240 deaths occurred every week from cancer of the uterine cervix, which was at the time the second most common cancer in women and not a murmur to suggest that the community cared, or the world's finest health service might be found wanting.

There was an outcry in 1963 because John Profumo, a government minister of war had lied to the House of Commons over an extramarital tryst with Christine Keeler, a call girl involved in a relationship with a soviet naval attaché. Some might claim Prime Minister Harold MacMillan's Tory government fell to Labour's Harold Wilson the following year because of this sleaze. A minister's lies and sexual peccadillo's were of greater concern to the press and government than the disturbing numbers of preventable deaths from cancer of the cervix.

In 1997 a paper published in the BMJ (British Medical Journal) **(M15)** confirmed that screening was saving 1,300 lives each year. To my knowledge no Member of Parliament ever raised this issue and no minister in the health department was ever called to account. According to that BMJ article more than 44,000 lives had been needlessly lost in the previous twenty-four years between 1963 and 1988 when universal screening was introduced. A memorial should be erected in Parliament Square to the women who died needlessly from cancer of the uterine cervix due to the ineptitude of NHS planners.

There were further sets of astoundingly preventable mortality and morbidity figures affecting every member of the public, of which doctors were aware, as were successive governments and yet no legislation had been introduced. According to Dr Doll's 1954 ground breaking report, smoking was killing and injuring many tens of thousands annually and yet had seemingly been ignored. Road traffic fatalities and injuries could have been significantly reduced with the introduction of a few basic measures, known for many years and implemented in other countries; cars to drive on dipped headlamps, at night and when visibility was reduced by poor weather; speed limit restrictions; the effects of alcohol impairing a driver's judgement were documented. Since there is no 'safe level' of alcohol consumption for pilots when flying, the same should rationally apply when driving a motor vehicle, piloting a boat or swimming. The use of safety seat belts in vehicles and crash barriers separating contra flow traffic on motorways. Apart from the latter, most could have been introduced with minimal cost to the exchequer, yet no regulation, except the speed limit **(M16)** on derestricted roads introduced in December 1965, appeared for decades.

I was increasingly disillusioned and frustrated as a GP mainly due to the unacceptable delays in investigative and treatment facilities that had been swiftly available to my patients in North America and which were only obtainable promptly in the private sector or within the NHS when linked to an emergency admission.

In Saskatchewan, the fluoride content of water to provide for the development of good strong healthy teeth was extremely low. The optimal three parts per million was achieved by women taking fluoride as part of an antenatal package and young children receiving a minute daily dose added to a beverage. On my return to London I discovered the fluoride content of water was similarly low. Contacting the department of health I had preliminary discussions concerning ways of raising the levels of fluoride for children and expectant mothers. These talks were terminated when a senior civil servant explained that fluoridation and dental conservation costs per head would far exceed the seventeen-shilling (85p.) cost of extracting a diseased tooth and the scheme would therefore not be cost effective.

No doctor in Saskatchewan outside of a specialised centre in Saskatoon received payment for treating a patient with cancer. Every patient had to be referred to this facility, which developed as a centre of excellence. Patients accepted the inconvenience of distance, for the advantage of a better prognosis in the treatment of such ills. In the UK, a complacent shortcoming was a failure to recognise the need and advantages of such centres, which evolved only years later.

*　*　*

I secured a one-year lease on a ground floor room at 22 Harley Street at a modest rent. With the help of June, and a painter, we decorated and furnished it, following which the interminable wait for patients began, during which I continued with a succession of locum posts, in the process meeting behaviour from some medical colleagues that defied credulity.

The BMA (British Medical Association) recommended a salary of 35 guineas per week (£36.75p) for full time locum employment. I soon learned that 'Locum required, with a view to partnership.' advertisements in medical journals were little more than rhetoric, the suggested 'view' a sight of anything but a partnership and worse was to follow.

There was Dr. Mark H. a single practitioner in Oakwood, who in the spring of 1963 arranged over the 'phone to pay me 35 guineas per week for a fourteen days locum. At the conclusion, he mailed me a cheque for 50 guineas. I phoned and explained there was a £21 shortfall.

"The cheque I sent is correct. You must have misheard me."

"Dr H, the BMA rate is 35 guineas and that's what you definitely offered and I accepted."

"You need to get your ears syringed. I never said 35, it was 25 guineas and if you think you're getting more, then you can go to hell."

In Harrow, another doctor paid me £70 for two weeks employment and denied the arrangement had been guineas. Dr. C. in Maida Vale who'd broken his lower leg agreed to employ me for 3 weeks as his locum. In the midst of the first surgery he hobbled in on crutches, smoking a cheroot cigar, interrupting a consultation. Blithely he announced.

"I can manage with these crutches, so I won't need your services any more. You can buzz off."

A solicitor's letter drew his attention to the fact that our verbal 'phone contract had been for 3 weeks employment and he was responsible for any loss of income during that time, and so it continued.

One of my most amusing locum posts that year, was for a partnership of two doctors. Richard K and Bernard K who had a large successful NHS practice with a sizeable private clientele in North West London. At the end of my three weeks locum, both doctors agreed they would be pleased to offer me a full time junior partnership with a salary of £2,400 a year which would lead to a full partnership in a year, during which time I would be permitted and encouraged to build up my own private practice in my own time. I would be required to take morning and evening surgeries, except Sundays and attend to home visits and emergency calls on a rota. I explained that I found the offer acceptable; particularly the ability to expand my own private practice, since I'd leased rooms for this purpose some weeks earlier and could develop and attract a private clientele during my free afternoons, with no conflict of interest. Dr Richard asked that he might inspect this facility. Following his visit the partnership offer was amended to provide me with an income of £1,800 pa, since I would not be devoting all my time to their practice. I remonstrated that this was a reduction of 25% for the privilege of utilising my own time in which to develop the private practice they'd suggested. I declined the reduced offer, but continued as a locum for Dr Bernard taking Saturday morning surgeries, for a number of months, receiving £3 for each two hours surgery, while domiciliary visits were excluded.

In the second week, the receptionist, Bernard's mother in law sweetly requested at the conclusion of the surgery.

"Would you mind doing a house call, that's just come in? It's quite close and won't take you much out of your way on your journey home." A charming lady, she smiled and I could hardly refuse.

This continued, week after week, first with one house call, then two, finally increasing to three and four, turning what was intended as a two hours surgery into a task that was taking an additional two hours, in addition to the use of my car and fuel. Following a number of months during which I received no additional offer of payment for any of this unscheduled work I presented Bernard with a modest bill of £3 for my additional services over the previous month, charging five shillings (25p.) for each house call made during the previous four weeks.

His response was as though I'd presented him with a major part of the national debt. He reluctantly paid, stating.

"Arnold, it's most unprofessional that you should make such demands without prior notice. I'm paying you under duress and I certainly shalln't need your services ever again."

Bernard and I met occasionally after this and remained on cordial first name terms. I learned that he and his partner later took rooms for their private patients in Wimpole Street. Over the years I met several doctors who prior to, and after my experience, had received similar offers of partnerships in that practice, which had never materialised.

There were many psychologically difficult months throughout 1963 and 1964 as I struggled to establish myself, but slowly and with perseverance, my practice grew. Family and in particular my father in law, rallied round to recommend patients. Even my receptionist Mrs. O'Rourke, who was also the housekeeper, unbidden by me, walked up and down Harley Street to speak with her fellow housekeepers soliciting that they encourage patients to seek my medical services. I sat every afternoon for months, in isolated solitude, reading, as I waited for patients. During the second quarter a slow trickle of patients appeared, each prepared to pay one and a half guineas for a consultation and should the need arise, three guineas (£3.15p) for a home visit. Within six months, thanks largely to the public relation efforts of my father in law, family members and some of my first patients, I established a small nucleus of an expanding private practice.

One of my first patients was Mrs S, who arrived accompanied by her mother. Incredibly obese, she claimed that her meals were regular and modest in size and she was at a loss to understand the reason for her increasing girth. She appeared to have little insight into the relationship between the copious quantities of snack foods, pastries, cakes and chocolates she munched in between meals and her adiposity. In addition, even though in the fourth decade of life she was enthralled to her mother. I helped her shed layer upon layer of surplus weight during the summer months of 1963. Both mother and daughter were delighted, the mother more so than her daughter. Everywhere this effusive matron socialised in London's swinging sixties society of Carnaby Street and elsewhere, she chatted amongst friends and acquaintances praising the Harley Street doctor who'd just returned to London from America and was miraculously restoring her daughter to more normal dimensions.

Throughout 1963 I continued with my medical locum work whenever this was available. Through one of these locums, I met an older GP, Dr E Joyston-Bechal and at the start of 1964 joined him in Kilburn as a junior partner in his NHS practice. The practice cared for a predominantly Irish community of generous, good-hearted, mainly blue-collar workers and a small number of more recent West Indian immigrants. Few of these patients had refrigerators or washing machines and shopping was a daily necessity, with the complete absence of supermarkets. Every doctor in the area was a UK medical graduate, almost all men in single-handed practice. Each individual doctor provided his own out of hours emergency service. There were no commercial out of hours service providers and little co-operation between doctors for holidays and nights when not on call. My new partnership arrangement gave me the flexibility to continue with my private practice every morning from 9 to 11 am and every afternoon, since the NHS practice hours were 11.30 to 1pm and in the evening 6 to 7.30pm.

At the end of my first year in private practice in July 1964, with my lease at an end I relocated to more spacious accommodation acquiring a seven-year lease on a first floor two-room suite at 100 Harley Street, where my practice continued to expand and thrive. I employed a physiotherapist who used one of the rooms while I used the other.

Teddy Joyston-Bechal, my NHS partner had married shortly after qualifying and simultaneously purchased his medical practice in 1928, in Netherwood Street, for the princely sum of £3,000 from Dr. Jacobs who then moved to Church Street in Lisson Grove. He assured me that in the 1920's Brondesbury was an affluent middle class area, which had rapidly expanded at the end of the 19th century, providing upper class housing for merchants and professional men working in the city. Running diagonally from Marble Arch through the area of his practice was the Edgware Road, which followed the straight Roman 'Watling Street', north beyond Edgware. Every Saturday from the railway bridges at the bottom of Shoot up Hill, (the site of the last turnpike on that section of the road, which was demolished in 1872. An earlier turnpike had first appeared in 1710 at Kilburn Bridge.) Southwards there was a market with stallholders lining both sides of Kilburn High Road down to Kilburn Square with their banter and colourful bazaar wares. In time the local authority decided to restrict market trading to Kilburn Square. Licenses were revoked for stallholders trading in the main road. These traders held out for several years with a simple ploy. Providing they kept moving when requested by the police they could continue selling their wares. Handcarts and barrows were slowly moved with leg or arm so as not to infringe the law as they continued to serve customers and trade. London's unique example of a moving market vanished completely in the mid 1960's.

In 1930 he leased a property at 341 Kilburn High Road, just south of Brondesbury station in a former dairy, with an apartment above. He renovated the building and divided the shop into two. In one half he created a men's hairdressing salon, moved his practice into the other half and found tenants for the shop and flat, all of which shrewdly covered his own rent. With the outbreak of war he employed a locum to manage his affairs prior to entering the army where he was commissioned as a Captain in the Royal Army Medical Corps.

Demobilised in 1946 he returned home. There had been a loss of population as a consequence of bomb damage and patients moving to safer suburban areas. He commenced the Herculean struggle to rebuild his practice midst all the continued discomfort of a post war England with rationing and shortages of most consumables. He had not appreciated the extent to which the 'patient mix' had begun to change. In 1901 there was an Irish population of some 3% and a Jewish population of 1%. Fifty years later the Irish population had grown to 20% and the Jewish population to 3%. By 1961 a decline in the Irish and Jewish groups was noticed, replaced by 'colonial immigrants' mainly from the West Indies, who numbered almost 6% of the population. Ten years later, in 1971 colonial immigrants accounted for 13% of the local population, displacing many of the Irish and Jews who moved further north.

In 1947 discussions ensued at medical meetings concerning the proposed introduction by the minister of health, Aneurin Bevan of a NHS (National Health Service), to which the majority were opposed. Bevan split the profession, by offering senior consultants, who were the privileged leaders, salaries with covert 'Merit Awards' and confirmed they could 'still enjoy the fruits of private practice'. They indicated their acceptance and on those terms opposition to the scheme crumpled from the remaining consultants, to be followed shortly thereafter from the bulk of the GP's. The principals in general practice were offered compensation valued on the average of the previous three years 'reported' turnover. Those GP's who continued to oppose the scheme were notified that unless they signed their agreement accepting conditions and terms of service they would forfeit all rights to compensation.

Having arrived at an agreed reimbursement, this was to be provided only upon the retirement of the GP at age 65, or earlier if on grounds of ill health, or death. This settlement attracted a derisory annual interest rate of half of one per cent. GP's then surrendered any right to sell a medical practice or to appoint a successor. Dr Joyston-Bechal volubly claimed that this recompense penalised all those who had served their country during the war. In every general practice private care virtually ceased, as in unedifying haste the nations doctors stampeded to sign their agreement prior to the July 1948 start up date. The professions leaders had been no match for the wily Aneurin Bevan, nicknamed by disaffected doctors, Urinal Bevan, who later allegedly boasted to colleagues.

"I succeeded because I stuffed the consultant's mouths with gold."

On Christmas morning, 1964, I received a telephone call from Mrs S, an unknown patient living in Woodside Park, requesting an urgent private house call to see her sick child. I drove to her home and examined her little boy. He had a middle ear infection for which I prescribed an appropriate antibiotic. The mother explained that she had been fearful of calling her own NHS doctor and disturbing him on Christmas Day, although he lived in the same street and had chosen to disturb me, since she'd heard from a friend that I was good with children. I explained the child should be taken to see his doctor at the end of his course of treatment but at the conclusion of my visit the mother requested that I should see him, as opposed to her NHS doctor.

A colleague, Joe Holmes, who delivered our youngest child and with whom we became friends told me, when on a visit to his Winchmore Hill home, that he'd painted the exterior of his house and built his own garden shed. My attitude was that if he could do this so could I. Using my summer holidays plus other weekends I sallied forth up a ladder wearing rubber gloves to paint the house, in spite of a great aversion to heights, always prepared to dash out in response to a phone call, to visit any patient. Occasionally passing pedestrians would pause to chat and ask to my amusement, if I'd call to give them an estimate. I also constructed my own garden shed. Some years later Mrs Holmes confided to June that her husband had not been entirely forthright as he was assisted by a handyman to paint the higher levels of their house and to build his shed.

(M13) The purchase price in 1963 of a substantial 5 bedroom detached house in the North London suburb of Edgware was £10,000.

(1) Papanicolaou Test. Named after George Papanicolaou (1883-1962) a Greek American doctor who in 1923 published his findings of a simple test in which surface cells could be taken painlessly from the uterine cervical transformation zone to investigate microscopically whether there were any cellular changes to indicate precancerous or early cancerous changes that could be treated with the eradication of that disease. In 1928 a low cost test was introduced and in the US and Canada large-scale screening commenced in the 1950's.

More than 70% of these cancerous changes in uterine cervical cells is caused by the 'human papillovirus' and a vaccine is now available to immunise women against this viral infection.

(M14) Cancer of Uterine Cervix:

Cancer of Uterine Cervix: Deaths in England and Wales; Rates per 100,000					
Ages	20-34 yrs	35-49 yrs	50-64 yrs.	65-84 yrs.	Total all ages
1963-1967	163	2,898	4,481	4,451	11,993
1983-1987	605	1,773	2,916	3,995	9,289
1998-2002	278	1,100	1,262	2,252	4,892
A National Screening programme was commenced in 1988 for all 20 to 64 year old women.					

(M15) In 1997 the Imperial Cancer Research published in the British Medical Journal that screening had saved 1,300 lives per year.

Times Health Correspondent Sarah-Kate Templeton reported that just under 3,000 new cases of cervical cancer are diagnosed annually and in 2006 almost 1,100 women died from this disease.

Chapter 17

LONDON

1963 Onwards.

It was 8 am on Monday morning November 18th 1963 when I received a telephone call from Alfred Hyman our family doctor and friend, from my parent's home telling me that my father had suffered an acute myocardial infarction and had died. If death could be considered a merciful relief, then I believe, although just 63 yrs of age he would have chosen it that way. Always an active person, this put an end to the intolerable burden his life had become through illness.

Father had been severely incapacitated for 16 months by a left sided cerebral thrombosis which had deprived this once independent and eloquently articulate gentleman of his speech, the use of his right arm and leg and worst of all, his dignity. Formerly gregarious, he declined to see any but his immediate family following his CVA. He adamantly refused to be pushed in a wheelchair to be viewed 'as an object of pity', should he venture into the street for a little fresh air and change of scenery. As a consequence seldom did he permit himself to be taken out other than for outpatient hospital consultations and physiotherapy, which made little difference to his quality of life.

Born in Warsaw, he arrived in London in 1904 with his parents together with his father's youngest sister Hilda, to help with the children, and Harry and Anne, two younger siblings having been forced to flee from anti-Semitic persecution. A month after his 18th birthday his infantry unit was posted overseas and in the second week of November 1918, with a boatload of young conscripts, he disembarked in Belgium at the port of Ostend where they bivouacked over night before marching inland to take up trench positions on the allied eastern front. As they marched inland within sight and sound of deafening cannonades, the armistice was announced on the morning of November 11th, when all hostilities ceased, Compelled through economic necessity to leave school at 14 he had followed his parent's occupation and immediately after his marriage, when aged 23, he and my mother established their own millinery company.

A charming caring man with a handsome full face he had penetrating grey eyes, inherited from his mother. Well-read he was intelligent and endowed with a social and political conscience. In 1926, at the time of 'The General Strike' he had undertaken duties as a special constable and in the 1930's had joined the communists since they were the only political group to oppose the Nazi and fascist tyrannies of the extreme right. Paying monthly subscriptions to that party until the 1940's he was the antithesis to everything that they stood for except their opposition to fascism. In 1936 with co-religionists and left wing supporters he participated, with pockets bulging with marbles, in what became known as the 'battle of Cable Street' (1) blocking the entry of a large group of uniformed black shirted fascists marching through the immigrant area of London's East End, bent on increasing racial tension and recruiting followers to their cause, which had inadvisably been authorised by the metropolitan police commissioner.

His overriding joy was his wife and children and an intense love of classical music, ballet and in particular opera. Father son relationships are complex and my relationship towards my father was no exception. I owed him everything, yet while he deeply loved and cared for me as he did all my siblings, I was terrified of him from my earliest years, constantly fearful of those brief mercurial outbursts of his temper, often accompanied by abhorrent corporal punishment. Never did I greet or part from either of my parents without first kissing them, returning their love, as a filial duty, yet at times when young I hated him and have suffered endless remorse as a consequence. My father's mother Zosha passed away in May of that year in a nursing home, and so it was that I lost two of the prime motivators who helped shape my early life.

Father's interment was the next day, followed by 'shiva', the seven days of traditional Jewish family mourning. Three days later during Friday evening dinner at my mother's home we were stunned, with the appalling radio news broadcast. President J. F. Kennedy had been assassinated. If my life were to be recorded as a book, then a further chapter had just ended on a sorrowful note.

*   *   *

At the start of 1965 my NHS partner, who had become increasingly disillusioned with NHS practice, retired as soon as he was eligible, to concentrate on his private practice in Queen Anne Street and managing an investment portfolio of commercial properties. My formal written application to the Brent executive council to succeed him in the practice was successful. Initially I had wanted to become a NHS practice principle, but by the time this had become a reality, my private practice had expanded to the extent that I was barely able to manage my NHS commitments unaided.

With his retirement I undertook a much-needed renovation of the surgery premises during which I discovered a number of large bottles labelled, red, brown, green, and white containing various coloured liquids. Mrs Warner, who had periodically assisted him in his dispensary, explained that prior to the war the bottles had contained four different medications. There was the red cough linctus, a brown concoction with Kaolin to control diarrhoea, a green syrup that was considered a pick me up, and a white antacid for the ulcer sufferers. In pre-war days the dispenser would respond to the doctor's brief scribbled note, which gave the colour of the medication, and the dispenser would then fill a smaller bottle with the appropriate liquid attaching a label with dosage instructions.

The majority of dwellings in our practice area were overcrowded houses. Every floor had been subdivided into tenement flats in which there were families, where the main breadwinner was invariably a Caucasian male in some lower paid clerical or manual occupation. Divorce was stigmatised and rarely seen. There were no single parents with young families and married women with young children tended not to work. Few had access to a motor vehicle, other than on public transport and even fewer owned a telephone, although the majority had a radio and television. Most adults visited the cinema weekly and many regarded cigarette smoking and a few pints at the local as two of their few pleasures in life. There was never any difficulty in finding space for parking my car in the street when making house calls, and I was never fearful of being attacked by drug users or muggers at night.

In the same month my partner retired, all eyes were glued to the television coverage of Sir Winston Churchill's state funeral, while I was involved in interviewing a number of applicants to fill a one-year locum post for the assistant I needed. It was not until the following year that the BBC announced they planned to introduce a colour television service, although we had watched it years earlier in Baltimore.

At the start of 1966 I advertised for a replacement locum on a one-year contract. The replacement locum was Dr Gill, a young married woman from Uganda. Midway through her contract she was scheduled to take her annual vacation. Her husband had travelled ahead to Nairobi for a holiday, to visit their parents, before the days of Idi Amin (2) and she had arranged to follow one week later. During the summer, the surgeries were far quieter and in her three weeks absence I covered her workload, forgoing an annual holiday for yet another year.

The 30th July 1966 saw England defeat Germany 4 - 2 in the World Cup football series, by which time my private practice, with a steady flow of patients, had grown sufficiently to necessitate employing a full time secretary. The following weekend my locum flew to Uganda for her vacation, following her husband who had left a week earlier. On Tuesday morning the fourth day after wishing her bon voyage, my secretary, Barbara Brown, announced there was a policeman in the waiting room wishing to interview me on an urgent and confidential matter. At the first available opportunity he was shown into my office. I invited him to take a seat and without any preamble he enquired.

"Are you Doctor Powell?"

"Yes. How can I help you?"

"Have you ever employed a person by the name of Doctor Gill?"

"Yes; Dr. Gill is currently employed by me as a full time medical locum."

"In that case, we would like you to attend the coroner's forensic department, to identify her?"

"Officer, I think you're mistaken. The Dr Gill I employ is on vacation in Uganda where she flew to join her husband and family three days ago. I don't think I can really be of any help to you."

"On the contrary; we have every reason to believe that Dr Gill didn't fly to Uganda as you believe and we need your help in identifying her body."

"I'm sorry, but you're wrong. Dr Gill did fly out to join her family and if this is some kind of hoax I think it's in very bad taste."

"Dr Powell, I'm being deadly serious, if you'll excuse the pun. This is no hoax."

"Can you tell me what makes you believe this is the body of my assistant?"

"Well I'll be as brief as I can. At first light this morning, the police and the fire department were called to a house converted into three flats. Dr Gill occupied the attic flat. A family who lived in the flat beneath were just sitting down for breakfast when the ceiling caved in. On top of the debris were the burned springs of a mattress and metal bedstead on which were the remains of a body. It appears that there was a low-grade fire, that must have smouldered and burned for several days. Nobody had detected any smell of burning and it gave that family below, a tremendous shock. The fire department is endeavouring to find the cause but it looks very much as though Dr. Gill may have fallen asleep while smoking in bed."

Surely there had been some sort of mix up, a mistaken identity. Dr Gill, in her mid twenties had only been married a few months and was on the threshold of her medical career. It seemed like a horrible nightmare and the news filled me with dreadful apprehension.

"Do you know if she smoked?"

"I'd seen her smoke the occasional cigarette, but I'm certain she would never have been so foolish as to smoke in bed."

"Well the evidence seems to suggest that she must have stayed up late packing, and then sat or laid on her bed to have a rest and lit a cigarette, when she fell asleep. The smoke and fumes must have overcome her and then the fire smouldered on for nearly three days until the ceiling joists burned through and collapsed. Incredible as it may seem, throughout that whole time nobody saw any smoke, or smelt burning. The body's been badly burnt and there's not much left to identify, that's why the coroner would like your help."

I concluded the morning surgery as rapidly as possible and immediately rushed to the morgue where I was requested to view and identify the body. I was still hoping there'd been a mistake and I'd be shown the remains of some unknown person. Lying on the gurney was the unrecognisable burned head and torso of a body, the arms from the elbows downward, and legs below the knees having been completely devoured by the fire. I felt hot and clammy as I identified the skull by her distinctive upper incisor teeth, the only part that was recognisable.

There then followed the difficult task of locating Dr.Gill's husband in Uganda to communicate news of the dreadful accident and some days later, the Coroner's Inquest.

(1) The Battle of Cable Street. On the first Sunday of October 1936, Oswald Moseley the head of an extremist racist group who dressed his followers in black shirts, aping Hitler's Nazi SS, obtained permission to march through the streets of London's East End. Racism at the time was an unpleasant fact of life, but the residents, mainly working class Irish and Jews, helped by communist sympathisers decided to oppose this provocative move. Ten thousand police were drafted in to protect the 3,000 fascist marchers. In the afternoon Moseley arrived to lead his followers down Whitechapel High Street.

As they started their march, protected on either side by a heavy police presence, keeping huge numbers of protesters at bay on the pavements, the marchers were obstructed by a tram that had been left by its driver (a communist) at a road junction. Unable to pass, the black shirts were advised by the police to take a detour through Cable Street. The crowd rushed to obstruct this new route. Barricades were placed across the street, while the police attempted to dispel the crowd, both on foot and using baton wielding mounted officers. The crowd anticipating this tactic from earlier confrontations against Czarist Cossacks used marbles, which rolled in large numbers in the road destabilised horse and rider.

In Cable Street, hastily erected barriers obstructed fascists and police, while local residents from open windows of apartments lining the route pelted those below with old vegetables excrement from chamber pot and other missiles. Finally the police advised the black shirts to turn back. No deaths resulted and the fascists were clearly humiliated.

Moseley flew to Berlin the following day where his second marriage took place to Diana Guinness (one of the three Mitford sisters) in the home of Joseph Goebbels,

Nazi Germany's club footed Minister of Propaganda, in the presence of Adolph Hitler the Nazi Chancellor. Some weeks following the 'Cable Street battle' the Baldwin government introduced legislation banning political parties from wearing uniforms. Moseley and his wife spent the Second World War in jail, while in the post war period the newspaper proprietors association imposed a voluntary ban on reporting his activities, and thereby sealed his fate as a far right political leader and rabble-rouser.

(2) Idi Amin. A former army heavyweight boxer, who proclaimed himself Ugandan President for life, overthrew President Milton Obote of Uganda in a 1971 military coup. A dictator and a homicidal buffoon, he was responsible in 1972 for the expulsion of all Indian and Pakistani Asians from Uganda and through his terror regime the imprisonment and murder of tens of thousands of Ugandan citizens. In June 1976 a hijacked Air France 'Airbus 300' passenger plane, en route from Israel to Paris landed in Athens, where, in the absence of adequate security, it was hijacked by Palestinian Arab PLO terrorists, flown to Libya refuelled and then on to Entebbe airport in Uganda.

Under Amin's auspices further terrorists were permitted to guard the hostage passengers, all of whom were released except those who were Jews. With remarkable planning and daring the Israeli Defence Forces raided Entebbe on July 4th and released all but one of the passengers. Only three Israeli lives were lost; the commanding officer leading the raid, Colonel Netanyahou, whose brother later became prime minister of Israel, one of the hostages who unfortunately misunderstood instructions, and Dora Block, an elderly woman who had been hospitalised in Nairobi and was shot and murdered in her bed the next day on Amin's instruction. When removed from office, he gained refuge in Saudi Arabia where he remained until his death.

Captain Bacos the Air France pilot refused to leave his plane and his Jewish passengers. He was later reprimanded by his Air France superiors and suspended from duty for a period.

Chapter 18

LONDON

1967

In the early summer of 1963 I started a private medical practice, which committed me to 5 working days a week, while in 1964 there was the further obligation of a busy inner London NHS practice. Each week there were 11 NHS surgeries, which included Saturday mornings and I was on call at all times of the day and night. In order to obtain some leisure time, I arranged with a colleague, Dr. Gerald Capper, that he would undertake my surgeries and emergency house calls alternate Friday evenings and Saturday mornings, while I reciprocated in his Fleet Road, Hampstead practice in addition to my own. Saturday morning surgeries were abolished years later and later still those on Thursday afternoons. In addition I regularly saw patients at home most evenings. Except weekends I never stopped for a meal from breakfast until the end of the day, only snatching time for the occasional cup of coffee. Throughout this time, June diligently supervised the education and care of our children, occasionally filled in as secretary or receptionist when one of my key practice employees were absent on vacation, or unwell and always made home a pleasure to return to at the end of each day.

Following our return to London until the summer of 1967, the tenth anniversary of my qualifying in medicine, we never took an annual holiday. No time was ever lost through sickness in those first ten years and on more than one occasion I made my rounds more unwell than some of those I was visiting, once throwing up into a bowl in my car, but never ceasing work for more than a few minutes. I could neither be seen to be unwell nor could I spare the time. We took the occasional weekend break, but I was possessed by a constant insecurity that impelled me to secure our future, by nurturing my medical practice.

In those years rarely a day passed without seeing patients with chronic disabling maladies that today are more readily amenable to better treatment and often cure. There were the large numbers of peptic ulcer sufferers who were treated with antacids and a strict diet regime for weeks at a time and sometimes indefinitely. Relapse was common and in more severe cases, part of the stomach was removed in a variety of costly mutilating operations. Nobody would have envisioned the newer more effective acid inhibiting medications (H2 antagonists) available after 1974 and the later eradication of the scourge with an appropriate antibiotic. Many from mid-life onwards suffered from angina, indicative of serious narrowing of the heart's coronary arteries. Perhaps these were the more fortunate patients, since so many, particularly men in the prime of life suddenly succumbed and died from a 'heart attack'. None realised the significant correlation of raised cholesterol nor would have thought it possible to use angiographies and coronary artery by pass grafts.

A constant flow of patients mainly from middle age onwards suffering from the disabling discomfort of rheumatic joint pains associated with arthritis was seen daily. Joint replacement surgery was appearing in the mid 1960's and the first of my private patients travelled in 1964 to Wigan, where a hip prosthesis was successfully fitted. John Charnley was the orthopaedic surgeon who pioneered the successful replacement of a hip joint. Having evolved a clean air system with an engineering friend, his operating room was freed from the problems of infection, which made such pioneering orthopaedic procedures possible. Relatively safe anti-inflammatory medications did not appear until the 1970's.

Never a week passed without a woman appearing with her chronic paronychia, the infection at the side of a finger nail induced by having hands constantly immersed in water with the chores of dish washing, clothes laundering and floor scrubbing and cleaning, tasks more efficiently performed by today's machines, making the condition a great rarity. In winter there was the chilblain sufferer, which with today's central heating in home and office has relegated such conditions to the past. With immunisation, the scourge of poliomyelitis disappeared and only once did I ever see a diphtheritic membrane.

The effects of cigarette smoke inhalation were slowly becoming accepted, as was the control of hypertension in the prevention of heart disease, although passive smoking had yet to be indicted. The contraceptive pill had made its debut in 1958. In the 1960's a number of specialities that had not previously existed were evolving. Huge swathes of hospital beds dedicated to the treatment of pulmonary tuberculosis were in the process of closing.

The scourge of these and many other illnesses have been replaced by others, most notably in the 1980's by AIDS (auto immune deficiency syndrome) while Alzheimer's disease had not crept into popular usage, nor repetitive stress syndrome. With the introduction of a 'Scribner Shunt' from Seattle in Washington, successful renal dialysis commenced in 1964 for the very few, selected by committee at the Royal Free and Guy's hospitals. Successful organ transplants and prosthetic implants also first took place at this time. Advances in diagnosis and treatment taken for granted in the early 21st century were often mere dreams in the 1960's.

In mid 1967 Paul M, a successful middle-aged industrialist and his charming Church of England lady friend consulted me. They had lived together for many years, since he chose not to offend his elderly Jewish mother's sensibilities by 'marrying out'. She was pregnant and while unmarried, having a child out of wedlock was out of the question. There had been many attempts in parliament to introduce legislation to legalise abortion, but none had been successful. Those with money had the option of seeking a number of psychiatric opinions which would identify a mental health risk to the mother greater than permitting the pregnancy to continue. I referred them to a psychiatrist, Dr. Eustace C, in Harley Street, who for an appropriate fee assisted them in obtaining a legal abortion in a private London Clinic. The majority of my patients had no alternative than to permit nature to take its course increasing the size of their family, while a small number put themselves at grave risk in the hands of illegal abortionists.

Later that year a bill known as the 1967 Abortion Act (1) was introduced in parliament, becoming law the following year, which provided one further step upon the path of the emancipation of women.

While consulting, I made it a rule never to be interrupted other than in a dire emergency. Late one morning my receptionist phoned on the intercom to tell me that a teacher had just walked into the surgery. She was escorting a group of teenage schoolgirls by coach to a swimming lesson when one of them convulsed with an epileptic attack. Seeing a doctor's surgery she had instructed the driver to stop and entered to ask if the duty doctor would attend to the young lady. I explained that I was in the midst of examining a patient and would be out in a few minutes. A minute later there was another call. Could I come quickly, there was now a second child having an epileptic attack on the bus. I replied that I would be out as soon as I was able and asked my receptionist to enquire whether the bus was escorting a group of known epileptic children.

Within a few moments of replacing the handset there was a violent hammering on the door. I opened it and there stood an irate teacher demanding that I follow her immediately to the bus since a third child was now having an epileptic attack. With no alternative, and hastily apologising to my patient, I left my surgery and followed the teacher out into the street where a huge coach had stopped. Standing on the pavement was a group of three or four young adolescent girls in school uniform. In the bus there was absolute pandemonium with a perplexed coach driver in his driving seat and another teacher helplessly attempting to maintain some semblance of order while children were screaming and attempting to push past her to leave the bus.

I saw three pubescent girls near the front convulsing and others screaming and looking on, hyperventilating in fear and horror. I noticed that the afflicted girls were likewise hyperventilating with limbs contorted in tetanic spasms, yet were not comatose. Suddenly another child started to convulse, conscious and terrified, limbs contorting in typical tetanic contractions.

I turned to the alarmed senior teacher and insisted that she evacuate all her pupils currently in varying degrees of panic and hysteria on to the pavement to avoid more of them going down with hysterical convulsions. The teacher was reluctant to follow my advice but I forcefully explained that we were observing mass hysteria and that unless she acted promptly she would have every child convulsing. Within minutes there were more than 40 uniformed schoolgirls rapidly calming on the pavement, while on the coach a large group remained of hyperventilating girls exhibiting varying degrees of frightening tetanic seizures. I instructed that the pupils on the pavement should be escorted back to school by public transport while I would arrange with the coach driver to take the afflicted children to the St Mary's hospital A&E department, since unaided, one doctor couldn't cope with the situation, which would require each child to breathe in and out of a paper bag, to increase the level of carbon dioxide in their lungs.

Under my instruction the coach sped off with about a dozen school girls and an alarmed teacher while the other teacher escorted her charges, a group of normal excited teenagers, to the nearby Kilburn tube station for the return journey to school. I then phoned the A& E department at St. Mary's to warn them of the problem that lay ahead before returning to my disrupted consultation.

During one particularly busy evening surgery there was an interruption when the secretary explained that she had an urgent call from Mr. Williamson who needed to speak to me. This patient was an intelligent, but unemployed schoolteacher in his early thirties, who suffered from schizophrenia. A very pleasant man, he often sent me poetry he'd written, but because of his delusional state had lost his job and had remained unemployed for some years.

"Tell Mr. Williamson I'm busy and I'll call him later." Within a minute my secretary disturbed me once more.

"Mr. Williamson says it's urgent and he must speak with you right away."

"Would you ask him, with my compliments, to indicate what his urgent problem might be." Within a few seconds my secretary returned with the message

"Mr. Williamson says he's bleeding. He's cut off his testicles and wants to know what he should do?"

Not believing this tale of self-mutilation, I advised my secretary.

"Tell him that I'm far too busy to speak with him at present and he should stop making up stories." Within moments the phone rang a third time.

"Mr. Williamson says he's not fabricating stories. He's thrown them on the fire, but he can't stop the bleeding. What should he do?"

"Tell him to 'phone for an ambulance." I replied in exasperation.

I didn't take this exchange seriously until a week later when Mr. Williamson attended to have his sutures removed. He then explained, with his bizarre logic, that he felt he must never risk passing on what he believed was an inherited disorder and so had removed all possibility of this happening by performing an orchiectomy with a kitchen knife, without anaesthetic. There, this strange story might have ended, since I never saw Mr. Williamson again, although he did write to me from Broadmoor, which I thought most considerate, explaining his subsequent actions.

Mr. Williamson's social worker 'phoned, wishing to speak to me urgently and in person. He explained.

"Dr. Powell, I'm calling to tell you the facts of the case before you read about it in tomorrow's newspapers. Yesterday your patient went to visit his mother. He attacked her with a knife and stabbed her to death."

Mr. Williamson bizarrely wrote to me, explaining he was punishing his mother for having inflicted his illness upon him. With his weird machinations he also explained that he was simultaneously ensuring she would never pass this malady on to anyone else. In spite of her age he seemed unable to rationalise that she was too old for further children. The tragedy of this crime was the absence of those medications, which appeared about a decade later, to treat the delusional mental conditions of paranoia and schizophrenia. With the appearance of reliable medications to treat psychiatric maladies in the last two decades of the 20th century, some of the countries largest hospitals closed and vast wards of hospital beds used for the incarceration of patients with mental ills disappeared.

There have also been great changes in attitude in the medical and nursing professions. From my student days and continuing into the 1960's and 1970's doctors never mentioned the word 'cancer', or malignancy to a patient, always using concealed euphemisms such as 'mitotic lesion' or 'neoplasm'. A patient with a malignancy or life threatening disease was never informed of this condition, the next of kin being the sole recipients of these unacceptable tidings. T.B. was never mentioned in front of a patient, always 'Koch's disease', and never syphilis, but rather a 'Luetic infection'. In return the medical and nursing professions were treated with the greatest deference and respect that have now become a thing of the past. Patients would often stand when the doctor entered the room, men would doff hats, and consultants were treated as though kin to royalty on their ward rounds. An attack on a nurse or doctor by any sane individual was a rarity.

While the 1960's could be described as the years of 'the Beatles', the 'Flower People' and 'Carnaby Street', throughout the latter part of the 1960's there had begun a steady and slowly evolving enlightened attitude reflected in social trends towards the rejection of the stigma associated with divorce and illegitimacy, acceptance of married women in the work place, and integration of peoples of different colour and religion into the community. These were gradually evolving processes, which in the late 1960's were well under way. The NHS patient cohort I had been caring for were changing during this time. The number of foreign-born patients was gradually increasing, largely from the West Indies, and a new phenomenon was occurring.

In the post war years there was a great housing shortage, exacerbated by the shortage of rental accommodation due to the 1957 Rent Act and further rent restrictive legislation in the wake of the Rachman (2) landlord scandals. Numerous single Caucasian teenage girls discovered that one of the simplest ways to reach the top of a council house waiting list was as an unmarried mother with a young baby. Word of this phenomenon rapidly spread and large numbers of young immature girls deliberately placed themselves in this situation to leave overcrowded and unhappy home environments.

These young single girls were replacing temporary home discontent with unseen life long difficulties for themselves and a generation of underprivileged children. This was reminiscent of the struggles I had witnessed in Baltimore amongst the Afro-American teenage girls, who blighted their lives and those of the children they were raising creating enduring problems as school drop outs, with unemployment, criminality and spiralling problems of underachievers as 'have-nots' in the community.

Council flats replaced large tracts of Victorian houses, in an attempt to reduce an endemic housing shortage, but creating unrealised problems in high-rise dwellings. Myopic British town planners and architects failed to appreciate the difficulties they were creating, as councils permitted high-rise homes in London and other major cities to be designed and built. As these rose skywards in the UK, identical developments that had been created ten and fifteen years earlier in cities across the USA were being dynamited and levelled, as costly mistakes. British councillors and planners willing to enquire might have learned from well-documented housing authority errors in the USA.

The ethnic population changes that had begun in the 1960's accelerated in the 1970's and thereafter as tens of thousands of Indian people from Africa, with rights to UK citizenship vanquished, by Idi Amin, and joined by others from the Indian subcontinent entered Britain. Iranian refugees, with the fall of the Shah in the late 1970's swelled these numbers. Kilburn acquired its share of these immigrants, further displacing the incumbent Irish northwards to Cricklewood. Midst a profusion of languages, without the benefit of interpreters, patients appeared in increasing numbers to register in my practice, predominantly with the name Singh and then another name, while at the next visit the name Singh was given as a surname. It took years to sort out the resulting muddle in notes and registrations. As large numbers of new immigrants and refugees arrived in Kilburn the scourge of TB reappeared, as did malaria while the need for a variety of interpreters became a daily necessity. At the time of my retirement in 1997 conservative estimates revealed that more than 75% of patients in my practice were either first generation British, or of foreign birth, with a multiplicity of dress, language and culture. A failure by the government to require some basic medical examination including a chest x-ray as a precondition for those seeking to migrate to the UK, such as we experienced in Canada, could have helped to detect and avoid many of the new cases of TB and other health problems.

(1) Abortion Act 1967. In 1938 a girl of 14 years was viciously attacked and raped by two soldiers in a military barracks. The resulting pregnancy was terminated by one of the countries most eminent gynaecologists, Professor Aleck Bourne. The operation was performed without concealment in St. Mary's Hospital and Bourne was tried on a charge of procuring an abortion at the Central Criminal Court in July, 1938, under the Offences against the Person Act 1861 and was acquitted. Under this act, the only recognized justification for the operation was probable danger to the life of the pregnant woman should the pregnancy be allowed to continue. Had he been found guilty the punishment for unlawfully procuring an abortion was penal servitude for life. In summing-up counsel said: "If the doctor is of opinion, on reasonable grounds and with adequate knowledge, that the probable consequences of the pregnancy will be to make the woman a physical or mental wreck, the jury are quite entitled to take the view that the doctor, who, under these circumstances and in that honest belief, operates, is operating for the purpose of preserving the life of the mother."

David Steele introduced a private members bill in parliament, which was passed as the Abortion Act 1967 and in April 1968 became law. This Act briefly stated that no offence under the 1929 Infant Life Preservation Act shall be committed providing that two independent practitioners shall agree that a termination of pregnancy is necessary under provisions laid down in the act. The procedure may take place only in premises licensed for the purpose and that the pregnancy has not exceeded 24 weeks duration.

David Steele's liberal 1967 parliamentary Act together with the contraceptive pill that first appeared in the early 1960's were the two major defining steps upon the road of woman's emancipation in the United Kingdom.

(2) Rachman was a notorious landlord in London's Notting Hill. He purchased slum properties, intimidated and evicted tenants providing substandard housing at exorbitant rents to mainly 'coloured' West Indian tenants, who could not find accommodation elsewhere due to colour discrimination. Rent controls further exacerbated the lack of rental housing. Most low cost rental accommodation was only available through local councils. A tenants waiting list rapidly evolved and points were awarded that would ensure greater priority to climb higher in the list to obtain housing at an earlier date. Severe disability, chronic illness, lack of accommodation where young children were involved all provided extra points to gain access to a rented council home of ones own.

Chapter 19

LONDON

Loose Ends

Prior to our departure from Canada our goal had been to settle in London in proximity to our parents and we arbitrarily set three years in which to re-integrate into the UK. By 1967 we were living within commuting distance of our families, as we had intended, and with both a busy private and expanding NHS practice I had achieved some of the security I yearned for my wife and children. An ambition to build our own home and further explore our interest in overseas travel didn't materialise until some years later.

As one goes through life, one periodically meets an old school friend or colleague at a school reunion, or simply bumps into such a person when least expected. At such times there's a cursory exchange of information. We then indulge in a game entitled; 'Wonder whatever happened to?' We've all played it, or a variant that proceeds something like.

"Have you heard from so and so, haven't heard from him in ages, what's he doing now?", or

"Do you remember so and so, well…."

From time to time when memories were jogged, I would reflectively say to June.

"Wonder whatever happened to Barbara and Norman Green once they settled in Montana and their little boy who was five years older than Robin? Do you remember the time Barbara nearly had a heart attack when she removed that dish from the refrigerator door, lifted the opaque lid to take some butter when she discovered a crouching mouse, with whiskers twitching, that her 6 years old son had placed there for safe keeping?"

And blissfully each Christmas, or whenever something reminded us of those prairie days we would repeat.

"Wonder how the Greens made out in the USA, and whatever happened to the Fletchers?"

In 1996 we embarked upon a P & O cruise ship touring the Caribbean. One morning June had gone up on deck to have breakfast and where I soon joined her. When I arrived June was engrossed in conversation with an older American gentleman at the next table, a retired doctor from Helena, Montana.

In our brief conversation we happened to mention that some years earlier we had known Dr. Norman Green who worked in an adjacent town to myself in Saskatchewan and had migrated to North Dakota or Montana in 1962 to take state board examinations. Had he ever come across the name?

"Yes, not only did I come across the name, but Norman Green and I were in partnership."

"That's fantastic, what a marvellous coincidence." I replied enthusiastically. "Tell me are you still in partnership with Norman?"

"No, our partnership ended two years ago."

"Do you still see him and do you know where he is now?" I enquired.

"It's rather a sad story. Norman died in an automobile accident just over two years ago. He was driving along, when another vehicle came speeding over the brow of a hill on the wrong side of the road. The driver was under the influence of alcohol. Dr Green didn't stand a chance in the resulting head on collision. It was all very tragic and sad and a great loss to the community. Such a terrible waste."

"What about his wife Barbara, how is she?"

"They were divorced some years earlier and I don't know where she went or whatever happened to her."

"I can't recall his name but what of Norman's son. Do you know what became of him?"

"I believe he was killed like his father in a road traffic fatality a good two years before his father."

Greatly saddened, I thanked him for the information he had given me but felt too upset to continue any further conversation. How I wish I'd never learned of these dreadful tragedies that had struck such a fine caring colleague and his family.

*   *   *

What of Saskatchewan's semi arid Palliser's triangle? The farms have increased in size, the smaller farms proving uneconomical, with the small farmer being squeezed out. The young have tended to migrate to the larger centres of population, in search of perceived improved standards of living and the recreational facilities available in larger conurbations. The populations in the small prairie towns of Climax, Frontier, Eastend and Shaunavon have dwindled some having almost halved in the past 45 years, while Swift Current has grown correspondingly. Many of the once essential small cottage hospitals have disappeared, including that in Eastend and have been converted into, or replaced with retirement homes to care for an aging community, while the monumental grain elevators have likewise diminished in number.

A comprehensive medical health programme based on the pioneering 'Health Region No. 1' was successfully adopted in Saskatchewan in 1963, the year following our departure and was introduced with public approval throughout Canada some years later.

The hospitals in Frontier, and Val Marie have closed, the consequence of government funding retrenchment and in Climax the hospital is open but four days a week and one doctor shares his practice duties with Shaunavon. Jack's café remains as a cheerful focal point in Eastend, now under ownership of distant relatives of the Shourounis brothers. Glen Smith an excellent pilot and instructor in his prime, who gave me flying lessons way back in 1961 passed away in 2005 having spent his latter years, a victim of Alzheimer's disease.

The Canadian Wheat Board, a government body dating from the 1930's depression when many farmers were being forced to leave their farms, created a monopoly over wheat and barley purchases and sales to help the farming community. Stephen Harper the leader of the Conservative minority government has indicated that measures will be introduced in 2008 to end this control. It is likely that this will produce an interesting short-term gain for the farm owners, followed by later uncertainties dependant on the vagaries of world grain prices. In 1974 we visited Eastend with our children to show them where their parents had lived and where the two eldest were born. We never encouraged our parents to visit us when I practiced there, feeling that prairie conditions, were in many ways too Spartan at the time when I always had the feeling that stripped of the essential luxuries of the automobile, electricity and telephone this was how my forbears had lived for generations in those tiny 'Shtetle' (1) communities in Russian Poland.

In retrospect I believe that when I commenced my medical practice in Saskatchewan, in spite of two years postgraduate hospital training I had insufficient medical skill and knowledge for some of the tasks that unexpectedly confronted me and many problems were compounded by the lack of consultant advice. A reliable air ambulance service was very reassuring, but frequently depended on the vagaries of weather at the plane's departure and arrival points, 250 miles apart, the availability of a plane and the assumption that the patient's condition had been stabilised sufficiently to be moved. There were a minority of patients who refused to be treated elsewhere, or through some misplaced religious conviction declined medical intervention for themselves or even their children.

I found myself thrust headlong from one end of an emotional spectrum and back, week after week. At times it was an exhilarating experience, better than any roller coaster joyride. I was on call for weeks on end in every adverse condition, learning self-reliance and to be a more competent doctor. Regretfully some patient's lives were curtailed because of my inexperience, but there were many more who were helped and for whom life was made more bearable. Had I not acted promptly and effectively some might not have survived. There's Tommy S living somewhere in Alberta with a wife and family and in Saskatchewan a middle-aged grand mother with her family who I rescued by caesarean section and many more, although often helped in less dramatic fashion. I improved the quality of life for some, but perhaps not as many as I might have wished when a patient declined advice to refrain from the many forms of addictive behaviour such as overeating, smoking, alcohol or drug abuse and gambling. We can't win every challenge.

Life in my NHS practice was always a continuous rush. Problems had to be dealt with as urgently as possible, particularly where children were concerned. Lurking at the back of my mind was often the concern that unless prompt action was taken, my patient might, for whatever reason, be running out of time. Frequently I needed to struggle for my NHS patients arranging what I deemed urgent investigation or to gain admission to hospital. Often I resorted to subterfuge, when some junior doctor or nurse refused the help I was seeking by requesting the full name of the person who was being obstructive. I would then spell it carefully back to them with the rejoinder.

"If anything untoward happens to my patient as a consequence of your refusal on this date, are you prepared to stand in a coroner's court to defend your course of action, admitting you had never seen or examined the patient?" Never once was a patient turned away. "Do not go gentle into that goodnight. Rage against the dying of the light." **(2)**

I have recorded some of my experiences in Canada together with a few reminiscences concluding in 1967, the tenth anniversary in which I gained my medical degree. Throughout, I strove for my patients assisting them in their struggle with illness when beset with fear and worry. Frequently I needed to resist and circumvent many forms of red tape and bureaucracy in the process.

Inevitably there were illnesses and times where one could offer little more than words of comfort to assuage grief. I made many mistakes along the way; thankfully fewer as I gained experience and where I erred, I apologise and hope that in time there may be forgiveness.

(1) 'Shtetle' One of the small farming towns in the area known as 'The Russian Pale' predominantly in Poland, where a considerable proportion of the populace was Yiddish speaking.

262

(2) Dillon Thomas (1914-1953) A great 20th century Welsh poet, who drank to excess, wrote in 1951 'A Poem to my father', who was dying, "Rage against the dying of the light….."

***   ***   ***

I wish to record my gratitude and appreciation for the immense help and encouragement my companion June has given me. Her unflagging support, both through difficult years in Canada and equally tough early years in London and in the preparation of this book have been immeasurable. She has always been and remains a beacon of kindness, warmth and comfort to all who know her. She is an outstanding woman. I have been remarkably fortunate to have found and befriended her, ultimately persuading her to become my wife.

I owe a great debt to Mark Powell my father, a too rigid disciplinarian, who believed as did so many of that era "If you spare the rod, you spoil the child." who loved his wife and children deeply and made it possible for me to attend medical college. Belatedly my thanks to my brothers Peter, Maurice and Michael who were always helpful financially and in many other ways during my student and later years and to my many instructors and teachers who helped me to progress academically, in particular Zosha Podguszer, Rabbi Dr Rudy Brasch of the Southgate Liberal Synagogue, Mr Martin Hackett and Mr George Vernon Boer, my form master and principal at the Oakwood Secondary Modern School and Mr William Auger, Southgate County Grammar School principal without whose help I could never have triumphed over that insurmountable hurdle, the 11 plus examination.

I wish to convey my appreciation of that generous warm hearted gentleman and friend, June's father Frederick Fraiman and his wife Dora, who accepted me as a son and without whose help I would have been unable to overcome those obstacles sent to thwart my wife and I, when attempting to relocate in London following our return from Canada and for the constant friendship and affection of their children Brian, Peter and Wendy and their spouses.

My thanks to family stalwarts and friends who have always been supportive and encouraging and particularly to those who have helped recently with their suggestions and proof reading, most notably June, Robin and Frederick Powell, Michael Williams, Tristan and Sebastian Balcombe and David Powell.

Finally I extend my gratitude to my many, teachers, and colleagues, too many to mention individually, amongst whom in recent years, Dr. David Lipkin MRCP. Cardiologist, Mr. Edmondson FRCS. Cardio-thoracic surgeon, Prof. Peter Hoskins FRCR, Radiotherapist oncologist, and Prof

Roger Kirby FRCS, Urologist, for their assistance in keeping me in robust health to enable me write of my early years. As a consequence of the latter's endeavours, I undertake that any profit ensuing from the publication of this autobiography will be donated to cancer research.

I conclude this message to my children.

"Should you believe you have any obligation or debt owed to me, I would consider it amply discharged by your providing a better educational opportunity for your children and grandchildren than my wife and I strove to give you and my father granted me, provided it is always in a home filled with love, respect for all and good cheer."

Arnold Powell London March 2007

***   ***   ***

Printed in the United Kingdom
by Lightning Source UK Ltd.
120872UK00002B/9